NEOCLASSICAL MICROECONOMIC THEORY

What did the founding members of the Austrian school contribute to our understanding of markets as economic processes? Carl Menger, Friedrich Wieser and Eugen Böhm-Bawerk are acknowledged as pioneers in the development of neoclassical economics, as well as being recognized as the founders of the Austrian School of Economics. *Neoclassical Microeconomic Theory* examines their contribution and compares it with the other branches of neoclassical economics that emerged between the 1870s and the 1930s.

The author begins by exploring the initial stimulus provided by Carl Menger's work, and then demonstrates the complementarities and tensions between Menger's, Wieser's and Böhm-Bawerk's views on such issues as the scope and method of economics; theories of choice; price theory; competition; entrepreneurship; and capital formation and distribution.

Whilst the Austrian research project was subsequently isolated from developments in mainstream neoclassical economics during the mid-twentieth century, the ideas of the early Austrian economists were to emerge as an inspiration for modern, Austro-American market process analysis.

A. M. Endres is Senior Lecturer in Economics in the School of Business and Economics, University of Auckland, New Zealand. He has published more than 30 articles on the development of economic theory, in journals including: *European Economic Review*; *European Journal for the History of Economic Thought*; *Journal of Institutional and Theoretical Economics*; *Scottish Journal of Political Economy* and *History of Political Economy*.

FOUNDATIONS OF THE MARKET ECONOMY
Edited by Mario J. Rizzo, *New York University* and
Lawrence H. White, *University of Georgia*

A central theme of this series is the importance of understanding and assessing the market economy from a perspective broader than the static economics of perfect competition and Pareto optimality. Such a perspective sees markets as causal processes generated by the preferences, expectations and beliefs of economic agents. The creative acts of entrepreneurship that uncover new information about preferences, prices and technology are central to these processes with respect to their ability to promote the discovery and use of knowledge in society.

The market economy consists of a set of institutions that facilitate voluntary cooperation and exchange among individuals. These institutions include the legal and ethical framework as well as more narrowly 'economic' patterns of social interaction. Thus the law, legal institutions and cultural or ethical norms, as well as ordinary business practices and monetary phenomena, fall within the analytical domain of the economist.

Other titles in the series

THE MEANING OF MARKET PROCESS
Essays in the development of modern Austrian economics
Israel M. Kirzner

PRICES AND KNOWLEDGE
A market-process perspective
Esteban F. Thomsen

KEYNES' GENERAL THEORY OF INTEREST
A reconsideration
Fiona C. Maclachlamn

LAISSEZ-FAIRE BANKING
Kevin Dowd

EXPECTATIONS AND THE MEANING OF INSTITUTIONS
Essays in economics by Ludwig Lachmann
Edited by *Don Lavoie*

PERFECT COMPETITION AND THE TRANSFORMATION OF ECONOMICS
Frank M. Machovec

ENTREPRENEURSHIP AND THE MARKET PROCESS
An enquiry into the growth of knowledge
David Harper

NEOCLASSICAL MICROECONOMIC THEORY

The Founding Austrian Version

A. M. Endres

London and New York

First published 1997
by Routledge
11 New Fetter Lane, London EC4P 4EE

Simultaneously published in the USA and Canada
by Routledge
29 West 35th Street, New York, NY 10001

© 1997 A.M. Endres

Typeset in Garamond by
Pure Tech India Ltd, Pondicherry, India
Printed and bound in Great Britain by
Redwood Books, Trowbridge, Wilts

All rights reserved. No part of this book may be reprinted or
reproduced or utilized in any form or by any electronic,
mechanical, or other means, now known or hereafter
invented, including photocopying and recording, or in any
information storage or retrieval system, without permission in
writing from the publishers.

British Library Cataloguing in Publication Data
A catalogue record for this book is available from the British Library

Library of Congress Cataloging in Publication Data
A catalogue record for this book has been requested
ISBN 0-415-15209-7

This book has been sponsored in part by the Austrian
Economics Program at New York University.

CONTENTS

List of Figures	ix
List of Tables	xi
Acknowledgements	xiii

1 IN WHAT SENSES WERE THE FOUNDING AUSTRIANS 'NEOCLASSICAL' ECONOMISTS?   1
Introduction   1
Recent treatments of early developments in neoclassical economics   3
Founding Austrian economics as a branch of neoclassicism   7

2 THE FOUNDING AUSTRIAN CONCEPTIONS OF ECONOMICS   9
Introduction   9
Some historical considerations regarding the nature of economics   10
The scope of Austrian economics and its associated styles of reasoning   13
The starting-point of founding Austrian economic theory   19

3 CARL MENGER'S ANALYSIS OF CHOICE   24
Introduction   24
First principles   26
The Mengerian economizer   27
The scope of economizing behaviour   31
The structure of needs   33
The growth of needs   37

CONTENTS

4 WIESER, BÖHM-BAWERK AND THE GOALS OF ECONOMIZING BEHAVIOUR — 41
Wieser's logic of valuation — 41
Wieser on the purpose of economizing behaviour — 44
Böhm-Bawerk's appeal to 'pure' psychology — 47
'Measuring' subjective value — 50
Conclusions — 57

5 CARL MENGER'S THEORY OF PRICE FORMATION — 60
Introduction — 60
Methodological considerations — 61
Menger's notions of equilibrium — 63
The formation of product prices in a decentralized economy: five illustrations — 67
Conclusion — 82

6 BÖHM-BAWERK'S VALUE AND PRICE THEORY — 85
Introduction — 85
First principles: the nature of value — 86
The cause of value and economizing behaviour — 90
The theory of markets and exchange value — 94
Böhm-Bawerk's concept of demand–supply equilibrium — 100
Conclusion — 105

7 THE PROCESS OF COMPETITION IN FOUNDING AUSTRIAN ECONOMIC THEORY: I, MENGER'S *PRINCIPLES* — 108
Introduction — 108
Competition in Menger's 'Principles': behavioural aspects — 111
Competition in Menger's 'Principles': the theory of market structures — 120

8 THE PROCESS OF COMPETITION IN FOUNDING AUSTRIAN ECONOMIC THEORY: II, WIESER AND BÖHM-BAWERK — 126
Wieser on competition as social conflict — 126
Competition as a bargaining process: Böhm-Bawerk's version — 134
Conclusion: the 'Hayekian' flavour of founding Austrian conceptions of competition — 141

CONTENTS

9 CAPITAL IN FOUNDING AUSTRIAN ECONOMIC THEORY: MENGER VERSUS BÖHM-BAWERK — 146
Introduction: background to the debate — 146
On the definition of goods: Menger and Böhm-Bawerk — 147
Categorizing economic goods — 149
Wealth and its computation — 153
Competing concepts of capital — 162
The meaning of interest for Menger and Böhm-Bawerk — 172
Conclusions — 176

10 MENGERIAN DISTRIBUTION THEORY: WIESER'S CONTRIBUTION — 179
Introduction — 179
Wieser's concept of capital — 180
Capital and the imputation process in a stationary economy — 182
Interest on capital in a stationary economy — 190
Capital and the trend of interest in a progressing economy — 194
The place of Wieser's theory in the founding Austrian tradition — 201

11 THE FOUNDING AUSTRIAN VERSION OF NEOCLASSICAL MICROECONOMICS: SUMMARY AND CONCLUSIONS — 206
Austrian economics in the formative years of neoclassicism — 206
Comparing founding Austrian microeconomics with aspects of contemporary neoclassical economics — 210
Enduring continuities in founding Austrian economics — 221

Notes — 226
Bibliography — 249
Index — 265

FIGURES

1 An Edgeworth–Bowley reconstruction of Mengerian isolated exchange — 68
2 Demand relation for trader B_1 in Menger's auction — 76
3 Böhm-Bawerk's market supply and demand relation — 98
4 Böhm-Bawerk's representation of the time structure of production — 164
5 Hayek's delineation of alternative types of capital — 182

TABLES

1	Menger's table of needs-satisfaction	28
2	Bonar's Mengerian table of needs-satisfaction	29
3	Menger's auction	72
4	Solution to Menger's original auction	73
5	Böhm-Bawerk's auction	94

ACKNOWLEDGEMENTS

I acknowledge the comments and advice of the following individuals on various parts of the manuscript: Ken Blakey, Conrad Blyth, Simon Chapple, Bob Coats, Peter Earl, Barry Gordon, David Harper, Samuel Hollander, Ken Jackson, Steve Jennings, Israel Kirzner, Heinz Kurz, Laurence Moss, Takashi Negishi, Vineeta Prasad, Bill Reindler, Alan Rogers, Erich Streissler, Shigeki Tomo, Lawrence White and Kiichiro Yagi. Parts of the manuscript have also been presented in seminars and conferences at the Universities of Kyoto, Queensland, Toronto, Wollongong, at Australian National University and at Harvard University. I am obliged to numerous participants in these seminars for constructive comments. Thank you as well to the Routledge readers for helpful suggestions on improving the manuscript.

Jeanne Lee and Brent Miller gave much care and attention to editing earlier versions of the manuscript. Special thanks to Susan Horne, who provided quiet space in four different residences in Australasia without which I would not have envisaged completing this monograph (at least by the end of the millennium).

I have made liberal use of material which I have previously published in articles appearing in *History of Political Economy, Journal of Institutional and Theoretical Economics* and the *Review of Austrian Economics*. I wish to thank Duke University Press, J. C. B. Mohr and Kluwer Academic Publishers respectively, for giving permission to use this material.

1

IN WHAT SENSES WERE THE FOUNDING AUSTRIANS 'NEOCLASSICAL' ECONOMISTS?

INTRODUCTION

The founding era of the Austrian tradition in economic theory is the subject of this book. Serious students of Austrian economics will recently have found the intellectual heritage nicely outlined in the first volume of *Classics in Austrian Economics: A Sampling in the History of a Tradition* (1994), edited by Israel Kirzner and subtitled *The Founding Era*. It includes selections for English-speaking readers from the works of the three luminaries in the founding era of Austrian economics: Menger, Wieser and Böhm-Bawerk. These selections, among others, deserve to be expounded and analysed thoroughly. For Kirzner's comprehensive, stimulating introduction to the first volume of his *Classics in Austrian Economics* underscores the urgent need for a more detailed examination of the founding Austrian project in microeconomics. His samples and selections from the founding era give us the impetus to read more Austrian economics at source. For those who want a better understanding of the uniqueness of founding Austrian economics, and an elucidation of the meaning and significance of many articles contained in volume I of Kirzner's *Classics*, this book should be of help. We intend to investigate the ways in which the Austrians were developing an essentially unified project which was different from other founding neoclassical branches of economics.

The intellectual antecedents of modern Austrian economics date from Carl Menger's *Grundsätze der Volkswirtschaftslehre* (1871).[1] We shall hereafter refer to this book as the *Principles of Economics*, following the Dingwall and Hoselitz translation of that great founding treatise in 1950.[2] In the development of modern Austrian economics, the work of Hayek and Mises has been supremely

NEOCLASSICAL MICROECONOMIC THEORY

influential, although both economists have acknowledged their indebtedness to the early Austrians, particularly Menger.[3] Hayek (1994: 44) recollected that he 'really got hooked' on economic theory when he 'found Menger's *Grundsätze*', which was 'such a fascinating book, so satisfying'. Furthermore, for Hayek 'the decisive influence was just reading Menger's *Grundsätze*' (ibid.: 57). Similarly, Mises (1978: 33) admitted: it 'was the reading' of Menger's work 'that made an economist of me'.

In tracing their intellectual origins to Menger's work, modern Austrians are also recognizing, at least implicitly, a distant connection to the so-called marginal 'revolution' in economic theory beginning in the 1870s, to which Menger, Wieser and Böhm-Bawerk were significant contributors.[4] Moreover, in capsule summaries of the Austrian contributions to economic thought from the 1870s up to the 1890s, both Wieser (1891) and Böhm-Bawerk (1891) communicated to English-speaking audiences their conviction that the Austrians were a part of an international movement towards marginalist economics which took place from the 1870s. As Peter Boettke (1994: 1) argued, Wieser's and Böhm-Bawerk's 'self-image' positioned all the Austrians in the 'mainstream of neoclassicism'. The marginalist economics of the 1870s and beyond eventually gave rise to a full-fledged neoclassical movement in economic theorizing which was to dominate economic thought in the twentieth century. However, while the founding Austrians may have contributed much to marginalism understood as a fledgling form of neoclassicism, it is by no means obvious precisely in what respects Menger, Wieser and Böhm-Bawerk may be considered neoclassical economists. The term 'neoclassical' was initially applied retrospectively and rather loosely to a wide body of literature; the Austrians were only one among several groups of economists of different nationalities to have contributed to that literature.[5] The foundations of Austrian microeconomics were developed by Austrians in Austria. However, even lately, a leading historian of twentieth-century Austrian economics has not yet been persuaded that the foregoing 'national distinction reflected any sharp doctrinal differences with neoclassical economics' where the latter remained very broadly defined (Vaughn 1994: 10). It is absolutely critical for our purposes to distinguish between neoclassical microeconomic theory as it might now be conceived *and the history of the development of that theory*. In terms of the history of the neoclassical movement in economic theory we can safely state that there was nothing monolithic about its incipient developmental phase. The early neoclassical movement had included many prominent economists, and one modern neoclassicist was quite prepared to include among these leaders such diverse theorists as 'Böhm-Bawerk, Edgeworth, Gossen, Jevons, Marshall, Menger, Wieser and Wicksell' (Bliss 1987: 883).

RECENT TREATMENTS OF EARLY DEVELOPMENTS IN NEOCLASSICAL ECONOMICS

At a very high level of generality, many leading historians of economic thought in the twentieth century have placed Menger's *Principles of Economics* (1871) alongside Jevons's *Theory of Political Economy* (1871) and Walras's *Eléments d'économique Politique Pure* (published in two parts, 1874 and 1877), in marking the beginning of marginalist economics.[6] Ingrid Rima's survey 'Neoclassicism and Dissent 1890–1925' (1977), located the founding Austrians firmly in the company of Walrasians and Marshallians as fellow neoclassical economists. More recently, John Henry's *The Making of Neoclassical Economics* (1990: 193) referred to the 'Austrian economists' variation on a neoclassical theme'. Ostensibly the Austrian variation was insignificant, particularly with respect to general economic philosophy and ideology. Thus

> One could reproduce the same general position taken by Jevons, Menger and Walras through an examination of the work of any major neoclassical theoretician of the period. Since the neoclassical theory, based on a utility theory of value represents a general ideological perspective, any economist holding such a theory must, if consistent, reach the same general conclusions as to the substantial or essential social questions facing the discipline.
>
> (ibid.: 210)

Apart from maintaining that Menger's achievement lacked distinctiveness, this passage also broaches a subsidiary question: may the ideological content of Austrian economics, or for that matter any other version of early neoclassicism, be separated from its intellectual content? Our answer, following Israel Kirzner (1994: I, xxiv–xxv), is in the affirmative. According to Kirzner, to 'dismiss any portion of...intellectual history as merely the propagandistic pseudo-academic façade for ideological pre-judgments is not only to be grossly unfair to the economists concerned, but also to manufacture shoddy excuses for avoiding grappling with important theoretical argumentation'. This book's focus will be on the microeconomic-theoretic structure of the founding contributions to Austrian economics. Any ideological dimension will be set aside.[7]

Given our desire to find a place for the Austrians as contributors to the neoclassical movement, the more technical meanings of marginalism as an embryonic form of neoclassical economics also deserve consideration here. According to Campus, marginalism was founded on

> the condition of proportionality between prices and marginal utilities for each consumer after exchange i.e. the condition of maximum utility. This condition (which implies the hypothesis of substitution between goods for each consumer when prices vary) gave an analytical basis for downward sloping demand curves for goods, and, with them, to the idea that *given* the quantity produced, relative prices are exclusively determined by marginal utilities, independently of the cost of production of commodities.
>
> (1987: 20; emphasis in original)

An alternative, well-known characterization of early neoclassical economics which aptly summarizes the scope and content of the discipline was offered by Mark Blaug:

> After 1870.... economists typically posited some given supply of productive factors, determined independently by elements outside the purview of analysis. The essence of the economic problem was to search for the conditions under which given productive resources were allocated with optimal results among competing uses, optimal in the sense of maximising consumers' satisfactions. For the first time, economics truly became the science that studies the relationship between *given* ends and *given* scarce means that have alternative uses.
>
> (1978: 310; emphasis in original)

To be sure, rational reconstructions in the history of economic thought may lay claim to finding the equivalent content of some or all of the substantive ideas expressed in these passages in the writings of the founding Austrians. For example, Robert Fisher's

FOUNDING AUSTRIANS – 'NEOCLASSICAL' ECONOMISTS?

The Logic of Economic Discovery: Neoclassical Economics and the Marginal Revolution (1986: 138–54) includes a chapter on Menger which does just this; he concludes that the 'hard core' of Menger's theory reduces to the 'foremost proposition...that individuals attempt to maximize their levels of satisfaction by fulfilling them through the use of goods' (ibid.: 152). However, both Erich Streissler's (1972) programmatic article, which posed the question 'To What Extent Was The Austrian School Marginalist?', and William Jaffé's (1976) dehomogenization of the work of Jevons, Menger and Walras, opened the way for more detailed researches focusing on the differences in substance, for instance, between Menger's version of 'marginalism' and thence of 'neoclassicism', and the contemporary Jevonian and Walrasian versions.

In Sir John Hicks (1976b: 212) we have an explicit denial that a concept of the margin actually distinguished the economics of the 1870s from classical economics. For Hicks, the economists who supposedly originated neoclassicism

> are commonly called 'marginalists', but that is a bad term, for it misses the essence of what was involved. The 'margin' is no more than an expression of the mathematical rule for a maximum (or minimum); any sort of economics is marginalist when it is concerned with maximizing. (Ricardo himself could be quite marginalist at times.) The essential novelty in the work of these economists was that instead of basing their economics on production and distribution, they based it on exchange.

The founding Austrians may definitely be classed among those economists who developed exchange-orientated theories; they therefore played a part in the Hicksian version of the neoclassical movement in economic theory. That the Austrians formulated theories of production and distribution based on exchange relationships is now well accepted. For example, Klaus Hennings (1986: 222) followed Hicks's perspective and considered the work of Menger, Wieser and Böhm-Bawerk as forming a component of the 'analytical core of...neoclassical economic theory'. Thus, according to Hennings, 'supply and demand on markets are *derived* from postulates about individual economic behavior [and this] is the theoretical novelty which distinguishes the neoclassicals from earlier traditions in economic theory' (1986: 222; emphasis in original). In the following chapters we shall reinforce this reading, in particular, by demonstrating that the Austrians offered an approach to the exchange paradigm which differed from that of the other neoclassicists according to the specific assumptions that they made as Austrian economic theorists. The hallmark of economic theorizing in the Austrian tradition emanating from Menger embodied a distinctive vision of individual behaviour and its consequences as manifested on markets.

In his 'Introduction' to *Neoclassical Economic Theory 1870–1930*, Warren Samuels (1990: 3) drew back from expressly including the founding Austrians in his definition of 'neoclassical' economics for that specific period: 'My own general view is that neoclassical economics comprises the work in the tradition of Marshall, Walras and others on how the price mechanism of the market allocates resources in a context of the mechanics of choice from within opportunity sets.' This reluctance to distinguish the Austrians as a category (in a book which included Streissler (1990a) on Menger, Böhm-Bawerk and Wieser) is defensible given research since the 1970s which, partly motivated and informed by developments in modern Austrian economics, has tended, though not without equivocation, to differentiate the founding Austrian contributions from Walrasian and Marshallian streams of economic thought. Phillip Mirowski (1984: 370–1) argued that conventional histories of economic thought did not appreciate that 'the Austrians were not neoclassicals' in the rather special sense that the core of neoclassicism was linked to the rise of energetics in the physical sciences. In particular, Menger was unfamiliar with developments in 'the physics of his time'.[8] Lately, Mirowski (1994: 68) has offered a version of neoclassicism which establishes three exceedingly general criteria for inclusion in the neoclassical fold: '(a) the unapologetic use of mathematics; (b) the importance of concepts of potential from physics... and (c) the attendant variational principle displaying the maximization of a mental entity of uncertain character'. According to Mirowski, the Austrian school was a 'minor rival' of neoclassicism in these senses because it 'eschewed (a)–(c)', although it 'persisted in using a psychologistic language' common to neoclassicism. Nevertheless, recent histories of economic theory from 1870 to 1930 have correctly located the Austrians in a 'neoclassical' movement (Hennings and Samuels 1990), although not squarely in the mainstream of that movement (Streissler 1990a).

FOUNDING AUSTRIAN ECONOMICS AS A BRANCH OF NEOCLASSICISM

This book is the outcome of further research on these differences in both style and substance of thought between the Austrians and other branches of neoclassical economic thought. There are two main themes in the following chapters. The first and central theme relates to the distinctiveness of the founding Austrian approaches to economics as compared to contemporary Walrasian and Marshallian versions of neoclassicism. The second theme focuses on complementarities, unifying threads and differences in perspective among the founding Austrians on *selected* problems in economic theory, where those differences are deemed to be significant. Neither theme will gainsay the view that the early Austrians were in fact neoclassical economists.

Following relevant articles in the *New Palgrave Dictionary of Economics* (Eatwell et al. 1987), it should be noted that the Hicks–Stigler characterization of neoclassical economics, first formulated before 1945, embodied methodological individualism, a subjective theory of value, and a marginal productivity theory of distribution (Aspromourgos 1987: 625). In these very general terms, applying the label 'neoclassical' to the founding Austrian contributions would not be too objectionable.[9] A word of warning should, however, be entered at this point. Modern neoclassical microeconomics analyses individual economic units (consumers, firms and particular markets) and their interactions by building theoretical models of individual behaviour. Most of these models are mathematical and are built on the assumption of optimizing behaviour. Moreover, neoclassical optimization is usually identified with 'rational' behaviour (Varian 1987: 461–2). It would be exceedingly anachronistic to apply the term neoclassical in these strictly modern senses to the work of the founding Austrians. Lawrence White (1985: x) was apparently aware of the dangers which may arise from anachronistic interpretations of early Austrian economics when he remarked self-consciously on 'the "neoclassical" tradition which Menger's own *Principles* helped to launch'.

For the purposes of this study and for the special topics treated in each chapter, we shall take for granted that there were three branches of neoclassical economic theory *emerging* at the time the founding Austrians made their contributions: a Jevonian/Marshallian branch, a Walrasian/Paretian branch and, of course, an Austrian branch.[10] This broad tripartite division conforms closely with that supplied by Donald Winch (1972: 334), who carefully distinguished between 'the English, Austrian, and Walrasian versions of neoclassicism' which were developed and refined *subsequent* to the contributions of Jevons, Menger and Walras.[11] In this connection, while Lavoie (1994: 7) made reference to a 'Mengerian branch of neoclassicism', we shall refer throughout this book to the 'Austrian branch of neoclassicism' *and* to important differences within the Austrian branch. That individual Austrians may have absorbed ideas from other branches of economic thought, including Marshallian economics, Walrasian economics, and historical/institutional economics, will doubtless complicate and enrich our story. Indeed, at various points in the following chapters, differences in theoretical orientation within early Austrian economics will be found to have been due to individual founding Austrians modifying or discarding original Mengerian insights because they remained so open to the influence of other branches of economic theory, both classical economics and other branches of neoclassical economics.

2

THE FOUNDING AUSTRIAN CONCEPTIONS OF ECONOMICS

INTRODUCTION

In outlining overall conceptions of the discipline of economics or political economy from the founding Austrian point of view, methodological issues cannot be avoided, although we intend to give them only a background role in this chapter. Questions of methodology – relating to theory - construction and theory evaluation – have tended to dominate discussion of the historiography of the Austrian School. Here we shall take a different approach. Particular philosophical and methodological issues raised by Menger, Wieser and Böhm-Bawerk are best examined in relation to their context. That is, we will find it more fruitful to remark on the *implications* of early Austrian philosophy and methodology for the construction of specific aspects of Austrian economic theory treated in the following chapters.

The modern interpretative literature on Austrian philosophy and methodology has burgeoned since the 1980s.[1] Some of this literature has been motivated by Menger's contributions to the polemical *Methodenstreit* ('strife of methods') in the 1880s, especially his comprehensive methodological study *Untersuchungen über die Methode der Socialwissenschaften und der politischen Ökonomie insbesondre* (1883).[2] While some points raised by Menger in the debate with the German historicists, especially Gustav Schmoller, will be taken into account, detailed examination of the *Methodenstreit* will also be avoided in this chapter.[3] The principal justification for ignoring the minutiae of the *Methodenstreit* comes from Menger himself. In his obituary of Wilhelm Roscher, Menger ([1875] 1935: 279–80) argued that the real differences between German historical economics and Austrian economics related to their divergent views on the *objectives* of economic research, and the range of problems which the economist aimed to solve. Accordingly, this chapter will be organized around the following questions with respect to the objectives and scope of economic research from the standpoint of Menger, Wieser and Böhm-Bawerk:

1. What was the nature of economics and political economy?
2. How was the discipline to be divided into subdisciplines for the purposes of research, and what subdisciplines captured the founding Austrians' interests? What styles of reasoning did they favour in these subdisciplines?
3. What were the starting-points of economics and political economy? That is, in what *central* problem or problems were the Austrians interested *ab ovo*?

SOME HISTORICAL CONSIDERATIONS REGARDING THE NATURE OF ECONOMICS

Menger's *Grundsätze der Volkswirtschaftslehre* was translated as *Principles of Economics* in 1950. Literally, the German word *Volkswirtschaftslehre* is best translated as 'study of national household management'. As well, together with other founding Austrians, Menger was to use *Nationalökonomie*, *Staatswirtschaft*, *Socialwissenschaften* and *politischen Ökonomie* to refer to the subject-matter under investigation. Menger's *Untersuchungen über die Methode der Socialwissenschaften und der politischen Ökonomie insbesondere* (1883) was originally translated as *Problems of Economics and Sociology* (Menger [1883] 1963) but that was not strictly a literal rendition of the German. When New York University Press republished this work in 1985, a fuller more accurate title was produced: *Investigations into the Methods of the Social Sciences with Special Reference to Economics* (Menger [1883] 1985). Here the translation used the terms 'economics' and 'political economy' (*politischen Ökonomie*) as synonyms. This rendering seemed to accord with Menger's ([1883] 1985: 207) preference.

While the Austrians may have produced several titles for the discipline, depending on the publication, context of a debate, or intended audience, there is nothing to suggest in any of the nomenclature they used that the subject-matter under investigation was significantly different from English classical economics. When Lionel Robbins wrote in *Political Economy Past and Present* (1976: 1) that political economy or economics was concerned with the 'entire universe of discourse of economic science and the theory of economic policy', he was intending that this definition would describe the interests of leading English classical economists; he was also, perhaps inadvertently, describing the outlook of the founding Austrians, whatever variations in title they may have used to label the subject-matter. Menger ([1883] 1985: 207) remarked on the 'totality of theoretical-practical sciences which are included under the concept of political economy' and by 'practical' he meant applied, policy-related work. Menger was especially concerned that the ambit of his investigation embrace 'the science of human economy in general' (ibid.: 208) and he used the term 'economic science' (*Wirtschaftswissenschaft*) to describe the endeavour. Furthermore, the Germanic usages of *Nationalökonomie* and *Volkswirtschaftslehre* (both popular with the founding Austrians) implied that not too much weight should be placed upon distinctions between economies of individual, people, nation or state.[4] In order fully to understand the reasons for reluctance on the part of the founding Austrians to draw these sharp distinctions, we need to consider the pre-history of German and Austrian economic thought.

Any account of the founding Austrians' conception of economics must include recognition of the pre-history of the Austrian School. The precursors of Austrian economics may be located in the philosophy of Aristotle and in the vast medieval Scholastic literature (Kauder 1958 and 1965; Rothbard 1976). More immediate intellectual roots may be located in the cameralist movement in seventeenth- and eighteenth-century Europe. According to Silverman (1990: 69) it was especially the influence of Austrian cameralism that was 'important for the development of the Austrian School [of economics] on account of the way they framed economic questions, not on account of the answers they provided. These questions created the academic ethos in which Menger grew to intellectual maturity.' Exhaustive historical research on European cameralism has demonstrated that at its core was the problem of resource administration for a state: cameralism encompassed, at a rather low level of abstraction, theories of economic policy, and it designed administrative rules to put those theories into practice. The cameralists conflated the economic life of the individual in society with the economic life of the nation. Much of their written work comprised descriptions of institutions, events and policy problems. The practical appreciation of the functions of economic activities preoccupied the pre-nineteenth-century cameralists:

Indeed, the cameralists of the seventeenth century wrote largely independently of any comprehensive system of thought, concentrating upon recording practical maxims without much regard to the principles that might underlie them' (Silverman 1990: 77).[5]

The sceptical attitude towards long chains of abstract reasoning so common in cameralist literature was carried over into German economic thought in the nineteenth century (ibid.: 85). However, there also developed a more theoretically orientated stream of cameralism which influenced Carl Menger.

Menger had studied K. Heinrich Rau's *Lehrbuch der politischen Ökonomie* (1826) – a book which had a significant pedagogic role in German economics in the nineteenth century. (It was republished several times up to 1876.) Rau paid obeisance to the German cameralist tradition before attempting to establish a new orthodoxy within that tradition. He based this orthodoxy on 'the theory of economic life' which he called *Volkswirtschaftslehre* (Tribe 1988: 190–1). Furthermore, Rau did not identify *politischen Ökonomie* with the state. The study of *Staatswirtschaftslehre* was concerned with the revenue and expenditure of the state. Rau's *Lehrbuch* began with a definition of the nature and scope of *Volkswirtschaftslehre*: it 'develops those characteristic laws which can be perceived in the economic activities of peoples *regardless of the intervention of government*' (quoted in Tribe 1988: 194; emphasis added). This definition is remarkably consistent with the scope of Menger's *Principles* in particular, since the interplay between humans and their need for goods was, for Menger, the central problem for the theoretical discipline of *Volkswirtschaftslehre*. It was Wieser who extended this founding Austrian interest to *Staatswissenschaftslehre* in *Natural Value* ([1889] 1930) and later in his *Social Economics* ([1914] 1927). Rau primarily focused on the administration of resources (or goods) in a means–ends, economizing framework. Goods were defined in a subjective sense; human want-satisfaction was the centrepiece of economic theory, which was devoted to establishing the rules for acquisition, maintenance and utilization of those goods. So established, the rules directed economizing behaviour both for individuals and for a people conceived as a group, nation or state. All these elements of economic theory were bequeathed to the Austrian economists in the late nineteenth century (Silverman 1990: 88).

FOUNDING AUSTRIAN CONCEPTIONS OF ECONOMICS

The influence of German classical and cameralist economics, with its emphasis on the subjective character of resource administration, was supremely important for the structure and content of Menger's *Principles* (Streissler 1990a and 1994). Menger's well-known dedication of the *Principles* to Wilhelm Roscher was one important allusion to the influence of German economics on his work. There is also the remark in the 'Preface' that 'the reform attempted here of the most general principles of our subject is therefore built on a foundation which has been laid almost entirely by the efforts of German researchers' (Menger [1871] 1950: xlviii). Wieser ([1889] 1930: xxxiv) admitted candidly that the 'German school long ago formulated the conceptions, leaving for us [the Austrians] only the task of filling them out.... In this it has laid up a treasure from which all succeeding economic effort may draw indefinitely.' Böhm-Bawerk (1890: 268) praised 'the rich German literature on value which has lately culminated in the theory of final utility'. We will note the influence of particular German classical ideas on specific aspects of the founding Austrian contributions to economic theory in the following chapters.

THE SCOPE OF AUSTRIAN ECONOMICS AND ITS ASSOCIATED STYLES OF REASONING

In the course of the *Methodenstreit*, Menger exhorted its participants to concentrate on obtaining 'full clarity concerning the whole complex of problems requiring investigation in the field of economics'; otherwise, he feared the preponderance of 'one-sided attitudes', with deleterious consequences for the development of economic science ([1889] 1994: 3). While he was not explicit about these consequences, he appeared to view with great consternation the prospect that those practitioners of historical economics holding a 'one-sided' attitude would promote an imperialistic takeover of the entire discipline. The 'field of political economy' included three main branches of inquiry classified according to the methods of approaching reality:

1 historical and statistical economics, which of necessity presupposed a 'collective' or aggregative approach to economic phenomena;
2 the theoretical 'science of human economy', divided into two branches: 'exact-theoretical' and 'empirical-theoretical' economics;

3 practical or applied economic science, including the study of economic policy; resource administration for public authorities and the science of finance which had a didactic role for private individuals *and* governments.

(Menger [1883] 1985: 208–11; [1889] 1994: 4–7)

These three main branches constituted in their totality the science of 'national economy'. The third branch presupposed acquaintance with the second, viz. theoretical economics.[6] Now it was patently clear by the time of the last major founding Austrian contribution to economic theory, that is, Wieser ([1914] 1927), that Menger, Wieser and Böhm-Bawerk were primarily interested in developing the *theoretical* branch of the science of national economy. Nevertheless, Wieser ([1889] 1930: Book VI; [1914] 1927: Book III) completed some peripheral work on economic policy under 3 above. Menger took great pains to stress that it was one-sided, intolerant attitudes to any of these branches of economic science that he was railing against in the debate with the German historicists.[7]

Against the exaggerated claims of the historical school, Menger emphasized the importance of, and the methods and styles of reasoning required for, a theoretical science of economics. The analysis of 'complex phenomena', in particular the need to trace these phenomena back to their ultimate foundation blocks – to 'psychological causes or to ultimate component elements that would still be accessible to perceptual verification' (Menger [1889] 1994: 3) – was the task of Menger's theoretical economics. A genetic approach was also indispensable to theoretical economics because 'economic phenomena are temporal events and...show developments that...attract the attention of theoretical inquiry' (ibid.: 4). A veritable mass of statistics and laboured descriptions of concrete events would not substitute for Menger's theoretical branch of economic science.

It is important to recognize that Menger's theoretical economics was *part* of the 'search for an understanding of reality'. The mind, when concentrated in its theoretical endeavours, was capable of directly grasping the essential qualities of economic phenomena. To state rather plainly that Menger was proposing an X-ray technique for the study of economics would not be too much of a simplification. Whereas historical, statistical and policy-orientated branches of economic science were interested in concrete events in space and time, Mengerian theoretical economics sought knowledge of the 'general nature and... general interrelations (i.e. relations of coexistence and succession among generally determined phenomena)' (Menger [1889] 1994: 5). Theoretical economics has two principal divisions yielding exact and empirical laws. Lawrence White (1985: xi) neatly explained this distinction: exact-theoretical reasoning yields laws or propositions of the general form 'if condition A and B hold, then condition C must also follow'; and empirical-theoretical reasoning yields laws or propositions of the general form 'A and B are usually accompanied by C'. The two laws provided different types of information or knowledge about economic phenomena. Menger ([1883] 1985: 140) insisted that only a *combination* of these two types of theoretical reasoning would 'procure for us the deepest theoretical understanding' of economic phenomena.[8] In neither case should the two terms 'exact' or 'empirical' be understood as necessarily referring to measurable quantities. It would be premature at this point to assess, in the abstract, the advantages and limitations of Menger's division of theoretical economics into exact and empirical dimensions.[9]

Two comparisons with other leading contemporary marginalist 'revolutionary' thinkers in the 1870s are in order at this point. William Stanley Jevons used the term 'exact' in the sense of 'precisely measurable' (see Winch 1972: 330). Léon Walras's conception of theoretical economics superficially paralleled Menger's notion of exact economics. For Walras, pure economic theory studied 'the ineluctable conditions that are imposed by the nature of things. This part consists of an application of logic to economic propositions. In postulating any hypotheses, it must be asked, in pure science, what must necessarily follow from it' (Jaffé 1983: 127; his emphasis). However, the similarities between Walras's and Menger's conceptions are only superficial, since Walras proceeded to use mathematics exclusively to seek out the implications of theoretical propositions – propositions which were considered to be fundamentally relationships between quantities. Furthermore, Walras's propositions carried with them a conception of causality based on mutual interdependence which Menger could not accept. We shall return to this matter in more detail and to the founding Austrian conception of genetic causality (as opposed to mutual interdependence) when considering specific aspects of Menger's, Wieser's and Böhm-Bawerk's theoretical work in the following chapters.[10]

Wieser and Böhm-Bawerk retained the styles of reasoning favoured by Menger. Menger ([1889] 1994: 3) merely hinted that theoretical economics must trace economic phenomena back to their 'psychological causes'. Much later, Wieser ([1914] 1927: 3-4) expanded on what he believed to be the 'psychological' orientation of economic theory – theory which, it should be stated, paralleled Menger's 'exact' theory in most important respects. The '"psychological" theory of economics' was developed by introspection, that is, by 'observations concerning the inner life of man'. According to Wieser, no 'theorist will be able to ignore his practical consciousness of economic relations'. In Joseph Schumpeter, Wieser had found an author who had ignored this practical consciousness, to the detriment of theory construction. Thus in his first book, *Das Wesen und der Hauptinhalt der Theoretischen Nationalökonomie (1908)*, Schumpeter had supposedly ignored the lessons of 'inner observation' (Innere Beobachtung). Furthermore, Schumpeter's book had attempted to reconcile the irreconcilable – namely the central propositions and concepts of Austrian and Walrasian economics. His attempt failed because he neglected to appreciate that Austrian theory, unlike Walrasian economics, was founded on introspection.

Wieser ([1911] 1994: 290) also complained: 'Schumpeter wants to observe economic facts from outside alone... whereas the psychological method observes them above all from inside one's consciousness.' Important aspects of the economy are 'practically familiar to all of us' (Wieser [1914] 1927: 6). The boundaries of economic theorizing have the same limits as 'common experience'. Historical and statistical investigation were valuable branches of economic science but entirely separate from theoretical economics. All branches involved the task of observing reality. Indeed, even '[t]rue economic theory shuns speculation in a vacuum' (ibid.: 7).[11] Economic theory, however, is the outcome of a severe process of idealizing and simplifying, unlike other fields of economic science. Nevertheless, despite methodological differences, the character of knowledge yielded from each branch of economic science was different, yet complementary. In remarking on the inability of the economic theorist to 'show the full picture' of economic reality, Wieser concluded:

> Some details can result only from historical proof, statistical compilation or the insights vouchsafed to a statesman in uninterrupted contact with national life.... They may be inserted only when theory enlists the continuous labours of other scientific methods, of practical politics even.
> ([1914] 1927: 7)

FOUNDING AUSTRIAN CONCEPTIONS OF ECONOMICS

Wieser came close to expressing Menger's concern to reserve a place for empirical-theoretical research in the economic sciences. He registered dissatisfaction with the notion that simplification and 'extreme abstraction' on their own constituted the entire domain of theoretical economics. For the economic theorist also aimed, '[s]tep by step by a system of decreasing abstraction' to render the assumptions of idealized theoretical constructions 'more concrete and multiform' (ibid.). That is to say, Wieser favoured a form of successive approximation in economic theorizing, much as Menger had argued that only a *combination* of exact-theoretical and empirical-theoretical research would do justice to the subject-matter of theoretical economics. Later in the Austrian tradition, Richard Strigl (1923) nicely brought together these founding Austrian approaches to theoretical economics. For Strigl, the 'structure of theoretical economics...takes the form of a pyramid, whose apex is made up of pure theory. Making our way down towards the base, we reach ever more special theories with an ever broader content and an ever smaller field of application' (Haberler [1923–4] 1994: 224).

There were differences on matters of detail between Menger and Wieser on the precise nature and function of theoretical economics; they differed in so far as Wieser, unlike Menger, believed that the construction of broad 'special theories' (as Strigl called them), would have favourable feedback effects on the formulation of pure theories. Wieser implicitly rejected Menger's notion of exact theory, by insisting that it could be reformulated in the light of research on 'special theories' which employed empirical-theoretical constructs. Wieser used what he called the 'most idealized assumptions' imaginable to construct a theory of 'the simple economy' in Book I of *Social Economics* ([1914] 1927); he then allowed for the intervention of what Menger would have regarded as non-economic phenomena (that is, inequalities of power which Menger would have treated by empirical-theoretical reasoning) in the 'theory of social economy' in *Social Economics*, Book II. In his theory of social economy, disturbances to the 'ideal' brought about by the occurrence of power modified the results of Wieser's idealized (or 'exact') approach in the earlier part of *Social Economics*. We shall discuss at greater length Wieser's theory of social economy in some of the following chapters.

At this point it is pertinent to compare the formal differences between Menger's and Wieser's styles of reasoning implied by their respective conceptions of economic theory. In short, Wieser ([1911] 1994: 295) proposed that pure theory idealized economic phenomena using 'temporary assumptions which in the end have to be corrected'. By contrast, Menger believed that exact theories had universal, logical validity and transmitted unique insights into the structure, co-existence and succession of economic phenomena. For Menger, exact theories may well have limited applicability; they were not meant to predict, for the theorist, observable outcomes consequent upon the actual interrelations between *specific* economic phenomena. His expression of two laws of demand made this clear:

> The exact law states that *with definite presuppositions* an increase in need...must be followed by an increase in prices just as definite by measure. The empirical law states that an increase in need *as a rule* is actually followed by one in *real* prices, and, to be sure, an increase which as a rule stands in a certain relationship to the increase in need, even if this relationship by no means can be determined in an exact way. The first law holds for all times and all nations which exhibit a traffic in goods. The latter allows exceptions even within one definite nation, and for each market is easily a different one to be determined only by observation, as far as the *measure* of the effects of demand on prices is concerned.
> (Menger ([1883] 1985: 72; his emphasis)

Menger would therefore have objected to Wieser's adjective 'temporary' when applied to the assumptions of exact economic theory. The assumptions of exact theory would in no way have to be 'corrected' to suit specific, actual economic phenomena under study, for that procedure would be tantamount to formulating a completely different theory – in fact an *empirical-theoretical* construct.[12] Altogether, the differences between Menger's and Wieser's conceptions of economics, particularly their conceptions of theoretical work, may be regarded as terminological more than substantial.[13] In crucial respects Wieser can be said to have supplemented Menger's insights, especially on the importance of introspection in giving 'empirical' content to what Menger had obliquely referred to as the 'psychological causes' of interest to the economist.

Böhm-Bawerk's article on 'The Historical Versus the Deductive Method in Political Economy' (1890) was a consistent, if unsophisticated, attempt to show his allegiance to the founding Austrian classification of the economic sciences earlier offered by Menger. It was also a crude effort to reinforce his own preference to practise 'deductive' economics as against historical work; it was hardly a careful statement of his conception of economics. Böhm-Bawerk expressly defended Menger's notion of exact theory but he redefined it for his own purposes as the 'abstract-deductive' method of theoretical economics (ibid.: 247). Again, much might be made of this terminological emendation by those interested in Böhm-Bawerk's methodology of economics *vis-à-vis* Menger's (Alter 1990a: 226–7). It is contended in this book that matters of founding Austrian methodology – of theory construction and evaluation – are best considered in relation to their substantive consequences, if any, in the practice of economic theorizing. Menger, Wieser and Böhm-Bawerk accepted that their objective was to offer sounder theoretical foundations for economic science. Menger and Wieser (but not Böhm-Bawerk) distinguished different levels or styles of theoretical reasoning. Our concern is with the points of separation and points of commonality which can be discerned in their respective theoretical endeavours while taking these different reasoning styles as given.

THE STARTING-POINT OF FOUNDING AUSTRIAN ECONOMIC THEORY

The questions which Menger frames in the first chapter of the *Principles* have their referents in highly subjective individual purposes and economizing activities. He explained some time later in the *Investigations* that theoretical research in economics has to provide microfoundations for all economic phenomena and that these foundations are located in individual behaviour:

> Thus the phenomena of 'national economy' are by no means direct expressions of the life of a nation as such or direct results of an 'economic nation'. They are, rather, the *results* of all the unnumerable individual economic efforts in the nation.... Whoever wants to understand theoretically the phenomena of a 'national economy' and those complicated human phenomena which we are accustomed to designate with this expression, must for this reason attempt to go back to their *true* elements, to the *individual economies in the nation*, and to investigate the laws by which the former are built up from the latter.
>
> (Menger [1883] 1985: 93; his emphasis)

NEOCLASSICAL MICROECONOMIC THEORY

At the risk of oversimplification, in modern garb we may say that Menger's goal was to provide a microeconomics rooted in individual behaviour. However variegated in terms of the problems chosen for investigation, most of the founding Austrian contributions to economics, as we shall see in the following chapters, had a microeconomic orientation. The first impulse of the Austrians was to locate the starting-point of any analysis of the economy in the wants, decisions and activities, perceptions and opinions of individuals. We turn now to a capsule summary of Menger's point of departure as an illustration.

If we take Menger's *Principles* as the archetype, his well-known starting-point serves as a splendid example of the founding Austrian interest in individuals' subjective perceptions and valuation processes. The term 'processes' is entirely apposite here because there is a clear implication in Menger's theory of goods that human valuation takes place *in time*.[14] Given that goods are the determinants of human well-being, Menger investigated their nature from the point of view of the valuing individual whose purpose it was to use goods to satisfy wants. The four necessary and jointly sufficient conditions which have to be satisfied for a thing (or service) to become a good are then stated: (1) there has to be a human want or need (used as synonyms here); (2) the thing has to have properties ensuring needs-satisfaction; (3) the causal connection between a thing's properties and needs-satisfaction have to be *recognized* by the individual; and (4) command over the thing has to be guaranteed (Menger [1871] 1950: 52). Any qualitative attribute of a good was not a property of the thing itself, but merely a *perceived* relation between that thing and human wants. Knowledge is therefore a vital consideration for the economic theorist as observer – since the condition that makes the satisfaction of any individual's wants dependent on a good has a subjective character, viz., perception, recognition and understanding.

Menger proceeded to construct a hierarchy of goods, placing consumer goods in the first order, and various intermediate or producers' goods in the second, third, etc., orders of the hierarchy.[15] As before, Menger's classification has no objective basis; it is not pre-given by objective properties of the goods themselves. From the point of view of the individual, a good's place in the hierarchy depends on its subjectively perceived role in producing first-order consumer goods. The value of producers' goods is then deliberated upon; since production and deliberation take time, valuation is a prospective phenomenon derived from the potentially changeable expectation that the first-order consumer goods, once produced, will ultimately satisfy wants to a certain degree.[16] For the economist as observer, the relationship between goods and human wants is one of cause and effect: goods have a causal relation to their effect – that is, human needs-satisfaction and the primary causes are located in the human mind. A secondary cause resides in the ability of the human agent actively to command (a cameralist would have said 'to administrate') those goods over time to ensure needs-satisfaction.

In 1876, Wieser proposed that the economist would derive the maximum advantage in theory-construction by starting with 'the simplest form in which the economic process' was to be observed (Wieser [1876] 1994: 207). Accordingly, the individual 'engaging in economic activity' was the subject of Wieser's initial attention. His article 'On the Relationship of Costs to Value' ([1876] 1994) sought to demonstrate how the individual's use of producers' goods of higher order to produce lower-order consumers' goods led to a valuation being placed on those producers' goods. This process of valuation is later described by Wieser in *Natural Value* ([1889] 1930: xxx) as the 'essence of things in economics'. Wieser insisted that there are 'laws' underlying valuation processes which need to be ascertained; they are the basis for 'political economy' just as the 'law of gravity is to mechanics'. Purportedly, the Austrians offered a new foundation for the theory of value (Wieser 1891; [1889] 1930: xxxi). The 'starting point of the wider investigation' into valuation processes was founded on a fundamental insight that 'value falls as goods increase'. Wieser continued:

> the want for the same things – even in the same person and in given economic conditions – is of quite different strengths, varying according to the degree in which the want has already been satisfied through employment of goods. But since the employment of goods depends on the amount of goods which one possesses, the quantity of goods obtains a decisive influence on the valuation of wants and so on the source of value itself.
>
> ([1889] 1930: xxxii)

Wieser cast the problem of economics in the same terms as Menger: the act referred to as the 'employment of goods' is at the heart of the discipline known to both Menger and Wieser as

NEOCLASSICAL MICROECONOMIC THEORY

Volkswirtschaftslehre, or economics, or political economy. The Wieserian act of employing goods has equivalent counterparts in the cameralist notion of resource administration, and in Menger's 'command' condition for a thing to be classified as a good. The opening chapters of Wieser's *Natural Value* represented a continuation and elaboration of Menger's work on the theory of goods and their valuation. Wieser's excursions into valuation were more detailed than Menger's. We may enumerate the titles of some of Wieser's chapters in Book I of *Natural Value* to illustrate Wieser's broad vista on value-theory:

i   The Origin of Value
ii The Value of Satisfactions of Want
iii Gossen's Law of the Satiation of Want
iv The Scales of Satiation
v   Marginal Utility
vi The Value of Future Satisfactions of Want
vii The Value of Goods
viii Valuation of a Single Commodity
ix The Valuation of Goods in Stocks
x   The Paradox of Value
xi The Antinomy of Value and the Service of Value
                    (Wieser [1889] 1930: xxxvii–xxxviii)

Böhm-Bawerk ([1881] 1962) also began his career by studying the theory of goods and their valuation (see Chapter 9 for more details). In this early work, Böhm-Bawerk foreshadowed a pre-eminent desire to re-work the theory of production, and his monumental studies in the 1880s on the theory of capital and interest brought this desire to full fruition (Böhm-Bawerk [1884] 1932; [1889] 1923; 1959a; 1959b).

Böhm-Bawerk (1891: 379, 381) made the important point that the day-to-day relationship between an individual (a 'Crusoe') and the 'external goods' used to satisfy wants is a deceptively simple one. Underneath the mundane simplicities, however, are 'endless complications', which are subject to 'fixed laws' – laws which it requires 'all the acumen' of the theoretical economist to discover. It is notable that Menger also began his analysis of 'human economy' with what he called the 'simplest case'. This was a case where he supposed 'that an isolated economizing individual inhabits a rocky island in the sea, that he finds only a single spring on the island, and that he is exclusively dependent upon it for satisfaction of his need for fresh water' (Menger [1871] 1950: 133). It would nevertheless be a caricature to represent the founding Austrians as being preoccupied with the isolated Crusoe economy. For the prime task of the economist in the Austrian perspective was to discover the laws relating goods and wants; thereafter the economist was charged with the extent to which these laws were relevant to 'the conduct of men in economic interconnection with one another' (Böhm-Bawerk 1891: 381).[17] Similarly, in his *Social Economics* ([1914] 1927), Wieser investigated valuation processes in his theory of the 'simple economy' and then moved on to analyse an economy in which the relations between individuals modified the valuation and pricing processes observable for an isolated individual in a 'simple economy'.

True to the Mengerian foundations of Austrian economics, Böhm-Bawerk's starting assumption was that individual consumers evaluate consumption goods directly and producers' goods indirectly. Moreover, producers' goods have prospective values, depending on the valuations placed on consumption goods that are promised from production in the future. Values are transmitted from consumers' goods *to* the producers' goods used in their production. This starting insight provided the basis for all the founding Austrian approaches to the theory of production, of capital and of supply in general. In this connection, the Austrian research orientation was adumbrated by Böhm-Bawerk (1891: 371) in an article written for English-speaking readers. He sought to substantiate the rhetorical question 'Is cost, the value of materials of production, in spite of all contradictory appearances, the variable part, determined by the value of the product?' For Böhm-Bawerk, as for the other founding Austrians, it was no mere hyperbole to maintain that this question was 'as fundamental for political economy as the question between the Ptolemaic and Copernican systems was for astronomy. The sun and earth turn... but one cannot be much of an astronomer to-day without knowing whether the earth turns about the sun or the sun about the earth.'[18]

3
CARL MENGER'S ANALYSIS OF CHOICE

INTRODUCTION

For the founding Austrians, economic analysis always started from a study of individual choice-making or economizing. Their analyses of choice were constructed by specifying constraints on choice very loosely, at least by the standards of modern neoclassical microeconomics.

According to received historiography, Lionel Robbins's *Essay on the Nature and Significance of Economic Science* (1932), borrowing expressly from Austrian economics, defined economics as a science of choice. Economics was considered a study of allocative behaviour, of choices to distribute given scarce means among given competing ends. According to Robbins ([1932] 1984: 16), economics is 'the science which studies human behaviour as a relationship between ends and scarce means which have alternative uses'. This definition finally superannuated the older classical restriction on the scope of economics to the causes of material welfare (Robbins [1932] 1984: 21). Immediately upon stating his definition, Robbins acknowledged Austrian economists Menger, Mises and Strigl as precursors.[1] In a masterly review article on Robbins's *Essay*, Souter (1933: 377) perceived that Robbins had contributed a 'scholarly and succinct account of the main tenets of "The Austrian School"' in its contemporary state. It is now acknowledged that the influence of Menger on Robbins's definition was distant and diffuse, and that the treatment of the economics of choice as *exclusively* a study of the pure logic-of-choice was not fully established until the arrival of later Austrian contributions (O'Brien 1988: 26–7, 184 n. 45). Rather than Menger (1871), it was Strigl (1923) that forged strong links with Robbins's position in the *Essay* (Fraser 1937: 30; Hutchison 1981: 226).[2]

MENGER'S ANALYSIS OF CHOICE

To the founding Austrians, particularly Menger, is correctly attributed the establishment of 'foundations of what later has been called the pure logic-of-choice' (Hayek 1978: 276; also Stegmüller 1973: 286–7). Menger, Wieser and Böhm-Bawerk also suggested *additional*, although not identical, foundations for *broader* analyses of choice conceived as economizing behaviour which this chapter and the one that follows will explore.

Menger, Wieser and Böhm-Bawerk were open to including within the ambit of 'economics' various ethical, psychological and even biological matters. That is, they believed that the analysis of economizing was dependent for its further advancement on interdisciplinary insights which needed to, but might not be, developed *pari passu* if the boundaries of economics were drawn too rigidly. By contrast, it was precisely a desire to 'delimit the spheres of economics and other social sciences' that had motivated Robbins's quest for a new definition of economics as an autonomous discipline (Robbins [1932] 1984: xxxv). Contemporary reviewers of the *Essay* noticed that while the scope of economics had in one sense been broadened by Robbins's definition to include all allocative processes involving purposive behaviour, in another sense economists were called back from investigating so-called peripheral matters which rested on the frontiers of ethics, psychology, sociology and the like (Souter 1933: 378, 382–3; Fraser 1937: 29, 34). For instance, as is well-known, Robbins insisted that preferences or the desired ends of human behaviour be taken as stable, given data by economists. Moreover, in so far as the ends of Robbinsian allocative behaviour were regarded as desirable or conferring 'utility' for the economizer, these ends begged no ethical or psychological questions in Robbins's estimation ([1932] 1984: 32; 56 n. 2, 84–6). All this was entirely compatible with later Austrian preoccupations, for example those of Strigl (1923) and Mises (1949), who attempted to de-psychologize the utility concept with which the ends of economizing were associated.[3]

Here we need to specify a distinction between the general Austrian concern with theories of economizing, which had substantial identity with later, more refined formulations of the logic-of-choice, and the concern of Menger, Wieser and Böhm-Bawerk to go beyond a restrictive logic-of-choice framework. It would be misleading to draw the contrast too sharply, principally because Menger, Wieser and Böhm-Bawerk evidently did not see conflict between the two lines of inquiry. Nevertheless, the great founding Austrian triumvirate would have seen pure logic-of-choice analysis as too limiting. In ways which were not altogether uniform or systematic, they explored other approaches.[4] Accordingly, emphasis here will be placed on the more generously drawn boundaries for the analysis of economizing as conceived by Menger, Wieser and Böhm-Bawerk. We have been led perforce to offer a close textual analysis of much-neglected aspects of founding Austrian theories on the nature, scope, purpose and process of economizing behaviour.

FIRST PRINCIPLES

Economizing was described by Menger in the *Principles* (1871) as a complex of purposive human actions striving to achieve needs-satisfaction (*Bedürfnissefriedigung*) ([1871] 1950: 116).[5] No special motive such as self-interest was implied by his definition, although later in the *Investigations*, Menger ([1883] 1985: 87) maintained that self-interest was 'by far the most common and powerful' motive for economizing. Knowledge of a causal relationship between the ends of economizing and available quantities of goods was an important presupposition, otherwise an individual's activities would have no purpose. Economizing for the individual agent (*Wirtschaftendes Individuum*),involved: (1) a desire to possess units of a good which are perceived to be related to needs-satisfaction (possession and knowledge); (2) choice between the more important needs, and needs that must be left unsatisfied (needs ranking and choice); (3) satisfaction of needs 'in the most appropriate manner' with a given quantity of goods (non-maximization); and (4) conservation of a good's useful properties for the satisfaction of future needs (conservation and futurity) (Menger [1871] 1950: 95–6). By 'goods' in this discussion Menger meant economic goods, that is scarce goods relative to requirements for them. These goods are 'scarce means', and human needs can roughly be equated with 'ends' in logic-of-choice analysis. However, in ways that advanced beyond Robbinsian, logic-of-choice strictures Menger proceeded to delimit the nature of economic phenomena, to investigate the structure of needs, to speculate on the interrelationships between economic activity and the development of needs through time, and to retain the principle of non-maximization. We shall begin with the last issue, since the principle of non-maximization in Menger's work has caused confusion among historians of economic thought. Thosehistorians steeped in the Marshallian and Walrasian traditions have been especially perplexed by this principle.[6]

MENGER'S ANALYSIS OF CHOICE

THE MENGERIAN ECONOMIZER

Maximization in economic theory now has a strictly mathematical meaning. In elementary utility theory, to depict the maximizer's choice as one which is made at the minimum point of the relevant marginal utility function, and the maximum point of the corresponding total utility function, is to describe a state of rest in which consumption of a good is pushed to the point where its marginal utility is in fact equal to zero. Jevons and Walras, but not Menger, would have recognized marginal utility as the increment of satisfaction deriving from the last unit consumed – the first derivative of total utility with respect to the quantity consumed. In other words, Jevons and Walras would have given their approbation to the use of the differential calculus to describe economizing behaviour. Scarcity, of course, implies that for the individual economizer as a maximizer, the marginal utility will remain positive for some goods, given an individual's resource-constraint. The simple, well-known condition required for an individual to maximize utility for any pair of goods –

$$\frac{\text{marginal utility of good x}}{\text{price of good x}} = \frac{\text{marginal utility of good y}}{\text{price of good y}}$$

– is another way of stating that the individual will allocate resources so as to make the utilities gained from the last unit of resources expended (e.g. money) on good x and good y equal, given some resource-constraint.

That there was no such analysis of consumer maximization in Menger's *Principles* is plain from a reading of relevant sections of his analysis of consumer needs-satisfaction. There is no concept of continuity or of differentiability in his numerical delineation of scales of importance used to sketch needs-rankings (Noyes 1948: II, 1292–9). Menger's tabulation is reproduced below.

When Stigler (1937: 239) perused this table he expressed frustration at 'Menger's failure to develop generally the method by which the individual maximizes his want-satisfaction'. Even the notion of optimization (constrained maximization), with consumption taking place subject to an explicit resource-constraint, is absent from Menger's discussion of Table 1. The next significant interpretation in the literature of history of economic thought came from Hutchison (1953: 141), and here we find a somewhat more sympathetic reading: 'Menger is simply concerned to point out how needs may

Table 1 Menger's table of needs-satisfaction

Goods or classes of goods consumed by an individual, ranked according to their needs

	I	II	III	IV	V	VI	VII	VIII	IX	X
Additions to individual's well-being resulting from acts of consumption, expressed in scales of importance (Bedeutung)	10	9	8	7	6	5	4	3	2	1
	9	8	7	6	5	4	3	2	1	0
	8	7	6	5	4	3	2	1	0	
	7	6	5	4	3	2	1	0		
	6	5	4	3	2	1	0			
	5	4	3	2	1	0				
	4	3	2	1	0					
	3	2	1	0						
	2	1	0							
	1	0								
	0									

Source: Menger [1871] 1950: 127; annotations added.

be arranged in order and does not even formulate a principle of diminishing marginal utility.' Indeed, the tabulated data do not readily lend themselves to a straightforward, mathematical–marginalist interpretation.[7] Certainly Menger, unlike Jevons or Walras, did not take the subjective value or utility of goods as given; he derived it from the importance of the wants that the goods would be used to satisfy.[8] Nicholas Georgescu-Roegen (1968: 250–1) has advanced one of the most compelling interpretations of Menger's table of needs-satisfaction – compelling in the sense that it makes claims for Menger's ideas which the original text can bear. Thus, according to this interpretation, there is a weak sense in which Menger attributed a 'marginal' calculating procedure to the economizer. It was a simple ordinalist procedure going by the standards of utility theory as it developed in the twentieth century. For McCulloch (1977), Menger gave the initial impetus for the development of a theory of ordinal marginal utility, and this view has retained its plausibility in the light of recent evidence becoming available from Menger's 1876 lectures (to Crown Prince Rudolf). In those lectures he stated that the 'importance of certain goods is inversely proportional to a person's wealth' (Menger [1889] 1994: 37).[9]

As early as 1888, James Bonar produced Table 2 (below) which lends some weight to Georgescu-Roegen's interpretation. Bonar pointed out that the 'arithmetic of the table would not bear to be pressed. The difference in degree of importance between

Table 2 Bonar's Mengerian table of needs-satisfaction

Degree	I Food	II Clothing	III Lodging	IV Smoking
First	Necessary for life.			
Second	Necessary for health.	First suit, necessary.		
Third	Agreeable.	Second suit, convenient.	1 room.	
Fourth	Less keenly agreeable.	Third suit desirable.	2 rooms.	4 pipes a day.
Fifth	Still less keenly agreeable.	Fourth suit, unacceptable.	3 rooms.	8 pipes a day.
Sixth	Satiety.	Fifth suit, satiety.	4 rooms, satiety.	Satiety.

Source: Bonar 1888: 8.

one meal when it is the only accessible one and one meal when it is *any* one of five alternate meals is not as 5 to 1, but as infinity to 1' (1888: 8; his emphasis). In fact Menger explained that the economizer does not perceive the absolute but only the relative importance of wants ([1871] 1950: 128). It has been problematic for researchers that Menger's use of integers suggests that the economizer makes cardinal utility measurements. As a representation of the activity of economizing, Menger generally presumed that the mental evaluation process resorted to ordinal comparisons. We may also appeal to Hayek's (1934: 401) authority in interpreting Menger on this point:

> Although he speaks occasionally of value as measurable, his exposition makes it quite clear that the value of any one commodity can be expressed by naming another commodity of equal value. Of the figures which he uses to represent scales of utility...it [is] perfectly clear that he thinks of them not as cardinal, but as ordinal figures.[10]

None the less, in restricting his one example of utility measurement (above) to integer values it cannot be maintained that Menger conceived of satisfactions or marginal satisfactions in terms of infinitesimal magnitudes, as is the hallmark of a full-blown marginalist approach to economizing. Hence Jaffé's (1976: 521) remark that Menger's economizer was modelled as being 'incapable of making *finely calibrated* decisions in pursuit of satisfaction' (emphasis added). If Menger possessed a concept of marginal satisfaction or marginal utility, it was used to express broad 'estimates out of a given stock of goods, such estimates declining by leaps and bounds when more units were added to the stock' (Pribram 1983: 290).

Economizing behaviour conceived as 'maximizing' may be considered to have its counterpart in the rather loose Mengerian notion that individuals will take the most efficient course in pursuing their objectives. In that case Menger can be said to have had much in common with Jevons, Walras and Pareto. As we have already stated, the *sine qua non* for a marginalist approach to choice is a precise mathematical concept of the margin. However, Menger nowhere concerned himself with ascertaining relative maximum values of total satisfactions (in functional form), or minimum values of marginal satisfactions (in functional form). Menger neither referred to maximization, nor for that matter used mathematical terminology. Crown Prince Rudolf reported that in his early 1876 lectures Menger defined economic goods and then proceeded to explain how economizing individuals endeavour 'to employ the quantity of these goods available so as to satisfy needs with the smallest possible amount, thereby *satisfying the greatest possible number of needs*' (Menger [1889] 1994: 35; emphasis added). The phrases he used in the *Principles* included: 'to satisfy a person's needs completely' ([1871] 1950: 79); 'most effective satisfaction' (ibid.: 80); 'greatest possible satisfaction' (ibid.: 94); 'as completely as possible' (ibid.: 95) and 'fullest possible satisfaction' (ibid.: 114).[11] Now these expressions did not have the equivalent content of mathematical maximization as employed by Jevons, Walras or Marshall. By way of contrast, the very logic of a maximization problem in modern, textbook neoclassical economics (which traces its roots to Walras or Marshall) requires, *inter alia*, an economizer who acts under conditions of certainty (or static uncertainty, allowing for measurable risk) and infinite divisibility of goods, preferences and satisfactions.[12] Maximization is not, therefore, a procedure that we may confidently attribute to the Mengerian economizer.[13]

Menger does not go so far as to suggest that economizers examine all, or at least a well-sampled subset, of the full range of consumption opportunities open to them. All he admits is that 'this weighing of the relative importance of needs...is the very part of the economic activity of men that fills their minds more than any other' ([1871] 1950: 128). The extent of the economizer's deliberations over furthering a particular objective, and the precise content of that mental process, are not investigated in the *Principles*. Readers will not encounter a description of fine mental balancing acts which involve careful computation of the incremental returns to consumer well-being of particular choice scenarios. It would not be too far-fetched to report that Menger had no intention of implying that economizers maximize anything at all. Instead, economizers aim to make consumption choices which are thoroughly viable but which offer no assurance to Jevonians, Walrasians or Marshallians that the consumption activities which are being analysed in fact produce for the economizer the best of all possible outcomes. The nature of the Mengerian economizer's aspirations are such that failure to calculate globally, in the strictly mathematical sense of weighing up on the mathematical margin all relevant possibilities, should not be interpreted as an inherently imperfect choice-making procedure or one which deviates from an otherwise perfect procedure.

THE SCOPE OF ECONOMIZING BEHAVIOUR

Economizing was explained in Menger's *Investigations into Method* ([1883] 1985) as 'premeditative activity aimed at satisfying our material needs' – as activity which assured satisfaction of needs for final consumption goods. Producers' goods could also be considered to involve economizing since their use satisfied the four principles of possession and knowledge, ranking and choice, non-maximization, conservation and futurity, but economizing on this level only provided for material needs indirectly (Menger [1883] 1985: 216). Menger employed the terms 'material' and 'economic' interchangeably. Commentators have thus criticized his definition of the scope of economizing because it was still apparently in the classical, materialist mould.[14] Lachmann (1978) claimed that for this reason, among others, Menger was an 'incomplete subjectivist'. Passages in the *Investigations* suggest that Lachmann's interpretation deserves qualification. 'Political economy', wrote Menger, 'cannot provide understanding of human phenomena in their totality... *but it can provide understanding of one of the most important sides of human life*'. This statement was preceded by the assertion that, of all human endeavours, those involving 'anticipation and provision of material (*economic*) needs are by far the most common and most important' ([1883] 1985: 87; his emphases). The predominant, though not exclusive, attention of political economy is on material phenomena, and to this extent Menger's emphasis diverged from later Austrian views. Close textual study suggests that the materialist restriction on economizing was only a matter of emphasis. Already in his 1876 lectures to Crown Prince Rudolf, Menger signalled:

> Worrying about how to satisfy the most basic needs entirely occupies the minds of the large majority of men.... Only the smallest part of mankind is free of these hampering worries and in a position where it can devote time to intellectual endeavours... [whereas] the serious endeavours of the multitude... [are] matters of life and death.
>
> (Menger [1876] 1994: 29)

It was for Menger simply more usual that the purpose of economizing was satisfaction of basic material needs. In the *Principles* he had sensed the importance of a special class of relationships (*Verhältnisse*) and intangible goods – friendship, business connections such as goodwill, love, religious fellowships (ibid.: 54–5) – which may be subject to economizing. Menger complained that these goods may be mistakenly ignored. He did not agree with the 'unconscious working of the materialistic bias of our time which regards only materials and forces (tangible objects and labour services) as... goods' (ibid.: 54). It is therefore not so readily apparent that Mises, Lachmann and others are justified in doubting Menger's commitment to subjectivism.

Mises's ([1933] 1960) position was also founded on a putative 'notorious slip' in Menger's *Principles* – a slip all the more deplored by Mises because it was not excised from the 1923 edition of the *Principles*. Upon defining goods, Menger considered a special class of imaginary goods including most cosmetics, charms, divining rods and love potions. Despite being subject to economizing behaviour, these had imaginary-goods status because they 'are incapable of actually satisfying the needs they are supposed to serve'. Economizers misperceived these goods as being related to specific needs either because these needs were mistakenly assumed to exist or because the attributes were erroneously ascribed to things that did not really possess them (Menger [1871] 1950: 53). In Mises's interpretation this did not make imaginary goods any less economic goods, because it was the subjective opinions of economizers that something will satisfy their needs that were singularly important.

Menger ([1871] 1950: 53) argued that, as civilizations progress, improved knowledge of the connection between things and needs-satisfaction reduces the number of imaginary goods and increases the range of 'true goods' available. Thus one plausible interpretation is that Menger's theory of economizing 'required that he make room for error... and this meant that he had to judge some past beliefs as mistaken if there were to be any meaning in the notion of improved knowledge' (Vaughn 1990: 386; also 1994: 23–4). Comparatively shallow, if not erroneous, insights into the causal connections between goods and needs could still prove satisfying for economizers. More accurate connections between the specific attributes of things and particular needs would, of course, be far more satisfying.

The most accurate causal connections between needs and the attributes of things available for consumption were made by supremely rational economizers. These economizers benefited from knowledge gained over a very long period of economic and social development. As Silverman (1990: 91) explained, fully rational *homo oeconomicus* was for Menger 'an enlightened creature who understood his real needs'. Moreover, according to Silverman, the 'goal of the market process for Menger was the emergence of the enlightened individual who realized his true being through the powers of science, natural and economic'. One of the apparent objectives of the scientist and the political economist was to discover the true causal connections between things and human needs, and to instruct economizers accordingly.

THE STRUCTURE OF NEEDS

One element in modern Austrian disenchantment with Menger's work, following Mises's original critique, has remained intact. This concerns a patently objective structure of human needs postulated by Menger in the *Principles*.[15] The well-known table in the chapter on value depicts a hierarchy of needs ([1871] 1950: 127, and Table 1 above). A choice between a comfortable bed and a chessboard was said by Menger to result in forgoing a chessboard if a person did not initially possess a bed (ibid.: 123). Consumption of some things, often up to satiety, must take precedence over consumption of other economic goods. Menger's illustrative hierarchy was: water, food, clothing, shelter (including a comfortable bed), transportation, recreation (including a chessboard) and tobacco (ibid.: 122–8). It is not really that Mengerian needs had a physiological basis, as suggested in Lachmann (1986: 55) and White (1985: xiv), since Menger (1923: 4–5 n.) later provided a tripartite classification of needs. In the second edition of the *Principles* Menger listed physiological, altruistical and egotistical needs-categories, thereby revealing that he was thinking of much more than mere physiological requirements. It is more correct to interpret Menger's attempt to classify needs as consistent with his conception of economizing individuals who, not being furnished with the fruits forthcoming from the *full* progress of civilization, must make do with limited perception and are thus incapable of making finely calibrated choices across all needs-dimensions simultaneously. Menger's impressionistic scheme in which preferences are ordered lexicographically, where certain needs must be satisfied in varying degrees before others are contemplated, is designed for individuals with limits on their information-processing faculties, and individuals with limited knowledge. Unlike Jevons, Menger did not seek to restrict the subject-matter of economizing to some subset of the needs-hierarchy. Jevons (1879: 25–7) restricted economizing to the 'lowest rank of feelings' in the 'hierarchy of feelings', by which he appeared to mean physiological and materialistic needs. As one reviewer of Menger's *Collected Works* remarked, Menger so broadened the theory of needs 'as to take every...impulse to action of whatever sort' into the ambit of economizing behaviour (Sweezy 1935: 727). However, this was to oversimplify Menger's position. In the *Investigations* Menger maintained that a

> contrast does in truth exist between the specifically economic propensity (directed toward satisfying the need for goods) and others – the non-economic drives of humans from which and in the midst of which real social life arises, a social life whose reality should not be presented solely as the result of the economic propensity.
>
> ([1883] 1985: 75 n. 26)

In this passage Menger admitted that there were other non-economic propensities and other goals towards which human activity was directed. Economizing was not for Menger all inclusive, as it is in modern microeconomic applications of the logic-of-choice. The ultimate end of human activity in general, variously described by Menger as 'welfare' or 'well-being' and by later Austrians as 'utility', was not exclusively the result of economizing, since that would include all possible goals, whereas not all purposive actions satisfied the four principles of economizing.

Menger nevertheless gave the undeniable impression that, in conferring a structure of ordered importance on human needs, there was some objective, universal basis to this structure. It is in this specific sense that he may be regarded as an 'incomplete subjectivist'. In this Menger followed a long tradition in German classical and historical economics to which, *inter alios*, Kudler, Rau, F. B. Hermann, Schäffle and Roscher were significant contributors. Banfield ([1848] 1973: 11) communicated the message to English-speaking scholars when he explained:

> there is an inseparable connection between the bodily and intellectual wants and enjoyments of men. The important economical result to be deduced from this is the classification of our wants.... An examination of the nature and intensity of man's wants shows that this connection between them gives to political economy its scientific basis. The first proposition of the theory of consumption is that the satisfaction of every lower want in the scale of wants creates a desire of a higher character. If the higher desire existed previous to the satisfaction of the primary want, it becomes more intense when the latter is removed.

Menger would have endorsed Banfield's claim of an 'inseparable connection' between physiological and other needs. Georgescu-Roegen (1966: 201) went so far as to resurrect a 'Banfield–Menger' theory of wants upon which he constructed the foundations of a lexicographic preference model. Menger's analysis of wants was particularly sophisticated since it allowed for subjective complementarity between goods. He saw no one-to-one correspondence between needs and goods. 'Usually', he wrote, 'not a single good, but a quantity of goods stands opposite not a single concrete need, but a complex of such needs' ([1871] 1950: 129, also 301). Food may simultaneously satisfy physiological needs, and the type of food, its preparation and mode of consumption may serve altruistic needs for fellowship, or even egotistical needs for social distinction.

From two revealing comments it becomes clear that Menger was unhappy with lack of progress in the analysis of needs-complexes on the boundaries first of economics and biology, and second of economics and psychology. The first comment appeared in the second edition of the *Principles* and it directed economists to consider biological data in order that economizers' needs be understood: 'The theory of needs is of fundamental importance for economics, and at the same time the bridge which leads from the natural sciences especially biology to the social sciences' (Menger 1923: 1). Pribram (1983: 291) reported that Menger was interested in bringing the results of biological studies to the fore in the theory of needs so as to provide a stronger basis for the theory of economizing behaviour. Evidently time was not on Menger's side, and he was forced to rely on successors in Vienna who did not follow his programmatic suggestion to construct linkages between economics and biology.[16]

Menger's second comment, which his successors were to take seriously, concerned the weak psychological basis of the theory of needs. He defined value as nothing inherent in external things or goods, but merely a judgement economizing individuals made about the importance of goods at their disposal ([1871] 1950: 117, 121). He understood the necessity for more penetrating analyses of the psychological bases of individual judgements. The table of needs-satisfaction in the *Principles* which classified needs in a hierarchy, although derived intuitively and not from a formal psychological theory, was none the less suggestive of 'a difficult and previously unexplored field of psychology' (ibid.: 128). Here, while the allusions were no more than fragmentary, Menger foreshadowed the direction for further necessary research linking economics and psychology. Moreover, these hints are enough to conclude that Menger would have rejected a requirement of the pure logic-of-choice that hypotheses about economizing behaviour be stated independently of non-economic implications and insights.[17] Certainly, Robbins's ([1932] 1984: 84) claim that 'the Mengerian tables were constructed in terms which begged no psychological questions' cannot be sustained.[18]

It remains to be established what sort of psychology Menger envisaged. Some all-too-generous speculation has suggested that the Mengerian economizer's subjective judgement of valuation could be inferred or assessed, supposedly in a manner consistent with Menger's proposals for further inquiry, by analysing consumption data gleaned either from budget studies, or from psychological or physiological experiments, or from 'data' derived from introspection and/or the *Verstehende* method (Sweezy 1935: 730). Consistent with later developments in the Austrian tradition, Hayek (1978: 277) and Addleson (1986: 10) have seen in Menger's concept of 'observing' economizing behaviour the method of *Verstehen* (interpretative understanding in the sense in which Max Weber later developed the concept). This amounts to an excursion into social psychology, because it attempts to comprehend subjectively the intended meaning of human decisions in terms of tacit societal rules influencing them. Pribram (1983: 281) argued that Menger made the needs-hierarchy intelligible through 'psychological introspection'. Introspection is 'psychological' to the extent that it consists in examining, as a social scientist, one's own reactions or conscious experience in a given situation. Beyond the case of an isolated individual, a method would have to be designed to explain economizing as a social phenomenon involving interacting economizers. This method entails 'getting inside the thoughts' of economizers as well. Menger's (1888: 41–3) attempt to define the popular form and content of 'capital' which economists should adopt, provided a splendid example of his use of this method. Imagining himself in the position of a farmer, first, in a predominantly barter economy, and second in a highly developed monetized economy, Menger outlined how in both situations the popular, everyday concept of capital was a pecuniary calculation. However, the former excluded from the calculation possibly inherited, immovable property such as land, whereas the latter did not. Insights from introspection and the *Verstehende* method were crucial to the development of economic theory in the Austrian tradition. Therefore, it is hardly surprising that Menger's work gave impetus for further work in these contiguous fields among both his economist followers, Wieser and Böhm-Bawerk, and Austrian psychologists Meinong and Ehrenfels (Eaton 1930: 92–3, 113).[19]

THE GROWTH OF NEEDS

There is one further aspect of Mengerian economizing behaviour that deserves elaboration because it is not compatible with the logic-of-choice approach to the economic order as a medium of needs-satisfaction in which economic activities are reduced to a strictly defined mechanics relating means to ends. Menger's treatment of needs in a 'progressing economy' demonstrated the importance of economizing behaviour in developing an individual's awareness of new needs created by that behaviour. That is, Menger was interested not just in the organization of means relative to ends, but also in changes brought about by their continual interaction.

In the *Principles* economic progress is underpinned by growth in knowledge connecting economic goods with the satisfaction of human needs. The 'progress of civilization' empowered economizers with the ability to perceive more elevated needs, and novel connections between goods and well-being (Menger [1871] 1950: 74). Needs not only arose from recurring physiological impulses – 'our nature' – they also arose from 'our previous development' (Menger [1883] 1985: 217–18). Menger's economizer was not so constituted that the activity of economizing always left needs intact. Menger cited the 'penetrating' work of A. E. F. Schäffle with approval in this connection. On Menger's reading, Schäffle broached, but did not solve, the difficult problem of the reciprocal relationship between economizing *activity* and human needs (Menger [1871] 1950: 300–1).[20] Needs were often re-evaluated endogenously during the consumption process – a process that involved both conscious 'thought and experience' (ibid.: 109). Menger referred frequently to changes in human needs (ibid.: 52, 148); to the 'disappearance of human needs' (ibid.: 63); to changes in needs through an economizer's life-cycle (ibid.: 231–2); to uncertainty about whether certain needs will be felt in the future (ibid.: 81); to the capacity of human needs to grow infinitely (ibid.: 82–3) and to increases in human requirements as knowledge expands (ibid.: 102–3).[21]

The contrast between Menger, and Jevons or Walras on this matter is quite stark. For both Jevons and Walras the taste or desire for various kinds of satisfaction had the analogue of force in mechanics. Objects of choice were thought of as enacting a pull upon the economizer and so causing a response behaviour which led to satisfaction but *not* to any change in tastes. Tastes were original and immaculately conceived. As Thorstein Veblen (1920: 72–3) recognized in an oft-quoted passage, an isolated economizer is constituted by a self-contained bundle of desires that, during consumption activities, 'shift him about' and, when satisfied, 'leave him intact'. Menger's economizer is not so constituted that the act of living and consuming leaves tastes intact. Tastes cannot be generally constant for Menger because they are being re-evaluated within and through the economizing process. An adequate theory of economizing behaviour must incorporate this critical process.

If we view the bulk of the *Principles* as reflecting on the subject of economic *progress* over a long, secular period of history, the broad Mengerian conceptualization of economizing is easier to appreciate. Menger's remarks on changes in tastes that occur in the process of consumption in a progressing civilization also become intelligible. Economic progress meant that economizers perceived new needs and novel, more accurate connections between potentially consumable things and well-being. The act of valuation by economizers is cognitive; it is a judgement and as such changes with circumstances as learning takes place. Hence, in the chapter on 'Economy and Economic Goods' Menger discussed the origins and acquisition of needs. He not only argued that needs are 'a result of previous experience'; he also maintained that 'experience...teaches us that goods of the same kind...lose their economic character with changing circumstances' ([1871] 1950: 81, 102). So there is no basis whatsoever for claiming that Menger exclusively treated the case of constant tastes. Indeed, the constant-tastes assumption, reflected in an unchanging ordinal needs-ranking, seems to have been a special case reserved for an exact-theoretical treatment of economizing behaviour. Constant tastes, 'ever-constant self-interest' and the absence of error in choice-making rendered economizing behaviour fully determinate (Menger [1871] 1950: chapter 4 et passim; [1883] 1985: 84, 216–19). On the other hand, empirical-theoretical analysis must take a broader perspective on the development of human needs through the process of choice given ongoing economic and social development.

The assumption of a fixed ordinal needs-ranking, together with its corollary, constant tastes, would be difficult to reconcile with Menger's allusions to error in choice. After carefully reviewing the *Principles*, Jaffé (1976: 521) took the view that Menger's economizer was a 'bumbling, erring, ill-informed creature, plagued with uncertainty'. Menger formulated a notion of dynamic, variable tastes as an integral part of his theoretical corpus. At least in the empirical-theoretical conception of economizing, the actions of the choice-maker spring from less than fully informed reason. The further an economy progresses beyond satisfying physiological needs, and the stronger its economic development, then the less stable do both needs and the suitability of means for satisfying those needs become. In a progressing economy, needs and the economizing behaviour which they motivate constantly look towards new and more viable and evolved plateaux of well-being. Previous neglect of Menger's enunciation of the principle of needs-growth can be attributed to doctrinal convention in selecting, as the 'core' of the *Principles*, portions of his work on choice theory with their attendant adumbrations of a weak concept of marginal utility and static subjectivist or exact laws of economizing (*Wirtschaftlichkeit*), premised on conditionally fixed tastes or needs, omniscience and self-interest.[22]

In the more *dynamically* subjectivist variants evident in the *Principles*, economizing was not fundamentally a striving for given ends in the logic-of-choice sense; rather, it was the basis for further striving. The way to economic progress was through expanding knowledge in order to create a larger quantity, higher quality and wider variety of goods for needs-satisfaction. Knowledge expanded and assisted economizing in the dual sense of helping individuals understand causal connections between goods and well-being and of enabling greater 'control of the less proximate conditions responsible for human welfare' (Menger [1871] 1950; 74, 109). In an original reinterpretation of Menger's *Principles*, Streissler (1972) revealed emphatically its dynamic subjectivist bent. 'Dynamic subjectivism' as defined by O'Driscoll and Rizzo (1985: 24–5) presupposes some ignorance and learning. It incorporates the passage of real, historical change into the corpus of choice theory. For Menger the dynamic subjectivist, the goal of economizing was to modify restraints on choice and to elevate the human condition by growing through a process of needs-satisfaction on to successively higher planes of well-being.

4
WIESER, BÖHM-BAWERK AND THE GOALS OF ECONOMIZING BEHAVIOUR

WIESER'S LOGIC OF VALUATION

The openness exhibited by Menger to questions which in the logic-of-choice scheme of things would have been classed as non-economic was continued, though not necessarily in a manner Menger would have countenanced, by Wieser. In Wieser's work we find that, after some hesitation, Wieser settled on the ends of economizing behaviour summarized in his expression 'highest possible utility' as being wholly purified of philosophical or ethical connotations. Consistent with a concentration on the pure logic-of-choice the majority of Austrian economists from the early 1920s onwards eliminated philosophical discussion concerning welfare goals or, alternatively, the ends of economizing. Rosenstein-Rodan's survey of marginal utility theory, first published in 1927, epitomized the prevailing view when it stated that 'all modern economists refuse to discuss the purpose of human action' ([1927] 1960: 79). In the furore of the *Methodenstreit* Menger ([1883] 1985: 234–7) insisted on disjoining the domains of ethics and economics. In the *Principles* (especially, though not exclusively, in the 1923 edition), this interdiction was explicitly relaxed, since he distinguished between physiological, altruistical and egotistical needs (Menger 1923: 4–5 n).[1] Furthermore, there was no implication of the influence of Benthamite hedonism on Menger's theory of economizing. Hedonism, broadly defined, was a philosophical doctrine that turned on the attainment of pleasure as the highest good and aim of life. Such a notion would have been anathema to Menger.[2] In the second, posthumous edition of the *Principles*, Menger (1923: 62) did not equate economizing behaviour simply with the highest pleasure resulting from the consumption of goods. According to Menger, economizing involved 'perform[ing] an economic action inasmuch as we provide the means necessary for satisfaction of our needs and we thereby assure the possibility of consumption at a future date, but not through the very fact that we consume'. Consumption in itself was not the be-all and end-all for Menger's economizer; the objective of attaining the highest satisfaction from consumption was secondary to performing 'the economic action', which involves first perceiving, then supplying, the means of well-being.

It is not immediately clear how Wieser's work may be understood in relation to developments in Austrian economics post-1920, especially if his early work is considered in isolation. For example, Wieser's first contribution, originally presented before Knies's seminar in 1876 (and reprinted in 1994), was set in a deterministic, proto-logic-of-choice framework, where the logic of performing 'the economic action', as Menger called it, was enunciated at length. At an early stage in his career, Wieser became interested in the influence which decisions to use particular producers' goods would have on the value of consumers' goods. His point of departure is the isolated economizer, who has production decisions to make before being able to achieve satisfaction through final consumption of the output. His assumptions may be enumerated as follows (Wieser [1876] 1994: 207–26):

1 The higher-order producers' goods are given and scarce.
2 The time period available for production is given and specific to the nature of the consumer goods (outputs) required.
3 There is no uncertainty as to the success or otherwise of the production of goods in the present to satisfy needs at the end of the production process, i.e. needs in the future (ibid.: 226).
4 Consumption requirements for final outputs are fixed.
5 The rhythm of needs is stable and unchanging: that is, the same needs for production and consumption 'recur over specific periods of identical length' (ibid.: 218).
6 The economizer strives to procure 'the greatest possible need-satisfaction' (ibid.: 208).

Employing these assumptions, Wieser reasoned that successive acts of needs satisfaction occur initially through decisions to use inputs in a time-consuming production process. Resource-allocation decisions in production are taken with a view to the prior fixed 'importance' of final consumer goods for needs satisfaction. The acts of needs satisfaction which begin with production are in fact 'rooted in [the economizer's] nature' (ibid.: 212). For instance, 'preservation of life' will give the highest importance-ranking to a particular consumer good, which will thereby be chosen for production ahead of other goods. Wieser's repeated references to the notion that needs satisfaction is 'rooted in human nature' (ibid.: 215) is reminiscent of Menger's first impulse to give needs some 'objective', immutable basis. Wieser's examples of needs satisfaction in his early work seem to concentrate on the physiological requirements of the economizer.

Wieser's analysis distinguished a logic of valuation from choice. The logic of valuation conferred an importance-ranking on goods and it arose from 'given conditions of economic life' summarized in the list of assumptions enumerated above. The economizer always made correct judgements when valuing goods in these circumstances. Valuation was strictly independent of choice. Conclusions drawn from the logic of valuation might diverge from actual choice, so that 'the most important act which could and should be achieved by the good was in reality not achieved, either due to our own deliberately economic course of action or due to the intervention of external circumstance' (ibid.: 214). For Wieser, it was the logic of valuation that required certainty and given conditions, whereas the process of choice, either in production or in consumption, could sunder the relationship between valuation and the use of resources. In the act of 'directing their efforts toward realising the value' of producers' and consumers' goods, economizers' choices might be imperfect. According to Wieser, 'Mistakes and carelessness or clumsiness are ... obstacles to bringing the efforts [of economizers] to fruition' (ibid.: 233). Ideally, goods used in accordance with their values will return the greatest possible needs satisfaction.

The distinction between the logic of valuation and the act of choice is important only if some of the assumptions associated with the former are relaxed so that choice may be analysed at a lower level of abstraction. All this is much in the spirit of Menger's empirical-theoretical approach to economizing behaviour, which admitted error and uncertainty. Choice in Wieser's model is less mechanical than valuation; choice is not merely the outcome of given assumptions and given data. The calculating procedure which Wieser ascribed to all economizers and which systematically compared the relative importance of needs so as to value goods prior to choice in production and consumption, was unaffected by changes in circumstances or data. The intervention of variable non-economic influences was also ignored. The Wieserian calculating procedure – the economy of the human mind – was a permanent, enduring feature of economizing behaviour even if real choices were inconsistent with its perfect operation.

WIESER ON THE PURPOSE OF ECONOMIZING BEHAVIOUR

In *Natural Value* ([1889] 1930) Wieser explained that economic goods yield utility, which is to say that they satisfy the economizer's wants. Now the word 'want' signified 'every human desire whether...justifiable or unjustifiable, necessary or unnecessary, material or immaterial. Bodily well-being, idle delights, artistic pleasure, moral satisfaction may be all classed together as objects of human want' (Wieser [1889] 1930: 6). After outlining Gossen's law of needs-satisfaction, Wieser referred to something that Menger had previously recognized as being worthy of further investigation, viz. the relationship between economic activities and the growth of wants. Gossen's law only applied at a moment of time to 'wants which are entirely developed'. Wants may be observed in some circumstances to grow 'by repetition and exercise...and become purified and elevated'. In the latter case Gossen's law must be regarded as inadequate because an economizer's desire for 'satisfaction does not [necessarily] weaken but rather stimulates it by constantly contributing to its development, and particularly, by giving rise to a desire for variety' (ibid.: 8–9). Wieser was prepared, like Gossen, to reduce all wants ultimately to a common denominator – satisfaction or utility. There was presumably no limit to the scope of the economizer's marginal utility calculations. Thus 'higher wants' which came into existence after 'the necessaries of life' were secured were subject to the law of diminishing marginal utility (ibid.: 9). The needs for food and for vanity were 'classed together' so far as the application of goods to these wants gave rise to a value magnitude which was reducible to the common utility standard (ibid.: 12). Here Wieser endorsed a neutral utility concept: that is, one kind of utility applicable across all categories of want – from physiological to moral requirements – and purified of all utilitarian or ethical connotations (Kauder 1965: 127).[3] In this view an economizer's use of goods implied that they had the potential of being desired, not that the goods ought to be desired. The theory of economic value could therefore be developed independently of moral or philosophical considerations.

WIESER AND BÖHM-BAWERK ON ECONOMIZING BEHAVIOUR

In *Social Economics* ([1914] 1927) Wieser repudiated neutral utility. In the pure theory of the 'simple economy' which he propounded in that work, economizing activity was undertaken by a single, isolated mind which foresaw wants and weighed attempts at their satisfaction 'without error or passion'. Moreover, economizing proceeded 'without loss of energy' (ibid.: 19–20). Wieser advanced beyond Menger's brief references to psychology when explaining this curious statement. Wieser's choice principle was a corollary of the fundamental postulate of conscious economizing behaviour. It related the notion of purpose to mental motor stimuli. The first stimulus to economizing was *conscious* purposeful desire which drove human effort to satisfy wants. This was interconnected with *unconscious* kinetic impulse: 'an active motor stimulus that is massed under tension and strives to be discharged' (ibid.: 18). Desire for gain was necessary but insufficient to urge economizers to strive for needs-satisfaction. When co-ordinated, conscious purpose and motor stimuli produced volition, which was defined as 'impulse controlled by purpose'. In their economizing activities it was likely that a group of interacting individuals, whose volition moved them to exert their full power to attain goods, would generate friction, error, conflict and wasted effort as well as gains. It was in this sense that, in the idealized simple economy, the isolated fully informed individual avoided such losses of 'energy' (ibid.: 18–19).

For Wieser, economic analysis was concerned with market exchange and pricing. It was 'not concerned with the direct satisfaction of needs'; rather, it studied demand for marketed goods and services. The 'psychological nature of human needs' was therefore not part of the province of economics, but a problem for 'scientific psychology' (Wieser [1914] 1927: 22–4; 1929). Wieser's attempt to distinguish between pure or scientific psychology (*Wissenschaftliche*) and the casual, introspective psychology (*innere Beobachtung*) used by economists in order to analyse economizing behaviour was unconvincing. Frequently in *Social Economics* some pure psychology (and also the literature of psychology) was relied upon to give substance to the axiom of conscious economizing, which would otherwise have enjoyed an unacceptable elusiveness of content. His analysis of the structure of wants breached the boundaries of economics and scientific psychology ([1914] 1927: 22–5). Applied, introspective psychology was none the less useful in providing Wieser with grounds for rejecting the equimarginal principle. Like Menger, Wieser ([1889] 1930: 14–15) considered that economizers evaluated goods not in infinitely small amounts, but only in discrete portions. In Wieser's analysis this insight was derived from introspection into the psychology of the human mind.

Wieser crossed into the debate on ethics and economics by pronouncing on the appropriateness of certain activities on the demand side. His earlier position on neutral utility would have been untenable if economizers' goals were ranked and assessed for them. Yet this was precisely Wieser's procedure. A dualism of wants or needs (terms he used synonymously) was established: 'healthful vital needs' and those which were 'merely pleasurable'. The first required satisfying because they ensured 'sound continuance' of life. Such satisfaction led to 'strength and vitality'; it excited the motor stimuli and gave 'impulse to progress still to be achieved' (Wieser [1914] 1927: 31). By contrast, when the merely pleasurable needs were gratified the motor stimuli were dulled, all the more so if 'degenerative and luxurious desires' came to the fore. In the simple economy the economizer avoided 'gross excess', which was described as a lamentable outgrowth of striving for greatest possible satisfaction from an ever-growing expansion of the means of gratification. Such striving was uncontrolled, whereas Wieser set out to posit permissible boundaries of desire which would not be exceeded. 'It is assumed', he wrote, that throughout the structure of the simple economy and a well-ordered social economy, 'human activity is directed to wholesome, vital needs and to permissible needs of enjoyment' (ibid.: 32–3). What were 'permissible needs'? Wieser referred positively to the 'laudable sentiment of frugal contentment' and 'moderation in our simple needs', and negatively to economizing that incited 'excessive acquisitive efforts' or led 'to degeneration either directly or by the tempting, circuitous path of over-refinement' (ibid.: 32, 33). Of course, argued Wieser, the proper appraisal of needs was a task for philosophy and ethics, but this admission did not limit the intrusion of broad value premises into his economic theory.[4] He hastened to separate 'hedonistic philosophic views' from his analysis. The economic principle of maximum utility which was developed within the bounds of 'permissible' needs was, according to Wieser, harmonizable with 'ascetic views' (ibid.: 33).[5]

Menger's principle of conservation and futurity stated, without elaboration, that one condition for successful economizing was that a good's useful properties be maintained so that future needs could be served by them. How were future needs valued? Wieser maintained that this was an ethical problem, which he had no hesitation in pronouncing upon:

> Efficient economy requires that the future satisfaction and need shall not be deemed less important than the vividly experienced desire of the moment. It is essential that every strong person or people shall maintain a sense of enduring values. They may not be impaired by passing solicitation.
> ([1914] 1927: 36)

There is nothing in this example or in others provided in Wieser ([1914] 1927) to suggest that the ends of economizing behaviour were for the economist *à la* logic-of-choice theory, given data; that *de gustibus non disputandum est*.

In conclusion, in *Natural Value* we find an exaggerated emphasis on neutral utility. Wieser was motivated in his early work to remove the misleading association of hedonism with the ends of economizing behaviour. This is not to say that he rejected all ethical referents of economizing. Indeed, in *Social Economics* he connected utility theory with asceticism. This did not constitute an *ex post facto* apology for his earlier over-emphasis on neutral utility. Instead it was a more comprehensive and mature statement of 'founding' Austrian economics, untrammelled by the restrictions which were later placed on the domain of choice-theory.

BÖHM-BAWERK'S APPEAL TO 'PURE' PSYCHOLOGY

Böhm-Bawerk's *Positive Theory of Capital* (1959a), first published in 1888, provided further evidence for not conflating 'founding' Austrian analysis of economizing with later, narrower logic-of-choice theories. Böhm-Bawerk rejected the notion of economics as an autonomous science of allocative behaviour. He opened his study by re-affirming the unity of all sciences, referring *inter alia* to the importance of conducting economic theorizing with the assistance of theorems established in contiguous disciplines, especially psychology (1959b: 3–4).

Value theory is the subject-matter of the first part of Book III of *Positive Theory*. There Böhm-Bawerk prefaced the discussion with a distinction between intrinsic value (*Eigenwert*) and extrinsic value (*Wirkungswert*).[6] Some goods are valuable for their own sake and are therefore intrinsically valuable. Others are valuable as instruments for promoting ends – both material and psychic – lying outside themselves (extrinsic value). Economic values are extrinsic in that economizers' valuations of goods are 'a reflection of a more basic valuation which [they] accord to the life and welfare purposes which goods serve to attain' (1959b 121). Two issues arise from this statement. First, how much of a reflection of 'more basic valuations' are economic valuations? On this point Böhm-Bawerk remained silent. Evidently 'more basic' valuations do not come within the domain of economic analysis, in so far as they can be isolated at all. Economic value is not a *perfect* reflection of 'basic' valuation, otherwise Böhm-Bawerk's distinction between two different spheres of valuation – one relating to ultimate ends, and the other to means – would be unhelpful. As Böhm-Bawerk was obliged to concede, the value of all goods was intrinsic (ibid.: 121). It is not crucial that he realized the transparency of a distinction borrowed from the fledgling literature of pure psychology (notably Ehrenfels's work). What matters is that Böhm-Bawerk believed that value and price theory could not be written without reference to psychology. Second, what role do economists have in evaluating how well economizing behaviour, following principles laid down in the theory of economic value, actually accords with intrinsic 'life and welfare purposes'? Must economists analyse intrinsic goals, or is such an endeavour already implicit in the theory of economic value? Affirmative answers to either part of the latter question require consideration of deeper philosophical issues that Böhm-Bawerk eventually found unavoidable.

As Böhm-Bawerk's treatise proceeded, the economic value of a good was said to be determined by the magnitude of its marginal utility (ibid.: 143). Marginal-utility calculations were apparent in many seemingly incomparable activities:

> Everyone knows from his own experience that the fourth or fifth course of a banquet arouses far less appetite than did the first.... Similar sensations can arise in the course of a concert, a lecture, a walk or a game that continues for an unduly long period. This will apply, indeed, to *virtually all physical and intellectual enjoyments, as well.*
>
> (1959b: 139; emphasis added).

Selfish or altruistic actions also took marginal utility into account (ibid.: 424 n. 19). It was argued that marginal utility was the decisive point 'of every explanation of man's economic behavior'. The epithet 'economic' referred to any purposive activity that used scarce means to satisfy needs which, in turn, were ranked in order of precedence in the economizer's mind (ibid.: 140–3). Ranking may be in error. Economizing was affected not by the true importance attaching to goods, but by 'the *opinion* that we have formed of them whether right or wrong' (ibid.: 432 n. 93; his emphasis). While the possibility of Menger's imaginary goods was granted, Böhm-Bawerk noted that the intellectual demands of economizing without extensive error were reduced by memory and learning (ibid.: 200–4). However, he offered no formal theory of learning.

Chapter 10 of *Capital and Interest*, written on the occasion of the third edition (1912), is entitled: 'Some Psychological Considerations Supplementing Our Theory of Value' (1959b: 184). In that chapter Böhm-Bawerk abjured adherence to 'antiquated philosophy', specifically referring to hedonistic approaches which maintained that there were no extrinsic values, and no intrinsic values other than pleasure and freedom from pain. Nevertheless he vigorously defended as part of his marginal utility theory the use of terms reminiscent of hedonism, such as 'pleasure', 'displeasure' and 'satisfaction,' to describe the economizer's maximand (ibid.: 184–5). For the economist:

> it matters not whether it be only pleasure and pain, or whether it be in addition other things that are 'desirable' and 'worthy of being desired', 'odious' or 'worthy of odium'. The only thing that is important is that people do love and hate something.
>
> (ibid.: 188; his emphasis)

This admonition is far from being persuasive in its attempt to remove all vestiges of hedonism from his analysis.[7] Also, it did not obviate the necessity for Böhm-Bawerk to explain the scope and content of the economizer's maximand, viz. the 'life and welfare purposes' referred to indefatigably in *Positive Theory*.

If the tools of marginal utility theory described economizers' mental processes involved in 'striving after well-being' (ibid.: 189), what was the precise scope of marginalism? Usually, wrote Böhm-Bawerk, in contrast with his previous (1888) position (but consistent with Menger's earlier interdiction in the *Investigations*), marginal utility does not apply to activities concerning 'glowing enthusiasm for lofty ideas and elemental outbursts of the primal instincts'. It is not fit for analysing human behaviour in these domains. Further, it 'is not in the lofty and exalted strata of human endeavour, but rather in its low-lying regions, that marginal utility has its habitat and performs its function of determining the value of goods'. In short, marginal utility applies only to the satisfaction of 'banal and prosaic needs' (ibid.: 189).[8]

Eugen Slutsky (1927: 545–7) attempted to expose two distinct value theories in Böhm-Bawerk's work: one based on the pain–pleasure calculus, which was formulated in the 1880s, and one incomplete theory based on 'higher values', written at the turn of the century. Slutsky's proposal was speculative and unconvincing. It attributed more to Böhm-Bawerk's 1912 additions to *Positive Theory* than is warranted by textual evidence. Böhm-Bawerk's position was not, however, as 'perplexing' as Kauder (1965: 129) presented it. Böhm-Bawerk, like Wieser, prepared a response to criticism of hedonistic elements in his original value theory only to find in responding that he needed a substitute once hedonism was jettisoned.[9] As we saw, Wieser resorted to asceticism. Böhm-Bawerk's dualism of higher and lower needs which conveniently corresponded with Ehrenfels's spurious distinction between intrinsic and extrinsic value, was constructed to appease the critics.[10] It is therefore understandable why Böhm-Bawerk was so keen to 'carefully step over the boundary line' into the field of pure psychology for support. Böhm-Bawerk's appeals to a more practical, introspective psychology were substantially different from his use of pure psychological principles. (His use of introspection is discussed in the next section.) In his use of pure psychology we find his rationale for appealing to the authority of 'modern German psychologists' (1959b: 121, 193). It gave him an excuse, however weak, to retain an unadulterated marginal utility theory in the face of criticism. In his estimation, dating from the 1912 edition of *Positive Theory*, 'economic phenomena...have their roots in psychological ground and it becomes the province of economic science to trace those roots far enough into that ground to make the explanation which it evolves...convincing' (1959b: 192).

'MEASURING' SUBJECTIVE VALUE

Joseph Schumpeter (1954: 1060) made a controversial comment on the Austrian approach to the measurement of subjective value (or utility, as it became more widely known):

> in the beginning, utility, both total and marginal, was considered a psychic reality, a feeling that was evident from introspection, independent from any external observation... and *a directly measurable* quantity. I believe that this was the opinion of Menger and Böhm-Bawerk.
>
> (Emphasis in original)

Following this statement he added the following footnote:

> The meaning of direct measurability is best instanced by the measurement of length. It may be defined as the association, with every utility sensation, of a real number, unique except for the choice of a unit which is to be interpreted as a unit sensation. Nobody held that this could be done as easily as it can in the case of length. But some authors did hold that there was no difficulty of principle involved. The presence of a practical difficulty – that would reduce utility measurements to rough 'estimates' – was recognised by Böhm-Bawerk.
>
> (ibid.: 1060 n. 1)

No evidence can be found to support Schumpeter's contention linking Menger and Böhm-Bawerk on this matter. Menger did not approach the question of measuring subjective value by way of any cardinal measurement scale akin to length such as is used by Schumpeter as an analogy for the operation of the human mind. If anything Menger, and also Wieser, considered subjective value as intrinsically ordinal (High and Bloch 1989: 351–3; Yagi 1992: 100). As for Wieser, his early, scattered remarks vacillate over the question of measurement (1884: 180–1). By the time he had come to write *Social Economics*, it was clear that in terms of the economist's representation of the operations of the economizer's mind, the attribution of a process of ordinal comparisons of utility assessment was regarded as sufficient.[11]

Böhm-Bawerk certainly maintained at the very least that economizing involved intra-personal ordinal measurement of the satisfaction gained from consumption (1959b: 151–5, 1959c: 136). The interpretative complications are, however, compounded by some of his other statements. In some passages Böhm-Bawerk believed that economizers could measure utility, in principle, in a cardinal fashion.[12] For Böhm-Bawerk, the problem of measuring subjective value was connected with a mental process of calculation:

the value of a good is to be measured according to the magnitude of the difference in welfare, the difference of pleasure and pain, which goes with the possession or non-possession of the good. So it is ultimately magnitudes of feeling and of sensation with which we calculate, according to our theory.

(1959b: 196)

It is conceded in *Capital and Interest* that, while the ultimate aims of economic life (interests, aspirations) may not be directly 'commensurable' or 'mathematically determinable', economizing nevertheless requires some kind of mental judgement comparing the relative satisfaction of human needs. The magnitude of pleasure and pain resulting from economizing is regarded by Böhm-Bawerk as potentially measurable by the individuals whose behaviour is being described. Indeed, according to Böhm-Bawerk, the 'fact that we economize at all is the best proof of the fact that our feelings of pleasure and pain cannot be said to be inherently impossible to determine', although admittedly there is legitimate dispute among economists over the methods of determination used by economizers (ibid.: 197). Böhm-Bawerk then proceeded to make a stronger claim that 'we at least *undertake* to form numerically determined judgements on the magnitudes of pleasure' (ibid.: 198; his emphasis). This statement suggests cardinality. The examples which Böhm-Bawerk adduced show that timely 'economical deliberation' as opposed to the 'well-worn rut of everyday habit' in choice-making, must of necessity involve 'careful numerical computation' on the part of the economizer. Only such computations provided the basis for 'rationally practical decision'. His classic example runs as follows:

> Let us imagine two boys, one of whom has an apple and the other of whom has some plums. The latter would like to make an exchange by which he can acquire the apple and he offers the first boy some of his plums. The latter, imagining the amount of enjoyment he will derive from the taste of the plums, refuses to accept four, and five and then six plums. When he hears the offer of seven plums he begins to hesitate, and finally gives up his apple in exchange for eight plums. How can we regard this transaction, if not as a clear-cut numerical judgement that the enjoyment of eating one apple is more than seven times but less than eight times as great as the enjoyment of eating one plum?

(ibid.: 198–9)

Much later Böhm-Bawerk ([1912] 1994: 346) continued to maintain in the face of criticism that the 'formation of numerical judgements on the degree of intensities of desired gratifications [is necessary] ...if we are to act rationally'.

The preceding statements notwithstanding, Böhm-Bawerk moved to make some significant concessions to the objection that cardinality was not a necessary condition for rational economizing. The process of choice and subsequent consumption takes place in time. Thus economizers 'never experience *simultaneously* the emotions of pleasure which [they] compare as to degree' (ibid.: 200; emphasis added). Memory and imagination play a critical role in computing the utility of one action compared with another. The results of such mental exercises can be 'quite deceptive' (ibid.: 200). Böhm-Bawerk's 'extensive concessions', as he called them, amounted to a dilution of the possibility of cardinal measurement to the point that economizers are viewed as merely making 'judgements' or 'estimates' of utility. In summary, he admitted that 'it is obviously impossible in...[economizing] activity to furnish a mechanical and accurate measure, like a footrule or a surveyor's chain' (ibid.: 199). Böhm-Bawerk did not apparently ascribe to economizers the ability to perform a mental operation which would yield the equivalent of a cardinal measure of utility, at least in any practical case under consideration. Nor, for that matter, did he make the convenient assumption which asserts that economizers act 'as if' they made cardinal calculations. However, the principle of perfect numerical expression of mental magnitudes still stood as an ideal principle.[13]

Howey (1960: 158) observed:

> Böhm-Bawerk never committed himself on the problem of the measurability of utility. For the most part he restricted his discussion to the ordinal aspect of quantity, but his restriction follows more from his desire to present his analysis in the simplest possible terms than from any view that the cardinal aspect cannot fit the case.

Far from simplifying the analysis, however, if the economizer is modelled as having to resort to rough and ready ordinal estimates, the economist's task is rendered more difficult, especially if, as we would expect, choice is regarded as an open-ended, thoroughgoing, subjective process.

The issue of measurability is of some importance for our understanding of the place of Böhm-Bawerk's contribution *vis-à-vis*

Menger's work and the ideas of other leading contemporary marginalists. Georgescu-Roegen (1968: 251) was persuaded by Böhm-Bawerk's remarks on cardinal measurement to go so far as to claim that 'Böhm-Bawerk, by a verbal legerdemain, equated *Grenznutzen* with Jevons's marginal utility, and Menger's ordinal importance rating with Jevons's cardinal utility. Actually, Böhm-Bawerk used more words than any other economist in arguing that satisfaction has a cardinal measure.'[14] Unfortunately, Georgescu-Roegen's argument is made on the basis of an incomplete reading of Böhm-Bawerk's text; Howey's reading is the more careful one and in our view captures the spirit of Böhm-Bawerk's important qualifications on the subject. Since the economizer uses imagination, memory and estimates or judgements when assessing subjective value, the results will not have strictly equivalent counterparts in a physical measurement scale. That Böhm-Bawerk ends up reasoning like 'Jevons or, rather, like Edgeworth, without admitting it overtly' (Georgescu-Roegen 1968: 251) is therefore a misrepresentation in respect of Böhm-Bawerk's ideas on utility measurement.

Whether the suggestion of cardinal measurement is considered as a vestigial element in Böhm-Bawerk's work or not, Čuhel's critique of this suggestion was of profound significance for the direction of founding Austrian economic theory. Čuhel was a Czech economist and a member of Böhm-Bawerk's seminar. He rightly objected even to Böhm-Bawerk's watered-down idea that subjective value was cardinally measurable. In a sophisticated analysis which drew heavily on what would now be regarded as economic psychology, Čuhel ([1907] 1994: 306–7) coined the term 'egence' to describe the two-dimensional features of an economizer's existing subjective 'welfare desire'. The two dimensions comprised: (1) the intensity of the motive for satisfaction and (2) the imagined duration of the increase in welfare which is to be achieved following a choice. Čuhel discussed the implications of this two-dimensional concept at great length. He demonstrated that 'there is no exact proportional relationship between the intensity of desires and associated feeling' (ibid.: 322): that is, between dimensions (1) and (2) above. Böhm-Bawerk's examples asserting numerical determination of subjective value conflated (1) and (2) in such a way that the intensity of human drives for satisfaction, and the imagined duration of satisfaction, could be cardinally assessed at one instant by economizers. Čuhel conceded the possibility that the 'measurability of intensities of feelings [might be put] beyond doubt' (ibid.: 322), as suggested in some of Böhm-Bawerk's examples. But the two dimensions constituting welfare egence were not obviously commensurable since the working of the imagination *prior* to actual consumption activity was not reducible to a certain measurement scale. It was therefore advisable for economists to rely instead on the proposition of ordinal welfare *comparisons* rather than cardinal measures.[15] His remarks deserve quotation in full:

> the measurement of egences should not be confused with numerical determination of them. One such is, for example, the determination of the hardness of minerals by means of the *Mohs* scale of hardness, which enables us to state whether a mineral has the second, third, fourth, etc. degree of hardness or if it is harder than a mineral of the second, third, fourth, etc. degree of hardness. However, these numerical determinations of hardness cannot be termed 'measurements', as it is not possible to state what multiples of a hardness adopted as the unit of hardness the hardnesses to be measured are equal to. For in saying that talc has the first degree of hardness and gypsum the second degree of hardness, this certainly does not mean that gypsum is twice as hard as talc, but only harder to a certain extent.
>
> (ibid.: 322–4)

Böhm-Bawerk's reply to Čuhel, 'On the Measurability of Sensations' (Böhm-Bawerk [1912] 1994), underscores our view that Böhm-Bawerk only half-heartedly held the position that economizers assess subjective value in a rather mechanical, cardinalist manner.[16] There are many instances, according to Böhm-Bawerk, where economizers are happy to make 'simple comparisons' of utility. For example, a judgement may be made that two satisfactions are equal, or one is greater than the another (ibid.: 345). Attempts at numerical calculation should not, on observing the above instances, be dismissed. For 'observing' here we follow Böhm-Bawerk's meaning: we observe, as economists, by applying a practical, introspective psychology (rather than borrowing principles from pure psychology).[17] Böhm-Bawerk's introspective judgement on the economizer's mind suggested that cardinal measurement is in fact attempted despite the dearth of 'guaranteed objective tools of measure'. Cardinal measurement may take place 'merely through vague, subjective, perhaps even deceptive, estimates of the intensity of sensations which we may partially experience, but mainly reproduce in our imagination' (ibid.: 346). That there were difficulties in the way of economizers being able to measure in a cardinal sense did not gainsay the existence of mental procedures which continue to attempt to estimate subjective value, however 'erroneously and imprecisely' (ibid.: 352).

In replying to Čuhel, Böhm-Bawerk hardly modified any aspect of his earlier argument. That argument had already made substantial concessions to those economists (like Čuhel) whose introspections on the human mind produced different conclusions. Now we may wonder which introspective observation is to be deemed correct? And is a resolution to this issue of great import? The well-known problem with introspections is that they are inherently and unashamedly subjective in the sense that they are not obviously open and transparent. Furthermore, one observer may not be able to replicate the introspection of another, and therefore any checking of the 'data' of introspective observation remains entirely intersubjective. This issue is of some significance because a binding theme of Austrian economics from Menger was that the 'data' of the social sciences were subjective. Čuhel's propositions on the impossibility of mechanical measurement of subjective value would seem to be more consistent with this theme than Böhm-Bawerk's. Certainly, Böhm-Bawerk's views on cardinal measurement allow us to include him among those who contributed to the analysis of a crucial, deterministic component of the pure logic-of-choice. Nevertheless, at the same time Böhm-Bawerk allowed for imagination which, being highly individual-specific, played a vital role in measuring subjective value. He judged that sensation – both intensity and duration – was 'a distinctly psychical process' (ibid.: 348), and that economizers generally erred in their measurement attempts. These concessions keep Böhm-Bawerk firmly in the founding Austrian tradition because they offer a route which takes the economist away from modelling economizing behaviour exclusively in terms of a mechanical logic-of-choice.

The content of the act of measuring subjective value is not something the founding Austrians could evidently agree on: that is, if we include Čuhel as an Austrian theorist. Menger and Wieser had nothing to say on Böhm-Bawerk's reluctant and hedged-about cardinalism. Ludwig von Mises ([1934] 1981: 55 n.) came down firmly against the cardinalist elements in Böhm-Bawerk's work, but the Mises exposition gave no consideration whatsoever to Böhm-Bawerk's significant concessions. Mises was correct in remarking that Böhm-Bawerk's reply to Čuhel 'did not succeed in putting forward any new consideration that could help toward a solution of the problem'; the same sentiments were expressed much later by Kauder (1965: 198). In our view there was not really a 'problem' here, since Böhm-Bawerk's discussions on measurement allowed for two supplementary analytical perspectives on economizing behaviour: behaviour which was strictly mechanical and rooted in cardinal assessments of subjective value, and behaviour which, because it was dependent on ordinal assessments, was more open-ended, subjective and faltering.

CONCLUSIONS

Menger, Wieser and Böhm-Bawerk were aware of possibilities for ethically and/or psychologically *non*-neutral analyses of economizing behaviour. Menger advanced beyond the boundaries of what is now known as the pure logic-of-choice. He investigated both the hierarchical structure and the growth of needs. Although having different bases, Wieser and Böhm-Bawerk separately established dualism-of-needs concepts; these concepts enabled them to retain the authorization to discuss the scope and purpose of economizing and to counter the charge of hedonism. Wieser used his concept to link the ends of economizing with the ethical principle of asceticism, whereas Böhm-Bawerk defended his concept by drawing on a branch of pure psychology which he thought sufficient to distance his analysis from the felicific calculus. One leading second-generation Austrian, Ludwig von Mises, was uncomfortable with all this. He was apprehensive about the penetration of ethical issues into economics. He railed against the needs-hierarchy notion evident in the writings of Menger and Böhm-Bawerk partly because it was implied that needs exhibit an objective structure according to which economizers *should* act and also because some needs, especially in Böhm-Bawerk's analysis, were considered beyond the scope of economizing (Mises [1933] 1960: 167, 170; 1949: 95). While his cardinalism implied a mechanistic approach to economizing, Böhm-Bawerk kept the way open, in his extensive elaborations and reply to Čuhel, for a far less deterministic treatment.

The main focus of doctrinal investigations in attempting to discover the uniqueness of early Austrian contributions has been on the intentionality and purposefulness of economizing in contrast with Jevons, Walras and Pareto, whose impulse was to model choice mechanistically. Menger, Wieser and Böhm-Bawerk certainly approached the analysis of economizing by the well-documented route pointing in the direction of a pure logic-of-choice. In Chapters 3 and 4 we have identified further lines of inquiry, suggested by the early Austrians, which utilized a range of interdisciplinary insights from biology, psychology and ethics so as further to understand, in particular, the *process* of choice and the *ends* of economizing behaviour.

If the entire foundations of early Austrian economics were established in a static, deterministic, logic-of-choice framework, Menger and his followers realized that they would then have denied themselves fruitful opportunities for interdisciplinary research. This realization was apparent, for instance, in Böhm-Bawerk's (1959b: 193) comment that the study of economizing 'may be logically correct' but is nevertheless undertaken in an 'empty framework'. As a leading Austrian in the mid-twentieth century, Mises (1949: 12, 483–4) sought to separate his praxeological analysis of choice from other disciplines, particularly psychology. In this, his work had something central in common with later studies of the pure logic-of-choice following Robbins ([1932] 1984).[18] As Rothbard (1956: 230–1) so neatly expressed it:

> Psychology analyses the *how* and *why* of people forming values. It treats the concrete *content* of ends and values. [Praxeology]...on the other hand, rests simply on the assumption of the *existence* of ends and then deduces its valid theory from such a general assumption. It therefore has nothing to do with the content of ends or with the internal operation of the mind of the acting man.
>
> (Emphasis in original)

We have demonstrated in the last two chapters that Menger, Wieser and Böhm-Bawerk analysed economizing in ways that contrast sharply with the later, very restrictive Austrian praxeological study of choices associated with Mises and Rothbard.[19] The praxeological approach to economizing is another expression of the pure logic-of-choice where concerns for knowledge dynamics are downplayed and their further exploration with the assistance of psychology or any other social science is barred (Endres 1987b: 122).

We have already discovered that the founding Austrians wished to inquire into the content, nature, growth and structure of economizers' objectives. They also believed that marginal utility theory, as they variously understood the concept of the margin, had a psychological basis; and they were happy to make generalizations on psychological matters. The proposition that the internal operation of the economizer's mind is beyond the economist's purview would have been anathema to the founding Austrians. In short, they favoured a non-positivist or non-deterministic perspective on the fundaments of choice. We turn in the next two chapters to another component of the core of founding Austrian microeconomics – the theory of price formation, which, as we shall see, exhibited similar non-deterministic features.

5
CARL MENGER'S THEORY OF PRICE FORMATION

INTRODUCTION

The purpose of this chapter is to reassess some fundamental principles in Carl Menger's chapter on price theory in the *Principles of Economics* (chapter 5) – a chapter Hayek ([1934] 1976: 20) described as Menger's 'crowning achievement'. In the literature on the history of economic theory, Austrian (including Menger's) price theories are invariably interpreted and assessed from the vantage-point of putatively more advanced or robust species of neoclassical price-theory: either Walrasian approaches to price adjustment in a multi-market economy or Marshallian partial equilibrium analysis. The former interpretations were originally propagated by Stigler (1937), Schumpeter (1954: 913) and Samuelson (1952: 61). However, consistent with Jaffé's (1976) de-homogenization of the economics of Menger and Walras, Alter (1990b: 343) has recently asserted that Menger's general economic theorizing and his vision of the price system in particular, were opposed to 'the Walrasian approach' conceived exceedingly broadly. The Marshallian interpretative benchmark was evident in Moss (1978: 28), and, in a magisterial treatment of the origins of Menger's work, Streissler (1990b: 55) located Menger's price theory in a long tradition of German contributions, dating from 1825, which were 'partial equilibrium' analyses *'par excellence'*.

While the above interpretations shed much light on Menger's price theory, what aspects have they possibly attenuated or disguised? Blaug's (1990: 186) remark that the Austrians 'rejected Marshall's partial equilibrium analysis and the kind of economics that Walras advocated' suggests that more attention should be given to the unique and distinctive elements of the Austrian contribution and of Menger's in particular. Accordingly, we shall offer an exposition of Menger's theory of price formation on its own terms and avoid the conventional impulse to view Austrian price theory with strong Walrasian or Marshallian preconceptions.

To foreshadow for the reader what we intend to discuss at length in this chapter, our results may be summarized as follows: Menger's objective was to explain the most general processes of 'economic' price formation. 'Economic' prices are not just *ex post* quantitative magnitudes. Menger's perspective also allows for an account of such prices as they form from the actions of individuals and as they function as inducements to act. He theorizes about an equilibrating system where prices are formed in a potentially terminating process. Equilibrating tendencies in prices distributed within transaction-effecting ranges are treated at length, while discussion of equilibrium prices as point variables does not figure prominently. He considers, mostly imperfectly competitive cases usually with, *inter alia*, a finitely small number of agents bargaining over discrete units. Prices at which transactions occur are formed in 'price duels' and distributed within ranges of indeterminancy so that there is no unique market clearing price. Both Walrasian-type equilibrium price distributions and supply constrained distributions are identifiable in Menger's illustrations. Walrasian *tâtonnement*, Edgeworthian recontracting and Marshallian monopoly price discrimination are not strictly applicable to Menger's illustrations. Menger illuminates price formation with the concept of a step-wise demand relation rather than a Marshallian demand schedule. In the development of sellers' competition, Menger employs conjectural history to predict a slow downward secular movement of prices although final trading prices remain indeterminate. In short, his analysis of price formation is significantly different from *any* other neoclassical position on price theory in late nineteenth-century economic thought, and it set the foundations for further work by Böhm-Bawerk along similar lines.

METHODOLOGICAL CONSIDERATIONS

References in the literature to the theory of value and distribution in Menger's *Principles* have been profuse and exuberant compared with the paucity of attention given to Menger's price theory.[1] In the Introduction to a recent reprint of the *Principles*, Hayek ([1934] 1976: 16) explains that Menger's early experience as a journalist reporting on price movements on stock and securities exchanges significantly influenced the content of the *Principles*.[2] An examination of Menger's Preface confirms Hayek's judgement that *one* of the principal objectives of that book was to develop 'a uniform theory of price' (Hayek [1934] 1976: 17).³ Thus Menger:

> I have devoted special attention to the causal connections between economic phenomena [*inter alia*] for the purpose of establishing *a price theory based upon reality* and placing all price phenomena... together under one unified point of view.
> ([1871] 1976: 49; emphasis added)

Taken literally, the foregoing passage might suggest that Menger is intent on presenting particular, concrete cases of price determination, but this is not his meaning of 'reality' here. Menger intended the *Principles* to be a predominantly 'exact' theoretical contribution; his theory of prices in chapter 5 is no exception.⁴ Exact research produced idealizing theory which nevertheless claimed to be 'based upon reality' (Menger [1871] 1950: 49); it was not merely *a priori* or tautological. Exact research assisted in our understanding of reality. An exact theory of price, for instance, would provide understanding of price formation 'for all times and for all nations which exhibit a traffic in goods' (Menger [1883] 1985: 72).

In the *Investigations*, Menger ([1883] 1985: 71) uses the analysis of price phenomena to illustrate the contrast between *exact*-theoretical economics and *empirical*-theoretical economics. Exact research may posit for a given 'trade area' an inverse relationship between quantity demanded and price which 'can be determined exactly according to measure' (ibid.: 71). For such an outcome, definite assumptions must be stated. Market participants are assumed to be motivated by a need fully to protect their economic interests; act in the absence of error specifically with respect to their economic goals and to the appropriate means for attaining them; have full relevant ('as far as it is of influence on price formation') knowledge of the 'economic situation' and not be impaired by external force. With these assumptions, the direction and magnitude of economic price changes could be established by exact analysis.⁵ By contrast, empirical-theoretical research examines 'real' (non-economic) prices. Particular cases of price adjustment may deviate from economic price adjustment because they are subject to exceptions not permitted in the assumptions of exact theory. The real, empirical law of demand would 'as a rule' indicate the direction but not the magnitude of price changes in specific situations. Chapter 5 of Menger's *Principles* endeavours mainly to present the results of exact research, with modifications to the above assumptions depending on the trading protocols assumed in his illustrations of price formation.[6]

MENGER'S NOTIONS OF EQUILIBRIUM

In the introduction to the chapter on price, Menger defined price, outlined several propositions on the functions of price in an idealized economy, and subsequently absorbed these into the analysis of price-formation and adjustment. First, prices in most general terms are represented by 'quantities of goods actually exchanged'; that is, *ex post* quantitative ratios resulting from actual transactions (of which *numéraire* prices *à la* Walras may be one species). Second, prices are also 'incidental manifestations' of exchange 'activities' (Menger [1871] 1950: 191); they represent inducements to act in exchange, and they arise from the decisions of individuals. The latter allow for a temporal dimension in Menger's treatment – for prices to be formed in a decision process of some kind to be clarified later in his chapter on price. Furthermore, for Menger, theorizing about prices as incidental phenomena can have either an exact or an empirical-theoretical basis.[7] Therefore, the *process* of price formation may have an exact basis so long as exact theory does not result from observation of a particular process or address the real development of such a process.[8] Third, prices are 'symptoms of an economic equilibrium between the economies of individuals' (ibid.). This multi-faceted equilibrium notion is elaborated by way of a metaphor:

> If the locks between two still bodies of water at different levels are opened, the surface will become ruffled with waves that will gradually subside until the water is still once more. The waves are only symptoms of the operation of forces we call gravity and friction.
>
> (ibid.: 192)

Prices are overt symptoms of deeper endogenized forces (or causes/tendencies) *in action*; these forces direct the economizing of individuals, that is, the endeavours of individuals to satisfy their needs.

Markets are places and social institutions where the traffic in goods takes place. The opportunity for exchange activity leads to the generation of prices, and this dynamic was of primary interest to Menger, rather than the precise *ex post* magnitude of prices. The behaviour required to 'open the locks between two unequal bodies of water' is therefore of interest in explicating pricing and equilibrium tendencies, and it is this interest that distinguishes Menger's contribution from those of his contemporaries, some of whom also used analogies relating to water levels to explain the notion of equilibrium. For instance, Roscher (1878: 319) explained that every 'deviation from [the equilibrium of prices] immediately sets forces in motion which endeavour to restore the level, just as the water of the sea seeks its level, notwithstanding the mountains and abysses which the winds bring forth from its bosom'. And Walras's (1954: 380) 'continuous market' refers to the dynamic problem of a succession of instantaneous market adjustments always tending towards or 'seeking' equilibrium: 'the market is like a lake agitated by the wind, where the water is incessantly seeking its level without ever reaching it'. In developing their analogies, both Roscher and Walras avoid detailed investigation of what, precisely at any moment (if we may labour the metaphors), 'activates the wind' or, in Menger's terms, 'opens the locks and generates the waves'.

What is important about Menger's equilibrium concept is the idea that prices in an exchange economy are analogous to waves and therefore disappear in a hypothetical motionless situation. Yet prices are *also* 'symptoms of an economic equilibrium in the distribution of possessions between the economies of individuals' (Menger [1871] 1950: 192). Does Menger mean to say that *any* prices generated in exchange must be symptoms of equilibrium in this sense? If so, then Menger's equilibrium is better expressed as a present participle – an *equilibrating* system – rather than as a noun. An equilibrating system is more all-encompassing than merely signifying the limiting case of a motionless state where transactions have already been effected. Indeed, we could describe situations where there are no waves, which is to imply that there are either no new price quotations, or no plans to buy or sell or no exchanges generated by the underlying forces (viz., human needs which are the ultimate generative causes of exchange). All this sounds much like market behaviour on stock or securities exchanges: if there are no bid-offer pairs (no explicitly stated buy-and-sell price quotations) there will be no inducement to trading activity whatsoever and no possibility for movement. To paraphrase Menger's metaphor, if the locks between two bodies of water are opened the water becomes ruffled (prices formed), otherwise it would remain motionless and the underlying forces would remain inoperative. Stated buy–sell quotations, no matter how widely distributed, are symptomatic of human needs remaining unsatisfied, of communication of that very fact, and of potential for trade under given geographical and temporal conditions. Consider the following cases:[9] first and second, if *either* demand price *or* supply price is quoted (without a matching supply or demand price respectively), this would be a symptom of economic equilibrium in Menger's sense. In the former case, for example, suppliers were presumably satisfied with the distribution of the good in question and were not moved to quote a sale price; the last trade price would be referred to as an equilibrium price. Demand quotations or supply quotations *on their own* were not 'economic prices' in Menger's sense; the *ex post* ratio resulting from an actual transaction constituted the economic price which resulted in the said state of rest and could therefore be termed an equilibrium price. Such a price, like Walras's *numéraire* price, would not have a function.[10] In a third case, when demand price and supply price quotations for a particular good are considered by traders to be too widely dispersed there may be insufficient incentive for potential traders to consider altering their quotations (or plans), and transactions may not be effected. In this case the last trade price would again represent equilibrium in the Mengerian sense, since existing quotations would indicate that traders are already satisfied with the distribution of goods. Menger's concept of equilibrium captures these three possibilities as limiting cases where there is no inherent tendency for change: i.e. for ongoing trading *activity* at a mutually agreed price. Menger was not much interested in such 'points of rest' where an 'economic limit to exchange' had been reached ([1871] 1950: 188).

The Mengerian equilibrating system refers to a potentially terminating process, but the system is not obviously stable or determinate. There is a mutual consistency between the perceptions of willing buyers and sellers (who co-ordinate their plans through price quotation) that a potential for transacting (exchange or price movement) exists; those perceptions may be formed under conditions in which available knowledge is incomplete. The equilibrating system does not generally refer to a state in which mutual compatibility of various transactions has already been achieved, or where price quotations signal that no trading activity will be worthwhile.[11] As we shall demonstrate below, Menger's elaboration of price formation was integrated with, rather than separated from, theorizing about equilibrating movements in prices distributed within ranges. As Streissler (1972: 438) was moved to remark, 'Menger...could not even conceive of equilibrium as anything precisely describable.'

Equilibrium and equilibrating tendencies in prices do not subsist alone in Menger's chapter on price. It is possible that he was disinclined to treat these concepts separately because he wished to leave room for an empirical-theoretical treatment of the position of equilibrium as dependent on the path by which it is reached. There are, in short, traces of what Hans Mayer (1932) termed 'genetic-causal' equilibrium in Menger's *Principles*. This concept was refined later in the Austrian tradition, and it attempted to encapsulate the path of a trading process including the intermediate stages up to the attainment of equilibrium. The preferences, bargaining skills, traders' idiosyncracies and various constraints on trading in any one bargaining session are, in the genetic-causal account, seen as being changing and changeable by the events of the preceding session. The main implication for microeconomic theory is that the distinctive contribution of Austrian economists, beginning with Menger, is a price theory concerned with explaining how prices are actually formed. Mayer (1932: 224) referred to such theories as *Preisbildungstheorien* (theories of price formation). Theories of price formation contrast with theories of price determination (*Preisbestimmungstheorien*), which are concerned with finding a consistent set of market clearing prices along Walrasian lines and describing those relations between the elements of an equilibrium price system that must logically obtain if such a set of prices is to exist.

A necessary precondition for potential trading is a divergence between plans or between stated demand and supply quotations. If trades were reversible, all relevant market conditions and traders' valuations remaining unchanged, demand price and supply price would be equivalent measured either as a sum of money or as quantity of goods, and there would be no point in effecting the transaction. For Menger ([1871] 1950: 193) trade irreversibility is a ubiquitous 'general feature of social economy' that his theory of price formation attempts to encapsulate. Again, his prime interest is in equilibrating processes, in trading activity and hence in the pricing of 'even...the most saleable commodities' in 'highly developed conditions of trade':

> [Let] anyone buy securities on a stock exchange and try to sell them again before a change in market conditions occurs, or let him try to sell and buy separate units of the same commodity at the same time, and he will easily be convinced that the difference between supply prices and demand prices is no mere accident.
> (ibid.)

MENGER'S THEORY OF PRICE FORMATION

Menger's theory of price formation aims to sketch price setting behaviour, in which traders transmit divergent price indications to the market before exchange takes place, as well as the actions of traders that lead to some price bounds, within which transactions are eventually completed.

THE FORMATION OF PRODUCT PRICES IN A DECENTRALIZED ECONOMY: FIVE ILLUSTRATIONS

1. Isolated exchange

The first type of price setting involves 'price formation in isolated exchange' (Menger [1871] 1950: 194) where product prices result from bilateral bargaining between traders after initial quotations (proposed, but not actual, trading prices) from both sides of the market. This form of exchange is stated to be common 'in the early stages of the development of civilization'.

We enter Menger's economy of isolated exchange at a point in time; while some of the data of the situation (information, tastes) are not clearly stated, it is announced that a grain owner (A) wishes to exchange less than 100 units of grain for 40 units of wine with a wine-owner. The goods have already been produced; allocative problems on the production side have already been solved by the exchangers, and factor prices have already been formed in anticipation of relative product prices. Menger's temporal perspective admits a lapse of time between A's decision to exchange and A's attempt to *'find*... an economizing individual to whom a smaller quantity than 100 units of grain has a greater importance than 40 units of wine' (Menger [1871] 1950: 194; emphasis added). In other words, economic exchange and bargaining will only take place if a grain demander *can be found* at a demand price of less than 100 units of grain. At this point wine trader B is found and quotes a demand price of an amount just greater than 80 units of grain for what is presumably a 40-unit *indivisible* barrel of wine. There is potential for exchange, and Menger then hastens to specify data of the situation: the full recognition of price quotations by the traders, and *ipso facto* each other's preferences, and the absence of barriers to exchange. A 'price duel' ensues. The duel involves a sequence of price offers and counter offers (195), and no trades actually take place. In bargaining, the traders ostensibly go through the motions of testing each other's knowledge of the set of possible mutually beneficial allocations. While the bargaining protocol is not explicitly specified, it cannot strictly be conceived as an Edgeworth-type recontracting process. When Menger refers in passing to trader A having to *find* trader B, the search may take on something like recontracting, but the discovery exercise is of only minor interest.[12] That Menger is uninterested in any form of recontracting may be explained by his penchant for theorizing in an exact sense. He presupposes the existence of bargaining behaviour in price duels involving careful prior deliberation such that movement from the original endowment point to a Pareto-efficient agreement between the two traders necessarily follows. Menger is not concerned with 'particular exchange situations' (ibid.: 199), which may be

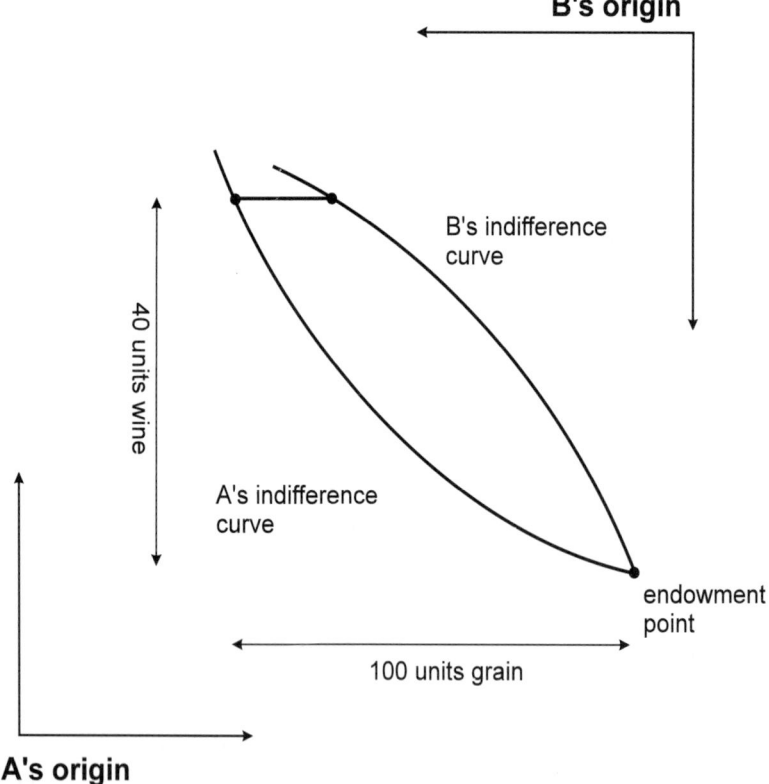

Figure 1 An Edgeworth–Bowley reconstruction of Mengerian isolated exchange

characterized by protracted searching processes; he is satisfied that the search for potential traders has been completed, although provision is made for a time lapse.

If we attempt to consider Menger's illustration of bilateral exchange in an Edgeworth box framework (see Figure 1 above), the post-trade allocation is a horizontal range, since Menger fixes the quantity of wine traded at 40 units. Indivisibility is alien to Edgeworth's treatment; Edgeworth also requires continuity of preferences along indifference curves, and, of course, a locus of tangencies between indifference curves is needed to construct the familiar contract curve. None of this can confidently be attributed to Menger's analysis. Nevertheless, Menger's final settlement range of between 80 and 100 units of grain for 40 units of wine is the analogue of Edgeworth's contract curve when one of the two goods is fixed. Furthermore, unlike Edgeworth, Menger considered only a single trade, leaving a free range only for the quantity of the other good.

In the next stage of his argument Menger intermingles exact and empirical-theoretical reasoning, and these need to be unravelled. So-called 'non-economic' influences on exchange – information asymmetries, 'human caprice', and factors founded on traders' unique personalities – could result in a final transaction price which is not the arithmetic average of the two price limits (where the limits are 80 and 100 units of grain for 40 units of wine). The transaction-price range (but not reasons for deviation within the range) may still be referred to as an 'economic' one so long as the price remains between 80 and 100 units of grain. Menger says that any real transaction price 'will sometimes prove more favorable to one and sometimes more favorable to the other of the two bargainers, depending upon their various individualities and upon their greater or smaller knowledge of business life and, in each case, of the situation of the other bargainer' (ibid.: 195). The range, and the final arithmetic average transaction price within the range, can both have an exact-theoretical meaning.[13] The range of prices is 'economic'; as Menger maintains, exchange at any price within the 'definite limits' of that range would have 'economic character' (ibid.: 197). Menger does not depart from exact theorizing in concluding that the final transaction price will not be a fixed (arithmetic average) point; rather, it will fall within a range. When the transaction price is not the unique, arithmetic average of the limits of the price range, empirical-theoretical research would then have to establish by observation which non-economic influences have been influential. That is, 'economic influences do not in any way, within this range of freedom fix the point at which price formation must, of necessity take place' (ibid.: 199). The extent of the range will depend on particular, concrete circumstances of the exchange situation.

Within the ambit of exact-theoretical research, Menger concludes unconvincingly that the transaction price – the arithmetic average – would be 90 units of grain.[14] The presuppositions are that non-economic influences are inoperative, that neither trader has 'an overwhelming economic talent', and that they are 'equally capable'. Both traders must be aware of their equal capabilities. All this is consistent with Menger's early 'Notes on Rau', which formed part of the drafts of his *Principles*. In those 'Notes' he gives much weight to the assumption of equal bargaining power in the analysis of bilateral exchange (Yagi 1993: 712). The price duel would then be 'mutually paralyzing' (Menger [1871] 1950: 196). It is notable that these assumptions, so far as they are elaborated, do not categorically rule out incomplete information; a mutually countervailing exogenous limit both on information and on information processing ('talent') is posited for both traders. Neither information nor the ways in which agents process information are necessarily regarded as perfect, but they are fixed *ab initio*. Menger is only theorizing in an exact sense about economic price formation at a conjectured stage in the development of markets or exchange institutions (or of what he calls 'civilization').[15] Within any hypothetical stage, Menger's traders do not change the ways in which they process information even if they are 'mutually paralyzed' by incomplete knowledge of the consequences of their bargaining. Traders' plans are nevertheless compatible and implementable given the data of the situation.

2. Competition among buyers for a single unit of a monopolized good

In the second type of price setting arrangement discussed by Menger the context remains a decentralized economy in which markets are organized independently of one another. There is, in other words, no suggestion of a Walrasian multi-market economy where general interdependence occurs. The following market situation is constructed: a selling agent who appears as a monopolist, who brings a single indivisible good (a horse) to market with no re-sale (implicitly) and who elicits *sealed bids* from buyers in a sequential process. The horse has obviously already been produced in anticipation of a buyer. On the buyers' side, there is a finite number of agents who are prepared to exchange varying amounts of grain for the horse. The *initial* information structure relies on the private-values assumption. That is, according to modern literature on auctions, bidders know their own valuations but not those of others, and sellers do not know the valuations of bidders. Each bidder knows what winning will be worth to him or her, but has no information on what it would be worth to others (Milgrom 1989: 4). For Menger, the maximum willingness to pay for each bidder lies just *below their valuations*, with the proviso that bids are restricted to integer values. The economic price at which exchange takes place is not a single price but a price range (in terms of grain) which is not known by potential traders in advance but emerges in a trading process. That range will narrow depending on the number of buyers who spontaneously 'appear on the scene' (ibid.: 202) and engage in a price duel. Consideration of buyers' offers takes time. A halt to this process occurs when the flow of buyers appearing on the scene is assumed to stop and a transaction is effected.

The transaction price will move towards and fall within a range of economic prices set by a lower bound – the buyers' commodity equivalent (grain) of the seller's horse that could be purchased by the individual with the lowest willingness to pay (i.e. with the least 'strength in exchanging', *Tauschfähigkeit*), but who still participates in the bidding – and an upper bound – the grain equivalent of the horse to the individual with the highest willingness to pay. This result is elaborated in illustration (3) below.

That Menger's result is robust to departures from the private-values assumption is evident in a footnote (ibid.: 201 n. 3). In the example of an 'auction sale', horse-seller A is faced with two bidders B_1 (valuing the horse at 80 units of grain) and B_2 (valuing the horse at 30 units of grain); Menger restricts the price outcome to a single point (30 units of grain) representing the bid of B_1, provided post-bidding negotiation is excluded. However, if A 'does not bind himself from the beginning with an auction contract', which is Menger's general presumption in the main body of the text, then relative bargaining talents will matter in an ensuing negotiation between A and B_1. In negotiation, the seller may develop better estimates of what the horse will be worth to B_1 and price may form anywhere in a range 30 units of grain $\leq$ horse price $<$ 79 units.

3. Competition for several units of a monopolized good

When there is competition for more than one unit of an indivisible monopolized good, the monopolist is assumed to fix the quantity (horses) offered for auction at the beginning. Buyers then settle quickly and systematically (rather than in a trial-and-error or *tâtonnement* process), the transaction price limits in terms of the buyers' commodity (grain) (Menger [1871] 1950: 203–7). Buyers are assumed independently of one another to value the seller's good prior to presenting themselves and their sealed bids to the seller. These bids are transmitted to the market by each trader before exchange occurs. As before, buyers would be willing and able to pay amounts up to (but not equal to) their valuations, but stated valuations in themselves do not ensure that buyers will achieve their desired trades (Menger has no concept of 'indifference').

The limits set on the transaction price (in terms of grain) will depend on the number of horses for sale, the number of buyers, and the schedule of buyers' valuations. The range of economic prices will be formed as in the foregoing illustration of buyers' competition for a single good; the possible ranges being illustrated by Menger in a table with up to 8 buyers and 8 horses for sale (ibid.: 207) (see Table 3 below).[16] As before, there is no hint that buyers will come to the market fully apprised of final transaction price limits. Notwithstanding the absence of perfect foresight, the private values assumption applies; the very existence of the institution

Table 3 Menger's auction

NUMBER OF BUSHELS OF GRAIN THAT ARE EQUAL IN VALUE TO AN ADDITIONAL HORSE ACQUIRED BY TRADE

	1st horse	2nd horse	3rd horse	4th horse	5th horse	6th horse	7th horse	8th horse
To B_1	80	70	60	50	40	30	20	10
To B_2	70	60	50	40	30	20	10	
To B_3	60	50	40	30	20	10		
To B_4	50	40	30	20	10			
To B_5	40	30	20	10				
To B_6	30	20	10					
To B_7	20	10						
To B_8	10							

Source: Menger [1871] 1950: 204.

of a well-organized market allows market participants to realize plan co-ordination without so much as a quibble. Some buyers are eliminated in the ensuing price duel within the now established price limits which are determined as soon as relevant data are stated (number of units for sale, the finite number of buyers). The buyers involved in the price duel are price makers; the transaction price is not parametric, and unlimited trading does not take place in the price range which is formed, as we might expect in a Walrasian auction market. Furthermore, as demonstrated in Table 4 below, Menger's price theory does not predict a unique price *ex ante*. The essential unity of his theorizing on price formation is to be found in the focus on price distributions rather than unique market clearing prices as point variables.

Table 4 Solution to Menger's original auction

Units brought to market	Horse price range	Excess demand
1	$70 \leqslant P_h < 80$	0
2	$60 \leqslant P_h < 70$	1
3	$60 \leqslant P_h < 70$	0
4	$50 \leqslant P_h < 60$	2
5	$50 \leqslant P_h < 60$	1
6	$50 \leqslant P_h < 60$	0
7	$40 \leqslant P_h < 50$	3
8	$40 \leqslant P_h < 50$	2
9	$40 \leqslant P_h < 50$	1
10	$40 \leqslant P_h < 50$	0

Menger ([1871] 1950: 208) states that buyers' competition for several units of a monopolized good would amount to an 'auction'.[17] Menger's auction in this case is a variant on the English style, where the buyers openly cry out their bids, but in this case successively higher sealed bids are solicited among the most eager buyers (given a known quantity of horses for sale). The most eager buyers will be left bidding in a price range which does not exceed their maximum willingness to pay but which excludes those less eager (ibid.: 205). Here Menger mentions the possibility that agreements could be made openly between the most eager buyers in the process of establishing equilibrating price ranges, but a more sophisticated Bertrand-type equilibrium solution escaped his grasp. The final, personalized transaction price is an empirical-theoretical matter and, as before, it depends on the price duel involving the bargaining talents and personalities of the remaining traders. Furthermore, in this illustration Menger does not assume that the seller has a reserve price, other than that it must be non-zero. The horses are sold to the highest bidders.

Facing buyers' competition, it is conceivable that the monopolist would have the choice of restricting the quantity offered for sale. However, in the present case, Menger analyses the impact of buyers' competition *in vacuo*, assuming that the monopolist places a certain quantity on the market, passively and all at once. In addition, the monopolist offers a quantity for sale before buyers' valuations are known. This is not, therefore, equivalent to presuming that a *tâtonnement* process is operative with the necessary changes for monopoly on the supply side. Prices are systematically bid up in Menger's auction; trading is not contemplated by the initial communication of random price bids/quantities offered as in a Walrasian price-auction market (Walras 1954: 242). There is one sense, nevertheless, in which 'false' transactions in the Walrasian sense do not take place in this Mengerian auction: the price limits are the unintended outcome of interaction among traders, and transactions must take place within these limits, although, as demonstrated in Table 4 below, the market may not clear in the Walrasian sense.

Two types of equilibrating price ranges are identifiable in Table 4. Market clearing in the Walrasian sense occurs for quantities 1, 3, 6 and 10 brought to market. For quantities 2, 4, 5, 7, 8 and 9, we have quantity constrained equilibrating price ranges (for a modern statement on these ranges, see Dehez and Drèze 1984). The latter are characterized by prices which cannot move outside the established range, which is to say that: (1) actual buyers within the established range would not bid up price beyond that range because they know that supply will not be augmented and (2) the seller is on the short side of the market; the seller could sell more within the price range but cannot bring more horses to market.

We would expect that in cases of excess demand (e.g. 7 horses, $40 \leq P_h < 50$) any bargaining will result in a price at the top of the range (i.e. $P_h = 49$) if prices must be integer. When excess demand appears in Table 4, the bargaining strategies adopted in the bidding game are critical for the distribution of horses after the auction. For instance, when four units are marketed, who gets to buy the horses and who is unable to purchase their required quantity within the prevailing price range? Menger does not offer an explanation, perhaps because a satisfactory answer would require the introduction of what he called non-economic factors such as an account of traders' different bargaining talents. Menger could have avoided the non-clearing problem if he had altered B_2's row to read '71, 61...', and B_3's row to read '62, 52...', and so on. That he was not moved to make such alterations reveals that market clearing by price adjustment was inessential to his theory of price formation.

The discrete nature of bids and goods in Menger's original table renders it impossible to construct a demand curve for each bidder of the ordinary kind (see the demand relation for B_1 in Figure 2 below). Indivisibility and satiation (since the relation meets the quantity axis) are responsible for the form of Figure 2. Strictly speaking, Figure 2 is not completely faithful to Menger's account; it is merely an approximation, because the solid-line vertical sections of the demand relation do not reflect Menger's belief that bids are restricted to integer values. It is precisely the discrete nature of Menger's auction market, in conjunction with the admittance of bargaining, that makes his analysis distinctive in late nineteenth-century economic thought. Most markets are discrete, although mathematical tractability made the transition to continuous cases tempting for Walrasians and Marshallians.

4. Active monopoly pricing

Menger's fourth case of price formation, active monopoly pricing, is formulated in an exact-theoretical manner in the sense that 'the entire course of economic events' in this class is 'capable of being reduced to definite principles' (Menger [1871] 1950: 215). He examines procedures adopted by a *fully informed* (ibid.: 216) monopolist who is not simply constrained within a very 'limited period of time' to sell the complete stock of a monopolized good (cf. Menger's previous case, ibid.: 208). In this case Menger makes some tantalizing allusions to the temporal structure of product pricing in a manner not previously encountered in his chapter on price theory.

The monopolist may, for instance, choose the price at which goods are sold. This choice is most beneficial to the monopolist if it is effected sequentially, with transactions arranged at successively lower prices over some hypothetical period of time:

> In the beginning, he will set the price as high as possible and thus market only small quantities of the monopolized good,

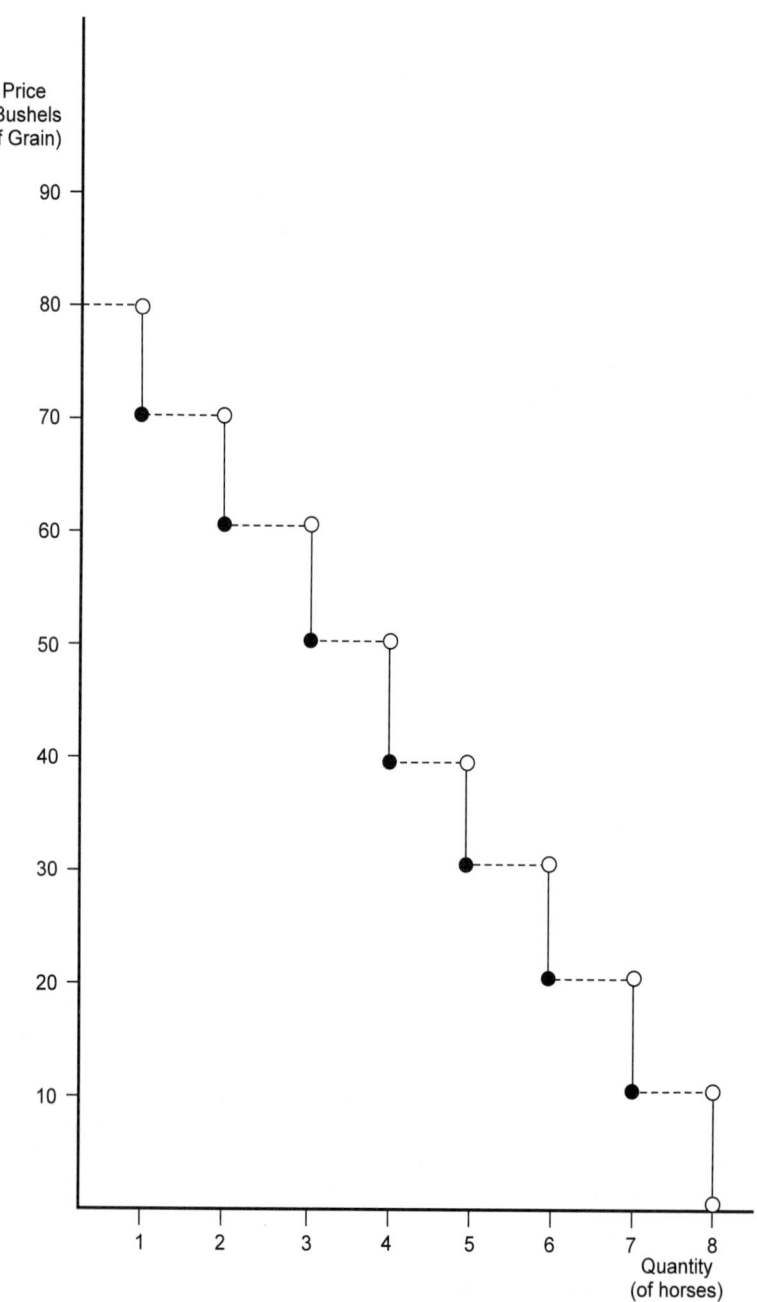

Figure 2 Demand relation for trader B_1 in Menger's auction

later lowering the price step by step to increase sales and thereby exploiting all classes of the population in succession – if he can obtain the greatest economic gain by following this procedure.

(ibid.: 212; similar strategies are described at 223, 234)

The market is a closed one, and all potential (finite) classes of buyers are present, although existing buyers may refrain from bidding if prices are unsuitable. The monopolist is on the long side of the market in the sense that the marketing plan will be to sell more at a higher price if there is sufficient demand.[18] Alternatively expressed, Menger's description of the monopolist's behaviour can be understood as a strategy in which the seller begins by asking a high price and gradually abates the price until different classes of bidders decide to claim some of the goods. For Menger's monopolist this is akin to adopting continuous sealed-bid, open Dutch auctions. The auctions take place over unspecified but successive periods of time, and the monopolist attempts to appropriate more consumer surplus than would be the case if all the goods were sold simultaneously. The private values assumption applies to buyers, and the most eager buyers will not, in this case, gain any information either about other buyers' intentions in the auction process, or the seller's stocks, or the seller's future sale intentions. The seller is fully informed about buyers' incomes and tastes. The outcome is a series of transaction prices over periods of time rather than either a single fixed-point price or an equilibrating price range, with the first horse in Menger's table selling when the price falls just below 80 bushels of grain. Strategic considerations are, unfortunately, avoided in the text.[19] Furthermore, demand and supply are not conceived as determinate functions of price in any mathematical sense.[20] Transaction prices are instead formed in an irrevocable, exploitative marketing sequence.

Unlike textbook Marshallian analyses of price discrimination, where everything occurs more or less instantaneously, Mengerian price discrimination is a temporally sequential process. Moreover, Menger ignores the effect of discrimination on total output (he would then have been required to consider cost conditions), possibly because he implicitly assumes unchanged output in the long run. Menger did not draw traditional demand curves but his demand relation illustrated in Figure 2 (above) evidently points to a need to reconstitute, in conformation, any aggregate relation that might be constructed for all the bidders in his original table, given that a monopolist's sales are sequential. A plausible interpretation of Menger's notion of sequential transactions is that demand relations for individuals or for various classes of individuals would appear as a series of simultaneous *alternative* maximum bids for quantities associated with each price.[21] It is not clear from Menger's description of the auction in Table 1 (above) whether the various alternative valuations could be considered independent and valid within a given unit of time. Does each lower maximum bid for a larger quantity depend on the assumption that a higher maximum bid for a smaller quantity was not realized previously? The time interval between successive transactions would have to be delimited; Menger's analysis is vitiated in this respect.

Menger nevertheless allowed explicitly for the case where a monopolist sells at consecutively lower prices, thereby 'exploiting all classes of the population in succession' (Menger [1871] 1950: 212). In the way Menger elaborates on monopoly price formation the selling agent is in a position to exploit, rather than passively to accept, the fundamental data of present and future by successfully predicting the level and timing of buyers' incomes and the intertemporal rhythm of buyers' wants. Price discrimination of a near perfect kind is then possible, especially if each consuming 'class of the population' bought discrete units of the product through time and can be required to pay just less than their maximum valuations for it.[22] For more than one unit per trading period (but still a limited number) some considerable discrimination is still possible for each consuming class arranged in a hierarchy of willingness and ability to pay. Provided that each class varied the amount purchased, both in a trading period which was exclusive to their dealings with the seller and within an initial price range which was high enough to exclude other classes lower in the hierarchy, then each class could conceivably be sequentially exploited in Menger's sense.

Menger envisaged demand in terms of discrete units and not infinitesimal amounts. If we relax for a moment the assumption of discrete quantities, it could then be claimed that Menger perceived heterogeneous classes of the population as having intramarginal demand schedules, in that alternative amounts are purchased to satisfy needs up to *present* satiation but nothing beyond, so that the corresponding demand relation meets the quantity axis. Buyers purchase what they need; if the price were higher they would bid for a smaller quantity. (A demand schedule would be 'marginal', as Morgenstern (1972: 1117) explains, if the price is so high that the maximum desired quantity is unattainable and the consumer's maximum bid is for a smaller quantity than what is desired for present satiation.)[23] In these circumstances it is doubtful whether an aggregate, market demand relation would have been a meaningful aid for Menger in his attempt to describe monopoly price formation. If an aggregate demand curve of the ordinary kind existed at all, it would have to be reconstituted after each irrevocable transaction, because, among other things, the number of buyers, and income availability, will not necessarily remain constant during the Mengerian trading process. At least in the short term, some classes of buyers are eliminated from the market. The elimination of buyers in a closed market, as Morgenstern (1948: 180) noticed, 'amounts to changing the entire structure of the market because – to speak now in terms of the theory of games – an n-person game has been transformed into an m-person game ($m \neq n$) and the theory [of games] shows that this entails very important consequences'. As Morgenstern insisted, these consequences cannot adequately be described by aggregate demand curves of conventional price theory. In Menger's early, tentative incursion into this field there is evidence of a desire not to submerge the micro-level complexities of demand through time by analyses which turn on static constructs such as Marshallian market demand schedules.

The first demand schedule drawn to interpret Menger's original horse auction appeared in Pantaleoni ([1898] 1957: 149). Our Table 4 and Figure 2 are sufficient to call into question Pantaleoni's conclusion that Menger's demand 'curve' 'coincides with the diagrams of demand of Cournot, Jevons and Marshall'. In reaching this conclusion Pantaleoni overlooked the importance of discrete bids and goods in Menger's auction; he also presumed that there was sufficient competition among buyers to eliminate positive excess demands. In a closed, time-segmented market where competition among buyers is limited, Pantaleoni allows for Menger's case in which the monopolist offered 'increments [of the good]...waiting for the first to be sold *before* he offered the second' (Pantaleoni [1898] 1957: 151; emphasis added). However, Pantaleoni does not realize that monopoly behaviour of this kind would lead to a shift in the Mengerian market demand relation, if one should be constructed, to a new set of market price-quantity relations with a buyer's demands (or classes of buyers' demands) successively dropping out. This is an implication of Menger's comment on temporally sequential transactions which Pantaleoni does not address.

We are now in a position to propose that Menger's account of the monopolist's temporally sequential actions makes Kirzner's injunctions against Menger's price theory appear as though they have been made too summarily. On Kirzner's (1978: 38) reading, 'in his chapter on price Menger seems unaccountably to lapse into a world in which equilibrium prices are instantaneously determined'.[24] Menger's formulation of the process of active monopoly pricing makes it clear that he was variously interested both in irrevocable transactions near the top end of each of the previously established price ranges, and in wide dispersion of prices for similar goods in circumstances where hypothetical time lapses are permitted, where sellers are fully informed and where there is insufficient information on the demand side.

5. Full competition with special reference to sellers' competition

In discussing the origins of competition as a preamble to analysing price formation under full sellers' competition, Menger reveals his interest in a further temporal dimension: the contours of product pricing in the very long run in relation to the 'economic progress of civilization'. Changes in population and income distribution, and increases in human knowledge, which are pivotal in economic progress, often carry with them secular changes in the pattern of competition. Monopoly is, 'as a rule, the earlier and more primitive phenomenon, and competition the phenomenon coming later in time'. Menger intends to examine 'the effects of the appearance of competition upon the distribution, sales and price of a commodity' ([1871] 1950: 217–18).

Menger concentrates on the 'appearance of competition in supply' (ibid.: 222) given a large number of buyers. With at least two suppliers it is considered that suppliers act independently and have no power over prices; they cannot increase profit by restricting supply, for fear that competitors will benefit. As Moss (1978: 27) points out, Menger observes that 'the demand curve facing an individual supplier is more elastic than the entire demand curve for the product'. Menger's examples implicitly presume (rather than deduce, *pace* Moss) that the elasticity of demand facing the individual supplier is greater than unity, otherwise it is possible that both suppliers could benefit from restricting supply. It should be proposed in Menger's defence that the situation he chooses to analyse is one of the above form and that his conclusion is valid given the assumptions. Two independent sellers under these assumptions would enter 'real competition' (ibid.: 221); long-run supply price would fall to something well below the price ruling in the case of a single seller. While the possibility of collusion among sellers is recognized, Menger's exact-theoretical reasoning strictly adheres to the foregoing assumptions regarding individual and market demand conditions.[25]

It is not so straightforward to dismiss uneasiness regarding the inscrutable position that Menger held on the cost conditions facing sellers. Wicksell ([1924] 1958: 199) made much of an apparent inconsistency in Menger's analysis of price: 'while [for] the individual seller under competitive conditions...production is subject to rising costs of manufacture so that seller's profit is a sort of quasi-rent...in the case of the monopolist...he is assured that the costs of production are constant'. Constant costs in the situation of seller's competition should lead to the elimination of economic profit. This is not, however, the final outcome of Mengerian sellers' competition, which, Menger ([1871] 1950: 225) says, leads to sellers producing on a 'large scale...with its tendency to make small profits'. Sellers' competition certainly leads to more extensive use of the means of production up to their 'natural' limits (ibid.: 222, 224), in which case increasing costs may be loosely rationalized; Menger's comments betray a rather primitive treatment of costs. He shows no interest in the problem of the determination of optimal output. Menger *is* clear on sellers' knowledge endowments. Sellers do not act in error and are fully informed as regards the entire quantity in their own and in their competitors' hands (ibid.: 224). It is in this specific sense that competing, independent sellers 'fix' their prices with full relevant knowledge. A general increase in the available quantity of goods follows (by contrast with the single-seller case), and prices fall in the process.

Notable in Menger's discussion of sellers' competition is that the argument is placed in a purely conjectural developmental perspective. It is a long-term outlook which endogenizes a tendency of market conditions and institutions to change under a hypothetical regime of sellers' competition. Initially, a single seller dies, leaving two potentially rivalrous heirs with equal shares (ibid.: 221). The heirs may decide to 'enter into a mutual understanding' to exploit buyers, but the *general* case is one of independent competitive behaviour causing an increase in supply, and a lower price. There is movement in price and quantity: 'more classes of society are able to consume the commodity at *falling* prices, and ... the provisioning of society in general *becomes* ever more complete' (ibid.: 224; emphasis added). Monopoly price discrimination 'becomes impossible' (ibid.: 223). Competition is a dynamic process, typically introducing itself gradually; it tends to 'descend with its goods to the lowest social classes' (ibid.: 225) and to increase the extent of exchange opportunities. With competition the available supply 'generally considerably increases', and 'reductions in prices are a consequence' (ibid.: 224). Here there is a suggestion, but no more than an oblique one, of a fall in prices in slow gradations, in response to supply augmentation consequent upon fuller utilization of the means of production. Thus competition 'not only causes the entire quantity of a commodity *actually* available to be offered for sale, but also has the fuller and much more important result of increasing significantly the quantity that *becomes* available' (ibid.: 224; emphasis added). Now all this is a form of conjectural theorizing consistent with exact-theoretical research. To paraphrase Menger's *Investigations* ([1883] 1985: 57), it treats typical phenomena by abstracting from all special, spatio-temporal circumstances. The transaction prices ultimately formed in full-fledged competition are not adumbrated by Menger. By dint of his concentration on the broad direction of prices to move in a downward direction upon the assumed 'appearance' of sellers' competition, he only refers to highly general, non-determinate results. He predicts falls in prices; the speed of downward adjustment is not specified, although his temporal perspective is evidently a long one.[26] Prices will nevertheless remain economic – in equilibrating ranges – as before. A multiplicity of sellers, and a large number of buyers, would create co-ordination problems overcome by the introduction of a class of speculators and *arbitragers* who would be interested in the re-sale of goods on auction. Economic prices would then be maintained, although the equilibrating ranges would be considerably narrowed compared with those established in some illustrations of imperfect competition (Menger [1871] 1950: 218–19 n. 7, 250–3).

CONCLUSION

Even in his fifth and last illustration of price formation under sellers' competition Menger analyses prices in a single market. As usual, he relegates to the background those aspects of the institutional organization of markets and exchange relations which may be regarded as preconditions for effecting viable needs-satisfying exchanges. As is well-known, in a subsequent chapter of the *Principles* Menger treats these organizational matters under the rubric of the 'degree of marketability of commodities' ([1871] 1950: 242–6).

From one point of view the scope of Menger's price theory is limited because he ignores the general interdependence of markets which historiographers with Walrasian preconceptions might expect. And there is no indication that he intended to analyse price formation in a single market under the presupposition of the invariance of conditions obtaining in other markets. Mengerian price formation takes place in an equilibrating bargaining process where both limitations on traders' bargaining talents and hypothetical temporal dimensions are evident in his five illustrations. Market clearing and supply constrained ranges of economic prices originate bargaining activities among a finite number of individuals buying goods in lumpy units in regimes of mostly imperfect competition. Mengerian individual demand relations are best characterized as 'intramarginal' in a restricted sense, while aggregate or market demand relations are not meaningful in Menger's illustrations, especially in the case of monopoly pricing. Mengerian price discrimination posits sequential selling through time to classes of less than fully informed consumers arranged in a hierarchy; the omniscient monopolist makes trading sessions exclusive to each class, and the law of one price does not apply. In Menger's illustrations there is no clearly defined role for the firm, and sellers' cost conditions remain obscure, perhaps because his focus is directed to the decisive importance of buyers' valuations in price formation.

In this chapter we have taken chapter 5 of Menger's *Principles* in isolation and produced some textual evidence of Menger's originality. He was responsible for developing a theory of price formation which did not simply absorb proto-Marshallian notions or correspond fully to Walrasian price-auction theory. His mode of theorizing yielded some rich insights, which were later refined in other contributions to the Austrian tradition, especially Böhm-Bawerk's (1959b) analyses of bargaining and of intertemporal price formation in a pure exchange economy. We shall explore Böhm-Bawerk's contributions in the next chapter. The distinctiveness and exemplary character of Menger's contribution on price formation may further be restored to view in additional exploratory work on the price theories of other leading first-generation Austrians. Mengerian price theoretic themes in modern economics may be found in aspects of game theory, in the literature on auctions, and in the Austro-American tradition of market process analysis.

6

BÖHM-BAWERK'S VALUE AND PRICE THEORY

INTRODUCTION

In this chapter we investigate Böhm-Bawerk's version of Austrian microeconomics. Böhm-Bawerk offered some ideas on the microfoundations of early Austrian economics which were elaborations on Menger's theory of price formation. We therefore draw some comparisons with Carl Menger's programmatic work on the principles of economic theory which originally established a distinctive Austrian tradition. Böhm-Bawerk's microeconomics is also considered against the background of contemporary Walrasian, Edgeworthian and Marshallian thought as well as twentieth-century work on the theory of games.

In reflecting on developments in game theory Oskar Morgenstern (1976: 805) acknowledged that he was 'constantly troubled' by Eugen von Böhm-Bawerk's early attempt to formulate a theory of price formation based on bargaining. Nevertheless, Morgenstern complimented Böhm-Bawerk for successfully treating 'fundamentals'. Indeed, in the *Theory of Games and Economic Behaviour*, Von Neumann and Morgenstern (1947: 9) paid tribute to Böhm-Bawerk's pioneering work in microeconomic theory. Furthermore, in the early collaboration between von Neumann and Morgenstern, Böhm-Bawerk's micro-analysis figured prominently: 'I showed him [von Neumann] the causal relationships in [Böhm-Bawerk's] price-theory, where...one obtains different results, depending on the assumed knowledge of the other's position'.[1] It is therefore surprising that Böhm-Bawerk's microeconomics has not attracted careful analysis by historians of economic thought. Our warrant for this study also comes from Böhm-Bawerk (1891: 380–1) himself: 'We must not weary of studying the microcosm if we wish rightly to understand the macrocosm of a developed economic order.' Accordingly we shall give special attention to his ideas on value, exchange, markets and price formation, which we consider were elaborations and extensions of Menger's ideas on these matters. Where relevant, as we proceed, any game-theoretic elements will be elicited later in this chapter.

Our primary concern is to establish precisely what was distinctive about Böhm-Bawerk's version of Austrian microeconomic theory; a secondary objective is to reflect on his ideas against the background of contemporary Walrasian, Edgeworthian and Marshallian thought. Our secondary objective is particularly relevant in the modern interpretative literature on the Austrian School given Max Alter's (1990a: 228) unsubstantiated proposition that Böhm-Bawerk's work can be 'locate[d] quite firmly in the camp of today's general equilibrium theorists, at least...as far as his theory of prices is concerned'. Earlier commentators proposed otherwise. For example, according to Nyblén (1951: 72), it 'must not be forgotten...that a critical attitude towards the Walrasian central theory, linked with more or less systematic alternatives to it, has been presented during the course of the science of economics. We mention...Böhm-Bawerk.' Howey (1960: 160) concurred: 'Böhm-Bawerk discovered Jevons's *Theory*...and had looked at parts of it, and he probably knew something about Walras's *Elements* too. But he never followed their procedure in any way in the consideration of price.'[2]

It should be emphasized at the outset that there is nothing especially Walrasian, or for that matter Marshallian, about Böhm-Bawerk's microeconomics. In particular, to anticipate one of our conclusions, the Böhm-Bawerkian emphasis on intentionality and imagination in value creation, the avowed scope for bargaining and strategic behaviour in his theory of markets, and the indeterminacies and equilibrating tendencies in his theory of price formation are not only entirely consistent with other first-generation Austrian contributions; they are also evident in aspects of modern Austrian economics and in the theory of games.

FIRST PRINCIPLES: THE NATURE OF VALUE

Before a theory of price formation on markets could be considered, the concept of value deserved careful examination. For Böhm-Bawerk, the market price of a present consumer good was not a relevant question prior to the acceptance of individual, evaluating minds which placed subjective valuations upon that good. Such valuations would differ between individuals 'according to their very various wants and inclinations on the one hand and their property and income on the other' (Böhm-Bawerk 1891: 367). Different subjective valuations between individuals give rise to a willingness, indeed provide the impulse or motivation for exchange; price formation is the resultant.

Positive Theory of Capital is replete with illustrations of the nature of value which is treated in isolation from value in exchange. Böhm-Bawerk was imbued with a distinctly Austrian general value theory, and particularly with the work of Austrian psychologist-philosopher C. von Ehrenfels.[3] In this tradition intrinsic value (*Eigenwert*) is distinguished from extrinsic value (*Wirkungswert*). Things possess intrinsic value if they are desired for their own sake; they possess extrinsic value if they are desired as means for promoting an individual's ultimate objectives. All *economic* value is of an extrinsic character, where the epithet 'economic' denotes that the means are scarce and have to be allocated carefully in order to achieve objectives (Böhm-Bawerk, 1959b: 121).[4] Scarcity implies that a good will have some perceived 'significance' or 'importance' for the individual economizer's 'well-being'. Thus we have extrinsic *subjective* value which refers to the 'significance which a good... possesses for the well-being of a certain subject' such that 'the good satisfies some want, provides some gratification, affords some pleasure or spares...some pain', and which would be forgone if the subject was denied possession of the good (ibid.: 121–2).[5]

Extrinsic subjective value is analysed by Böhm-Bawerk (1891: 379 et passim) as a matter for the isolated 'Crusoe'; it reduces to a personal interest in goods. Moreover, in a formal sense this subjective value concept is substantially equivalent to marginal utility: 'the value of goods produced, which for Crusoe have no price, but merely a subjective value, will equal their marginal utilities to him' (Böhm-Bawerk 1894: 330). That there is an intrapersonal, cerebral exchange in operation here, whereby Crusoe estimates value, by no means exhausts the meaning of exchange; for Böhm-Bawerk the more interesting and complex value estimates arise out of exchange relationships involving interpersonal interaction in market contexts.

Compared with subjective value, extrinsic *objective* value is purely technological; things are adjudged by convention (e.g., measurement) to produce certain effects. To use Böhm-Bawerk's examples, two chords of beechwood have equal fuel or heating value; specific foodstuffs have objective nutritive value, and fertilizers have fertilizer value in the sense that they have measurable effects on soil fertility. If, therefore, we claim that 'beechwood has more fuel value than pine' then we are asserting 'that a definite quantity (by weight let us say) of beechwood will release a larger number of thermal units than an equal quantity of pine' (1959b: 122). Extrinsic subjective value and objective value are both mental acts or 'judgements', but the former has a rabidly individualistic reference, whereas objective value is grounded in social or technical conventions. The bearing upon the well-being of an individual of some technical result (e.g. number of emitted thermal units) will not necessarily be the same for another individual. Finally, goods which are in abundance (e.g. wood) to the point that they might be regarded as 'free' may still have objective value but no subjective economic value or allocative significance for anyone's well-being (ibid.).

From a discussion of value in general, Böhm-Bawerk proceeds to a discussion of exchange value, which he considers a species of objective value. From the point of view of the outside observer, exchange value is a quantitative magnitude; it refers to 'the capacity of goods...to command a certain quantity of other goods as an equivalent in exchange' (1959b: 123). In short, objective exchange value or price is a quantity of goods; it is the capacity of goods to produce effects: that is, purchasing power over other goods in an interpersonal context. The economist-observer has no special authority to judge exchange value for individuals who intend to apply those goods as a means to satisfying their well-being after exchange has taken place. According to Böhm-Bawerk, 'we are saying nothing [in this instance] about the influence those goods exert on the well-being of any individual' (ibid). Indeed, from the individual economizer's viewpoint Böhm-Bawerk suggests by implication that exchange would not lead to the transfer of goods of equivalent value, where value is the purely personal, perceived subjective significance of a good for well-being. By contrast, exchange would always appear to the observer as an exchange of equivalents in objective value terms.

When Böhm-Bawerk maintains that the purpose of economic science is to 'delve into the laws which govern exchange relations of all goods' his exposition proceeds on two different planes. There is in fact, a 'double task' for economics (1959b: 123, 124). On one level of thought the laws of price formation are established and they should explain how and why a good can command a certain price expressed quantitatively. On the other level of analysis, the economist is ultimately driven to launch into a study of the laws of subjective value formation with the assistance of theorems developed in contiguous disciplines, especially psychology (1959b: 3–4). Böhm-Bawerk (ibid.: 192) was adamant that

> economic phenomena...have their roots in psychological ground and it becomes the province of economic science to trace those roots far enough into that ground to make the explanation which it evolves understandable and convincing as a unified whole.

For Böhm-Bawerk, by far the most important problem for economists was to investigate the laws governing objective exchange value but they should not be preoccupied with the objective results. Objective price outcomes are the resultant of the interplay of individual economizers' deeply held personal valuation processes. Market exchange ratios or prices have an 'objective' function in so far as they make subjectively held assessments of trade-offs or opportunity costs into transparent 'data' which still remain to be interpreted by market participants. Böhm-Bawerk would assuredly have subscribed to Menger's view that exchange value was an institutional creation, viz. the unintended or non-deliberative outcome of social interaction among economizers.

In emphasizing the objective aspects of exchange value, Böhm-Bawerk was affirming what he regarded as commonsense usage of the term in real market situations, but he was not departing from Menger's concentration on the subjectivist foundations of value, including exchange value.[6] There is only a change in the focus of attention in Böhm-Bawerk's version of Austrian value theory. Superficially there is a conscious neglect of the subjective foundations of price in *Positive Theory of Capital*. In an important review of *Positive Theory*, Green (1895: 57) considered this

> relapse [by Böhm-Bawerk and Wieser] from the subjective standpoint...[as] unfortunate. The Austrians have given us the vision of a theory of value resting upon the substantial basis of importance to human well-being, but in the field of exchange value where we have the greatest need for some substantial basis, we are left with the old idea that value is an expression of a quantity of goods rather than of subjective importance – a relation of goods to each other instead of their relation to human welfare.[7]

As we shall see later in this chapter, Böhm-Bawerk's supposed incomplete, reluctant subjectivism assumes other guises when he turns to the epistemic conditions necessary for individual traders who are involved in the price formation process in an auction market setting. Nevertheless, as we shall maintain below, Böhm-Bawerk did not abandon the subjective standpoint simply because he identified objective exchange value with the quantitative (e.g. barter ratio or monetary price) effects of interpersonal interaction on markets.[8]

THE CAUSE OF VALUE AND ECONOMIZING BEHAVIOUR

Literature in the neoclassical tradition on value and price theory is replete with criticisms of Böhm-Bawerk's attempt to explain price formation in causal rather than functional terms (e.g. Kuenne 1971: 35; Brems 1986: 11; Niehans 1990: 228). Generally stated, the Austrians rejected any Walrasian notion of strictly mathematical, simultaneous price determination in a static general equilibrium system. The character of prices in the Walrasian view is best described mathematically using calculus-based first-order conditions to define prices in equilibrium. Carl Menger originally averred, in correspondence with Walras, that 'the object of economic analysis was to discover the fundamental laws governing market prices which can be located in the ultimate genetic determinants of human nature; this was something a mathematical exposition could not do' (Jaffé 1976: 521–2). Some leading contemporary economists did not understand that the Austrian approach was fundamentally different. For example, in a review of William Smart's English translation of *Positive Theory* Edgeworth (1892: 330) wrongly characterized the Austrian method as the mere verbal, *simplified* version of Walrasian and Jevonian value theory. Thus, 'the Austrian exposition of the subject is not embarrassed by the symbols and ideas of the differential calculus. There is much to be said for thus presenting a conception which is essentially mathematical in a form free from scientific conventionalities. It may be expected that the general reader will derive [an]...advantage from this simplification.' Böhm-Bawerk (1890: 263; 1891: 369) was sympathetic to the Mengerian outlook, although, unfortunately, his remarks on methodological matters were not as systematic as Menger's. None the less, the charge that Böhm-Bawerk presided over the 'dissolution of

Menger's methological framework' (Alter 1990a: 227) does not find support in the following discussion.

We need to elaborate on the causal laws which lead to price formation and which formed the centrepiece of Böhm-Bawerk's microeconomics. He treated causes at the level of *intra*personal valuation processes.[9] For instance, the economizer uses means (goods) intentionally to satisfy ends (wants). Strictly stated, from the earliest beginnings of the Austrian tradition, value formation requires an intention to economize, and this presupposed accurate perception of the ends–means framework within which economizing takes place (Kirzner 1973: 33). Now,

> in the relationship between means and ends it is the end that lends the means its importance, not vice versa. It is self-evident that a man who is shipwrecked values a life-belt more highly if and because he values his life highly which he hopes will be saved by the life-belt; of course nobody will assume that he values his life highly because of the life-belt. There cannot be any doubt that there is a causal relationship between the importance of the end and that of the means.
>
> (1959c: 111)

The 'causality chain' emanating from the source of value is uni-directional; it is an asymmetric, serial chain running between ends and means, where the ends (or wants) have causal priority in logic and in time. Value originates or has its genesis in human wants.[10] The value or 'importance' attached to means is derived from the intended ends of economizing behaviour (1959c: 110–12). Mutual, contemporaneous means–ends value determination (e.g. between the values of producers' goods and that of final consumers' goods) is not meaningful in this context. In a critique of Marshall's formulation of demand and supply as mutual determinants of value, Böhm-Bawerk applies this causal notion and obtains an important result: 'the valuation of consumers' goods has causal *priority* over the valuation of producers' goods'. By contrast, Marshall's 'scientific investigation of the *causae causantes* reveals no priority whatever, just complete parity.... In traditional manner he presents "utility" and "cost" as the rivals for causal priority which he then denies to each one of them' (1959c: 104, 106).

Economizing involves the intentional 'gratification of wants', where wants are presumed to be embedded in the human psyche.[11] Wants also reflect 'various factors of a physiological, moral, cultural, [and] historic nature' (1959c: 108). Wants are also experienced and provided for in time; they are potentially changeable. There are potentialities in the present for behaviour leading to satisfaction of future wants. It was precisely Böhm-Bawerk's 'causal' theorizing that enabled him to include within the scope of his analysis the problem of sequential choice-making by individuals who have the future in mind. There are connotations of irreversibility in Böhm-Bawerk's conception of economizing but they are not made explicit (and they are consistent with the principle of asymmetric, serial causality from which his understanding of microeconomic processes derived).

Individuals are motivated to undervalue future goods relative to present goods, and Böhm-Bawerk accepted that individuals who economize over present and future have *some* relevant 'knowledge of causal progressions' so that they are able 'to depict in advance and with accuracy the form, the quantity and the fruition of those goods which will result from the...activities which [they] are initiating in the present' (1959b: 263). At the core of the matter here is knowledge of causal relationships between activities and outcomes. What is particularly unique about Böhm-Bawerk's treatment *vis-à-vis* other early Austrian contributions is his emphasis on the role of imagination in the intertemporal valuation process:

> It can hardly be maintained...that we possess the gift of literally *feeling in advance* the emotions we shall experience in the future. But it can certainly be said that we possess that other gift of being able *to imagine them in advance*.... Hence economizing imposes on us continual choosing, continual selecting of those wants which can and shall be provided for.... Such a selection proceeds, of course, from a comparison of the importance and urgency of wants.... [And] we are compelled to base our comparisons...on the imaginary representations which we make for ourselves of emotions that lie in the future.
>
> (1959b: 260–1; his emphasis)

Thus, by intending to achieve ends economizers imagine causal relations; they predict in the present how a flow of purposive actions will provide for future needs.

Economizing is learned behaviour; it is a forward-looking process which 'babes and sucklings are entirely incapable of, and which a child and barbarian can perform only quite inadequately' (1959b:

263).[12] To depict the most mature form of economizing Böhm-Bawerk offered the rudiments of an expected utility model of choice under uncertainty, and a theory of certainty equivalents.[13] Furthermore, Böhm-Bawerk provided a discussion of futures contracting, which he regarded as a means of making provision for future needs while hedging against inevitable imperfections in knowledge which were associated with an exercise of the imagination 'even among the most advancing peoples' (1959b: 263). Ultimately, knowledge of the future can never be perfect, so that economizing may in general lead to 'opinions' of the 'true importance attaching to the aims and objects with which economic activities deal...whether right or wrong' (1959b: 432).

While Böhm-Bawerk only offered adumbrations on such matters as the behavioural foundations of choice, his appreciation of intertemporal problems and the role of imagination and knowledge, and his consideration of the appropriate responses to uncertainty, went far beyond that which might be discovered on these matters in the work of other leading late nineteenth-century economic theorists, especially the Marshallians and Walrasians (including Schumpeter).[14] In this connection Böhm-Bawerk's correspondence with Walras (Walras 1965: 180–2, 193–5, 260–1) is unhelpful because it lacks specificity. The closest Böhm-Bawerk comes to expressly venting his disapproval of Walrasian methods used to theorize about choice and value determination is in a criticism of Schumpeter's procedure:

> Even those who would like basically to eliminate the thought of causality, resort to it in some form or other as soon as they start to theorize. Under the admitted influence of a certain epistemological school of the natural sciences Schumpeter... wants to avoid the concept of cause and effect and substitute for them the 'more perfect' mathematical concept of 'function'.
> (1959c: 228).

Schumpeter (1954: 908 n. 47) later acknowledged that the Austrian analytical procedure differed from the Walrasian method, but he showed no enthusiasm for the former in his own work. By contrast, Böhm-Bawerk did not resort to using tractable functional forms as summary mathematical tools to theorize about choice or the results of choice (or about the equilibrium price outcomes of choice on markets, as we shall see below). The first principle of Böhm-Bawerkian economizing was that valuation is an *intra*personal genetic–causal process logically originating in, and generated from, an individual's creative imagination. In this, the pedigree of Böhm-Bawerk's contribution is entirely Mengerian. We turn next to consider price formation on markets where economizers interact and where, *ipso facto*, prices are the result of the play of an *inter*personal valuation process.

THE THEORY OF MARKETS AND EXCHANGE VALUE

In summarizing the contributions of the Austrian economists for English - speaking readers, Böhm-Bawerk (1891: 379) maintained that the Austrians endeavoured to formulate 'the laws according to which we pursue our interests when they are entangled with the interests of others'. The objective of what he called the 'first part' of price theory was to develop a general theory which assumed a given property-rights structure and the wholesale quest for 'selfish economic advantage' among market participants. The 'second part' of the theory of price was more 'applied' in that it incorporated variations in 'highly concrete institutions' (1959b: 208, 213–14). In his own work on the 'first part' of the theory of price formation, Böhm-Bawerk constructed several cases of market situations where exchange value is explored in a stationary and in an intertemporal context. The well-known stationary horse-auction case shades into the more general case involving exchange of present for future goods; at least, all the *main* conclusions applying in the former are relevant in the latter.[15]

Table 5 Böhm-Bawerk's auction

Willing buyer	Valuation of one horse	Willing seller	Valuation of his horse
Aa	$300	Ba	$100
Ab	280	Bb	110
Ac	260	Bc	150
Ad	240	Bd	170
Ae	220	Be	200
Af	210	Bf	215
Ag	200	Bg	250
Ah	180	Bh	260
Aj	170		
Ak	150		

Source: Böhm-Bawerk 1959b: 220.

Böhm-Bawerk's illustration of a two-sided auction market involves ten buyers and eight sellers of horses over some hypothetical period in time; the horses are homogeneous and indivisible. Traders are not separated in space and they are able to communicate freely with one another. His data is presented in Table 5 above.

Edgeworth (1925: 39) described this table as a summary of market conditions in 'an exceptional sort of auction' which amounted to 'riding a one-horse illustration to death'. Indeed, in Böhm-Bawerk's market, buyers and sellers wish to trade only one horse. Their behavioural inclination is to obtain direct benefit through exchange – either a horse, or a monetary amount in return for a horse (1959b 215: 221–2). The traders listed have coincident wants and there is no place provided for an auctioneer. The tabulated data do not strictly represent individual *schedules* of demands or supplies in a mathematical sense, because each buyer and seller does not continuously vary the amounts of a horse (or money) that they would be willing to trade over a *range* of prices.

Similarly, conventional market schedules of demand and supply would be difficult to construct from these data since we are given what might be termed strictly individual reservation values. Hennings's (1987: 255) attribution of schedules to Böhm-Bawerk's discussion of price formation in the horse-auction market applies a Marshallian construct towards which Böhm-Bawerk was in fact quite hostile. Note also Maloney (1987: 103), whose rough transcription reads: 'Böhm cited a horse fair: the buyer's utility from acquiring a horse and the seller's utility from keeping his horse played not just an equal but an identical role in determining price. Hence only a demand curve can be drawn; at the equilibrium price, it crosses the vertical line representing the fixed stock of horses.' This is a plausible Marshallian reconstruction but, as we shall demonstrate below, another reconstruction is possible which is more in keeping with the way the community of first-generation Austrian economists would have understood putative 'horse fairs'. The Austrians placed considerable weight on the role of individual reservation values in the market pricing process. We turn now to a more detailed discussion of these values.

On the demand side, bidders form an 'opinion' or guess 'an ideal "true" value' of a horse (1959b: 432). That is, in the terminology of the modern literature on auctions, their stated valuations are private valuations (Milgrom 1989: 4). Böhm-Bawerk uses the term 'subjective valuations' (1959b: 220). According to the private values postulate, differences among valuations are idiosyncratic to the bidders; bidders have access to different information or possess different imaginative capacities about the unique or true value of the horse to them. Therefore, each bidder does not need to be interested, at least *ab initio*, in competitors' valuations when forming a private valuation (1959b: 433 n. 8). The supply-side quotations are also private valuations. The offer of eight horses by sellers up to certain amounts is an actual quantity brought to market and potentially saleable, although there is no requirement to sell *all* horses to the highest bidders.

The information structure in this auction is critical to understanding the process of price setting and to establishing the final trading price range and quantity. Böhm-Bawerk's discussion is opaque in this respect, and readers of *Positive Theory* have to search between the lines for his implicit assumptions regarding epistemic conditions. The traders do not know in advance the final trading price and quantity; they are not necessarily fully informed on market conditions when entering the auction context. There may be dispersed information. Thus,

> [the] more...familiar with the state of the market the people are who are seeking to do business on the open market, the more quickly do they terminate the preliminary 'sounding out' by means of reserved or intentionally inadequate bidding. In a market where the action moves in 'deep well worn grooves' the participants will dispense entirely with extreme bids that have no prospect of acceptance at all; their very first offers will at least approach a zone within which the market price will ultimately fall.
>
> (1959b: 433 n. 9)

Böhm-Bawerk evinced no knowledge of Edgeworth's *Mathematical Psychics*, yet a recontracting process is suggested in the above passage where market participants freely communicate their bids and offers in the style of a (weak) co-operative game until they become sufficiently familiar with market conditions. The procedure which Böhm-Bawerk calls 'sounding out' is reminiscent of the making and cancelling of provisional contracts in Edgeworth market games. Moreover, the 'zone' of actual trading may be determinate and parallels Edgeworth's contract curve and the core of a co-operative game.[16] However, the final trading price in any Böhm-Bawerk auction is indeterminate, since it will depend on bargaining among some small number of traders. Indeterminacy was not problematic for Böhm-Bawerk given the level of abstraction being applied in his price theory. To be sure, a Walrasian price-auction market where the number of competitors is sufficiently large, where traders are faced with parametric prices and where equilibrium price is determinate implied reasoning from a level of abstraction well beyond Böhm-Bawerk's purview.

The procedural rule for each buyer in the Böhm-Bawerk auction is to remain in the bidding until the price rises to his or her own valuation of a horse and to exit as soon as the price reaches this point. Buyers will not pay their stated valuations since there would be no profit in the exchange.[17] Similarly, for each seller the strategy is not to make an offer at any price equal to or above their stated valuation. Böhm-Bawerk allows for multiple rounds of bidding which continue so long as it 'is commonly perceived by all parties' that those desiring to buy exceed those willing and able to sell (1959b: 222). A market clearing price–quantity configuration is sought by the traders, and no trading takes place until it is found. In the horse auction depicted in Table 5 above, as the price is bid up above 150, weak buyers are eliminated and more sellers are added. At a price of (say) just below 180, the quantity demanded (8 horses) exceeds the quantity supplied (4 horses). The pressure to bid up among buyers dissipates when price-offers reach the 210 mark. Trader Af drops out on the demand side so that five willing buyers now face five willing sellers. The faction of five buyers then co-operates in a self-enforcing manner, since they now become aware that their individual advantages will not be served by driving each other out of the market by raising bids: 'it is their common interest, as against the sellers, to close their transaction at the lowest possible price'. The 'marginal pairs' (*Grenzpaar*) of buyers and sellers have the strongest influence on the formation of the final trading price – a price which is always uniform, non-discriminatory and marginal. According to Böhm-Bawerk (1959b: 225), 'every market price is a "marginal price" and is limited by the economic condition of those competing pairs who are situated at the very limit or margin of the "capacity of exchanging"'. The final market clearing price must be equal to or greater than 210 to exclude Af, but not higher than 215 to include Bf. Given the small number of traders remaining, the price-forming 'zone' or 'bound' for horse trading is 210 $\leqslant$ horse price $\leqslant$ 215. This price bound is demonstrated graphically in Figure 3.

NEOCLASSICAL MICROECONOMIC THEORY

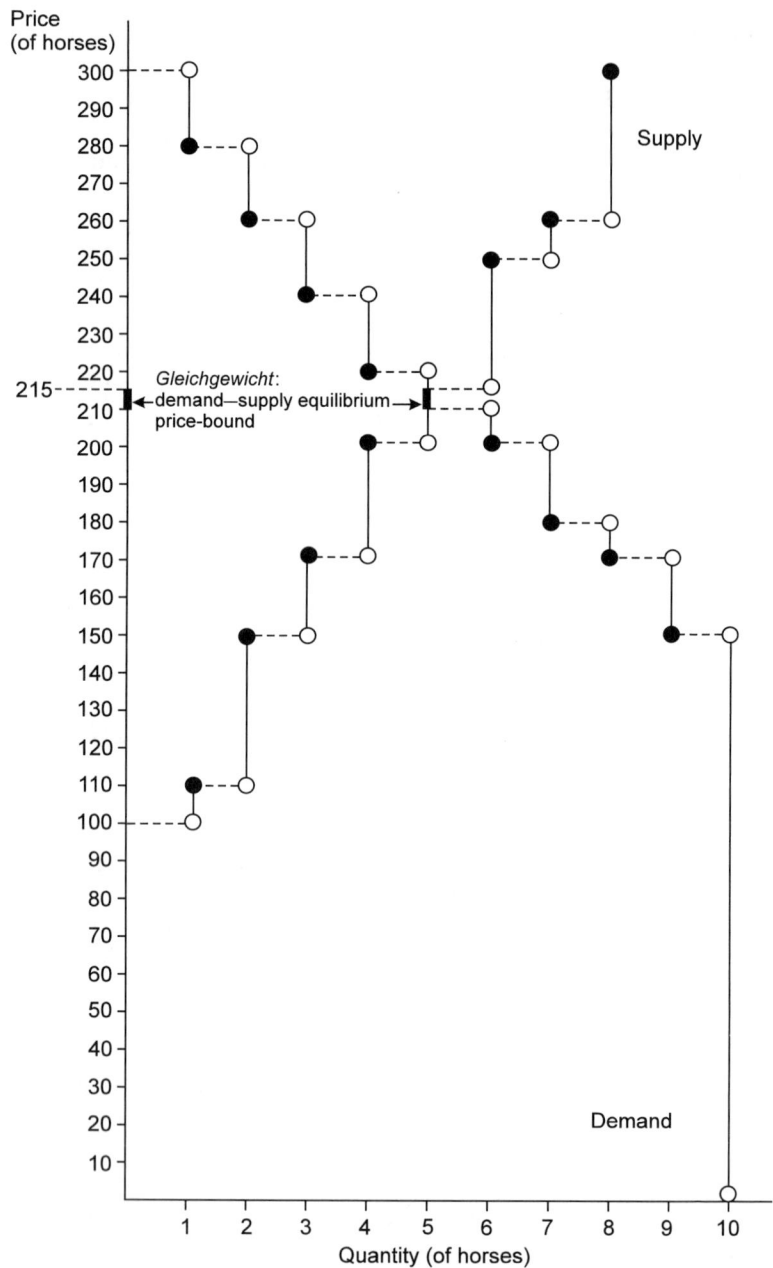

Figure 3 Böhm-Bawerk's market supply and demand relation

The figure illustrates discontinuous demand and supply relations constructed from Böhm-Bawerk's data and depicts the price bounds for each potential transaction.[18]

Böhm-Bawerk neglected to consider coalition-forming behaviour of all kinds on both sides of the market because his focus was on the 'first part of...price theory exclusively', without reference to institutional variations (1959b: 213). However, his analysis is not strategy-free. Sellers may play an offer game which attempts to squeeze more profit out of the remaining five buyers on the presumption that the buyers are not fully aware of sellers' bargaining power. So Böhm-Bawerk allowed for a situation where, as a group, 'sellers can be stubborn' (1959b: 222); they may develop some self-enforcing, mutually advantageous joint strategy and perhaps refuse to sell five horses at a market clearing price of 210, thereby forcing the price up to something closer to 215. The game-theoretic weaknesses of this classical Austrian 'core' solution are doubtless obvious to modern theorists. For instance, weak players in the game receive no consideration for their efforts, and the strong buyer in desperate need of a horse is at a disadvantage (provided such a need is known), since it invites collusion among sellers. And, as Shubik (1987: 230) argued, the 'seventh buyer might argue that his participation in the bidding tends to limit the sixth buyer's threat value; if he should refrain, then the latter might be able to command a "bribe" for remaining on the scene and making the bids that force the price up into the Böhm-Bawerk range'. In Böhm-Bawerk's defence, this is to ascribe some patently 'irrational' behaviour to market participants, at least on Böhm-Bawerk's terms. As we have already mentioned, Böhm-Bawerk submitted a general theory of price formation in its 'purest form', in which market participants were interested in their 'direct advantage'. That is to say, it was presumed common knowledge in the market that all participants were perfectly rational – which, for Böhm-Bawerk, ruled out threats to behave otherwise (1959b: 212, 215ff). Threats are not an acceptable standard of behaviour in Böhm-Bawerk's community of horse traders and this, of course, contributes to the stability of any price–quantity outcome. Furthermore, weak buyers, for example, 'can exert no effective influence in the way of external results' (1959b: 229). We could, perhaps, conceive of Böhm-Bawerk's traders as being exceedingly myopic about their outlook on the menu of advantages emanating from exchange. One thing is certain – traders are single-minded; they are interested in their *direct* advantage, be it a horse or a monetary sum in return for a horse, and do not seem to be interested in some compensation for not having their desire satisfied.

Modern variants of the Böhm-Bawerk market could just as well derive both non-uniformity of pricing and profit-sharing with weak players (Shubik 1987: 241). The introduction of specific auction rules and an active, non-costless auctioneer into Böhm-Bawerk's market can drastically alter final prices and the allocation of horses sold (Schotter 1974: 201–3). Overall, these modern reconstructions indicate that there is a certain arbitrariness in the institutional form of Böhm-Bawerk's two-sided auction market. Obeisance should nevertheless be paid to his pioneering effort; he came to the brink of perceiving the significance of bargaining and strategic behaviour in price formation, even if he did not elaborate on cases where the solution concept to apply in a given 'game' situation would depend on the institutional context, which could vary widely. For example, there are some oblique comments in his footnotes (1959b: 434 nn. 12, 13, 16, and 437 n. 34) where institutional variations are suggested but not pursued. And in the text there is the following comment: 'Once oriented as to essentials we can find it difficult to advance... to an understanding of the situation as it changes by reason of the subject matter becoming more variegated and complex' (1959b: 230). At a very high level of generality, in so far as a 'game describes a problem situation where agents interact knowing that their different moves and plans may affect each other' (Bianchi and Moulin 1991: 179), Böhm-Bawerk's horse auction, for all its limitations, must be counted as one early game-theoretic prototype.

BÖHM-BAWERK'S CONCEPT OF DEMAND–SUPPLY EQUILIBRIUM

Price formation has a strategic dimension in Böhm-Bawerk's auction, even if he fails to explore that dimension systematically. Multilateral exchange in this context is not anonymous, since at certain points in the bidding process both buyers and sellers deliberate on their 'common interests'. The equilibrating character of the auction assumes the form of a *tendency* towards price uniformity after a bargaining process between the successful marginal buyer Ae and seller Be. The marginal pair Ae and Be consider their positions in conjunction with other potentially successful buyers and sellers respectively before consummating an exchange at any equilibrium price; they determine the bounds within which the final trading-price falls. A range of possible equilibrium prices (rather than a unique point) is predicted by Böhm-Bawerk's analysis; the final trading price depends on the relative bargaining strengths of the traders. As Wieser (1891: 117) was to explain, from the point of view of the Austrian School taken as a whole, actual market trading prices 'cannot be taken without qualification as the social expression of the valuation of commodities; they are the results of a *conflict* waged over those commodities in which power besides need, and more than need, has decided the issue' (emphasis added). And there is nothing in Böhm-Bawerk's analysis which would suggest otherwise.

The conceptualization of a demand-supply equilibrium (*Gleichgewicht*) in terms of price bounds or zones was originally presented in Böhm-Bawerk's early Innsbruck lectures (Tomo 1987: 10). It bears the imprint of earlier work in German classical economics.[19] The *Gleichgewicht* notion seemed especially suited to investigations of intertemporal price formation and equilibrating processes – where equilibrating tendencies can be compared not with 'the balance of a quietly standing man, but with the balance of a walking man, who, with every step, leaves and loses his present balance, to regain it with every step, to lose it again etc' (1959c: 101). The equimarginal principle, which was so central to choice theory based on marginal utility, was not sufficient to explain choice at a point in time and over time. The 'perfect levelling of all marginal utilities and product values' is 'most pronounced' when there are no co-ordination problems in an exchange context. The equimarginal principle was originally formulated and most suited to 'an isolated economy' (1959c: 100, 228 n. 9). Price formation in the multilateral context cannot usually be so deterministic. For one thing, the structure of wants and supplies can change. Producers' responses to changing consumption requirements 'do not take place so gradually and equally in all kinds of products that they gnaw evenly at our product supplies and tear tiny gaps with equal marginal utilities' (1959c: 101).

Citing Menger, Böhm-Bawerk argued that the value of producers' goods is 'not determined by the value ascribed to [consumers'] goods *in the present*, but by their *anticipated* value in the future periods when today's producers' goods will have ripened into ready products' (ibid.: 230; his emphasis). The transmission of value from consumers' goods to producers' goods takes place as 'a causal sequence of events' (ibid.: 113); the possibility of disturbances, divergent responses among consumers and producers to change, and lags in the value-transmission process loom large. In particular, depending on the structure of their anticipations, market participants may employ 'tactics which may perhaps retard the causative factors that are broadly effective' (1959c: 230). Divergent anticipations between the traders in Böhm-Bawerk's market imply less than full information on future prices, and divergent views on the behaviour of competitors; therefore, the scope for price formation within broad price bounds is widened. In situations where widely different subjective valuations are observed between present and future goods, auction market processes can be useful institutions, acting as a 'levelling influence'. As before, in the stationary case, price bounds are the equilibrating outcome as long as a small number of bargainers is involved in exchanging present for future goods (1959b: 286–9).

Commentators have attempted to fit Böhm-Bawerk's theory of markets into a Marshallian scheme without much success. Rather than continuous demand and supply schedules, Böhm-Bawerk conceived of markets in terms of discrete bids and offers within specific price bounds. Furthermore, market conditions in the original horse auction suggest temporarily fixed supplies faced by variations in the intensity of demands. Marshall and Edgeworth interpreted Böhm-Bawerk's theory of price formation as a special case – an Austrian version of the 'English theory [which] is limited to "market values" or "short periods"' (Edgeworth 1892: 335). To be sure, superficially in Böhm-Bawerk's analysis there is no concept of multi-market equilibrium, so he is closer to Marshall than Walras. Furthermore, the horse auction takes place in a situation where the quantity brought to market and the demanders' purchasing power is given for the period of the auction. The parallels with Marshall end there. Böhm-Bawerk fulminated against Marshallian conceptions of demand and supply and responded to comments on Austrian analysis in the fourth edition of Marshall's *Principles*. The Austrian case went well beyond rejection of infinitesimals, schedules, functional forms and continuities. According to Böhm-Bawerk:

> Marshall levels at the opinion of myself...the indictment that...one-sided consideration [is given] to the 'causes of temporary changes and short-term value fluctuations'. [W]e do not at all consider the supply as 'fixed' as Marshall alleges

in the presentation of our one-sidedness. On the contrary, the problem for whose discussion we earned Marshall's critique emerged in the very analysis of the causative and changing influence which production constantly exerts on the changing magnitude of 'supply'. It emerged amidst our endeavour to analyze to their ultimate bases the secrets of the concurrence between the value of consumers' goods and that of their producers' goods, which in turn is the condition of a relatively *permanent* establishment of a certain price. We were reproached with assuming 'fixed' supplies just when we demonstrated their formation and flexibility.

(1959c: 115; emphasis added)

We might demur that Böhm-Bawerk offered a thoroughgoing process analysis of long-period value formation and of factor supplies, but it is unmistakable from the above passage that he believed otherwise. 'Supply' is a result of some dynamic equilibrating process going on behind the scene in Böhm-Bawerk's analysis of market adjustment. He was not thinking in terms of continuous variation of supply (whether of goods or of factors) along a supply schedule; each auction situation represented or assumed a discrete change in supply. Compared with Marshall's short-period analysis, supply meant quantity brought to market *after* changes in supply conditions had had time to work themselves out in response to initial changes in demand. If reconstructed in Marshallian terms, cases where Böhm-Bawerk discusses the formation of the *Gleichgewicht* must be treated separately by locating supply as points on different market supply curves. Supply in Böhm-Bawerk's microeconomics is the outcome of a dynamic process beginning with ultimate generative causes on the demand side. Only then can we make sense of Böhm-Bawerk's microfoundations, in which supply has 'flexibility'.

In the traditional reading of nineteenth-century concepts of equilibrium a Ricardo–Mill–Marshall line has been distinguished from a Böhm-Bawerk–Clark–Wicksell line (Robbins 1930). In the former, supply varies throughout the movement towards a stationary equilibrium state; whereas in the latter supply is rigidly fixed by presupposition, and equilibrium is achieved by holding the amounts of labour and capital constant. Both lines of thought characterize stationariness by unchanging conditions on the supply side. However, constancy in the former is an *outcome* of a dynamic equilibrating process, while in the latter it is a *condition* of stationary equilibrium. In a recent appreciation of Robbins, Weintraub (1991: 17–18) demonstrated that 'the distinction between holding something constant and establishing the features of equilibrium' was the centrepiece of Robbins's 1930 article. What, then, is the most useful way to conceptualize constancy on the supply side? In fact, perhaps inadvertently, Böhm-Bawerk offered two answers, which were tantamount to a dichotomization of microeconomics and macroeconomics. First, when considering the economy as a set of independently operating auction markets, he viewed the microstructural details as potentially changing and changeable by dint of bargaining and ultimately by the operation of subjective or causal factors emanating from the minds of economizers. In this perspective, price and quantity adjustments are ongoing. Second, at the macroeconomic level (for example, in Böhm-Bawerk's theories of production, capital and interest), the Robbinsian link between Clark's and Wicksell's thinking on 'constancy' and that of Böhm-Bawerk is entirely apposite. It would be misleading to draw the distinction between Böhm-Bawerk's microeconomics and his macroeconomics too sharply. Time preference, which has its basis in individual decision-making, provides one key link between his microeconomics and his macroeconomics. And Böhm-Bawerk's reasoning relied on the phenomenon of interest as an omnipresent intertemporal variable inherent in all valuation processes and all buying and selling on all markets. Nevertheless, it is evident that Böhm-Bawerk abstracts from microstructural dynamics and avoids discussion of ultimate generative causes of pricing in markets when elaborating on production, capital and interest. Microstructural elements are submerged beneath aggregates such as the totality of wage goods, *the* rate of interest as a macro-phenomenon, total output and the average degree of roundaboutness, or period of production. It is scarcely surprising that Robbins and some other leading historians of economic thought neglected Böhm-Bawerk's microfoundations – foundations which may have been considered too fragmentary. These foundations may also have been completely overshadowed by Böhm-Bawerk's exemplary macroeconomic theorizing. As Schumpeter (1954: 997–8) argued, Böhm-Bawerk may well have 'started with a theory of individual behaviour and with a theory of exchange based upon it, but on the highest floor of his building *there is almost nothing left but aggregates*' (emphasis added).

A word of caution is in order at this point, because there is an elision in Schumpeter's foregoing comment which is common to many histories of economic thought. There is a tendency in these histories automatically to expect in a writer's work a coherence which is not historically present (Weintraub 1991: 19). Modern readers should not be so expectant of coherence in Böhm-Bawerk's thought, for there is a tension between his macro-theory of capital and production and his microeconomics.[20] This is not the place to review his macroeconomics. But helpful in this connection is Streissler's (1969: 254) description of the early Austrian conception of economy-wide equilibrium as the 'bastard stationary state'. It is a state

> in which aggregates remain constant while their structures change, in which only variances but not aggregates are parameters of thought (Böhm-Bawerk's capital theory is a good example). Unhappily, this is likely to be a model self-contradiction in the last resort, because a change in economic variance tends to reflect back on the values of the averages.

Böhm-Bawerk permitted structural change in his theory of markets, and this gave him scope to ignore price determinateness in exchange; also to allow for bargaining and, as we mentioned earlier, principally to consider *equilibrating* market processes – hence his definition of equilibrium in terms of the metaphor of a 'walking man' who continuously 'loses his present balance' only to 'regain it with every step'.

CONCLUSION

A prominent feature of Böhm-Bawerk's work was his interest in microfoundations: that is, in the theory of individual valuation and behaviour. He investigated the nature and cause of value, and he demonstrated that economists could analyse value on two different planes, in terms of both its objective and its subjective dimensions. His discussion of the cause of value dealt at length with issues in economic philosophy and placed him firmly in what was later known as the genetic–causal tradition in economic theorizing. Böhm-Bawerk founded economizing behaviour on the intention to satisfy human wants arising in the future, and that behaviour must perforce employ imagination in order to effect needs-satisfaction by carefully structuring present allocative activities.

NEOCLASSICAL MICROECONOMIC THEORY

Böhm-Bawerk chose to analyse markets where final trading prices were regarded as imprecise; he generated predictions of equilibrating price bounds or ranges rather than single-point equilibria. The auction market institutions he chose to consider traded indivisible goods, and the number of traders was finite and small. So, in short, individual market participants *could make a difference* to market outcomes. Trading prices were not fully arbitraged equilibrium prices. Böhm-Bawerk allowed scope for bargaining and the design of 'tactics' among relevant traders who recognized their 'common interest'; elementary game-theoretic notions suggested themselves to later readers of his two-sided horse-auction market. Böhm-Bawerk constructed a dynamic micro-structure for his theory of markets, but it promises to modern readers much more than it delivers in terms of an analysis of the effects of a variety of procedural rules under which the horse auction might be played.

There was nothing unique in approach about Böhm-Bawerk's elaboration of microfoundations, because it was in many respects similar to Menger's. Like Menger, he viewed the economic system from the vantage-point of its component parts, where there were hypothetically separate markets everywhere and ongoing bargaining within those markets. This was his 'partial' method and it turned on microeconomic questions – value, economizing, exchange, price formation – *par excellence*. Böhm-Bawerk's exploration of these questions did not impinge on his macroeconomic analysis of the economy as a process of production in time. And this 'macro'-analysis was conducted without explicit reference to microeconomic foundations.

Altogether, it is unjustified to claim that Böhm-Bawerk's ideas can be located 'quite firmly in the camp of today's general equilibrium theorists' at least so far as his microfoundations are concerned; it is not easy 'to see how the step from Böhm-Bawerk's restatement of Menger's theory can be made to Walras's theory' (Alter 1990a: 228). For we have maintained that Böhm-Bawerk's microfoundations present another example of some fundamental ideas which members of the early Austrian school held in common *and* in opposition to those working in the Walrasian and Marshallian traditions.

Consistent with their positions on price formation, the founding Austrians developed conceptions of market competition which stressed the importance of bargaining behaviour. In the following chapter we consider the nature and functions of competition in early Austrian microeconomics. Again, as we shall demonstrate, the Austrian conceptions had no substantially equivalent counterparts in the work of Walras, Jevons or Marshall.

7

THE PROCESS OF COMPETITION IN FOUNDING AUSTRIAN ECONOMIC THEORY: I, MENGER'S *PRINCIPLES*

INTRODUCTION

In this chapter, and the following Chapter 8, we recover and enlarge upon some neglected conceptions of competition in the work of the founding Austrians. It should be remarked at the outset that we shall not be presupposing a distinction between perfect competition and monopoly, or between perfect competition and imperfect competition, such as has been bequeathed to modern economists from late nineteenth-century Walrasian and Marshallian economics, and from Chamberlin and Robinson writing in the Marshallian tradition in the 1930s. Instead we take a position closer to each Austrian text which, as we shall demonstrate, neither adopted a rigid, formal taxonomy of market structures as if competition was a given state of affairs, nor analysed the properties of so-called competitive equilibrium states. The founding Austrians regarded competition as a highly personalized, faltering human process of rivalry and bargaining which had no substantially equivalent counterparts in the treatment of competition in the writings of leading contemporaries from other schools of thought, particularly, Jevons, Edgeworth, Walras and Marshall. By the close of Chapter 8 we should be in a position to demonstrate that when Hayek (1948) later expanded on the meaning of competition as a dynamic market process, whether conscious of the influence or not, his contribution acted as a conduit for the transmission to modern economists of some founding Austrian insights on the subject.

A broad concept of 'dynamic competition' is at the core of developments in modern Austrian economics (O'Driscoll and Rizzo 1985: 100–9, 130–1; Kirzner 1992: 85). That concept is co-extensive with the current Austro-American emphases on the subjectivism of market participants' knowledge and on entrepreneurial discovery. It is well known that the scope and content of Austrian 'dynamic competition' was systematically treated by Hayek in his essay on 'The Meaning of Competition' (1948: 92–106) and again thirty years later in his 'Competition as a Discovery Procedure' (1978:179–90). Less directly, at least on the subject of competition, the contributions of Schumpeter and Mises should not go unnoticed. Kirzner (1990b: 248) stated that 'for each of these two scholars, this attention to the process of dynamic competition must have appeared entirely consistent with the common training they had received in Vienna'. The Austrian 'scientific milieu' before Hayek's post-war contributions had always 'stimulated the growth of independent thinkers' (Haberler 1951: 29); it expressed rather heterogeneous visions of the economic process and of competition in particular, which diverged from mainstream neoclassical orientations in their conventionally accepted Marshallian and emerging Walrasian forms.

Mark Blaug (1992: 33) maintained that 'Hayek's appreciation of the learning and discovery aspects of the dynamic process of competition, as distinct from the static properties of *end-state* competitive equilibrium...strikes us today as remarkably original and perceptive' (his emphasis). Modern Austrians would doubtless agree that Hayek was 'charting a whole new territory from that of the Walrasian mainstream of economics that was beginning to emerge in the late 1930s' (ibid).[1] That Hayek's insights on the meaning of competition were in many respects anticipated by earlier luminaries in the Austrian tradition is something yet to be fully documented. We shall be interested in the perspectives on competition provided by Menger, Wieser and Böhm-Bawerk. We exclude consideration of minor Austrian contributions for reasons of space and submit that Menger, Wieser and Böhm-Bawerk offer a representative sample of principal early Austrian ideas on the subject of competition. Other minor Austrian contributions to this subject came from H. von Schullern-Schrattenhofen and G. Gross, and, on the cognate subject of bargaining, Hermann and Schäffle were important influences on Menger (Streissler 1972: 437–8). We shall have occasion to mention Schumpeter's work in passing.[2] However, we concur with Hayek (1934: 393) that the reputation of Menger and the Austrian school 'in the outside world...[was] due to the efforts of his brilliant followers, Eugen von Böhm-Bawerk and Friedrich von Wieser'.

NEOCLASSICAL MICROECONOMIC THEORY

An investigation of the intellectual antecedents of modern Austrian conceptions of competition must have justification beyond mere antiquarianism. While the variegated intellectual background to the modern Austrian paradigm is important, the Austrian economic-theoretic foundations have been neglected.[3] It may have been the case that Austrian ideas were believed erroneously to have been absorbed without much difficulty into mainstream economics post-1945, or regarded as differing 'not very much beyond style' (Kirzner 1992: 84) from other leading streams of economic theory. However, in the case of theorizing on competition (and apart from a discernible Austrian strand in the work of von Neumann and Morgenstern) relative neglect of Austrian conceptions has been an important factor. To be sure, von Neumann and Morgenstern (1947: 9) do not neglect the Austrian influence on the theory of games. The fact that several Austrian economic classics were not available in English prior to 1950 (e.g. Menger [1871] 1950, and sections of Böhm-Bawerk 1962) is a rather weak reason for neglect. It is notable that over sixty years after publication of Menger's *Principles*, Hayek (1934: 393) was driven to lament that 'there must be few instances in economics or any other branch of knowledge, where the works of an author who revolutionised the body of an already well-developed science and who has been generally recognised to have done so, have remained so little known as those of Carl Menger'. For example, as late as 1961, in a treatise on *Competition as a Dynamic Process*, John Maurice Clark failed to mention any Austrian source (other than Schumpeter [1911] 1934 and 1942 *en passant*) yet his theme throughout was that in 'the field of theory the most challenging opening seems to be for an approach that would shift the emphasis from *competition as a mechanism of equilibrium to competition as a dynamic process* (1961: 2; emphasis added).[4]

In a recent study of different notions of competition in late nineteenth-century American economics, Morgan (1993: 566) presented a 'stylized version' of the early twentieth-century 'neoclassical analysis of competition'. In short, this version contrasted perfect competition with monopoly. Whereas the former category contains many price taking firms which 'do not actively compete according to any commonsense definition of the word' (ibid., citing Hayek), the latter contains a single-price monopoly which cannot actively compete with other firms. Accordingly, Morgan deduced that these 'limiting cases mold an analysis that is largely static and that portrays competition as a situation devoid of behavioral content... When neoclassical economists talk of the market, they often mean the competitive structure of the industry, not the relationship between buyers and sellers' (ibid).[5] Accepting Morgan's stylization, our objective will be to consider whether the Austrians from Menger onwards can be said to have treated competition in a 'neoclassical' manner.[6] More specifically, Jaffé (1976) successfully dehomogenized the economics of Menger, Jevons and Walras, and it therefore behoves us to inquire whether the early leading Austrians, as an amalgam of independent theorists on competition, continued to develop economics along non-Walrasian lines. In other words, with respect to ideas on competition, we shall put to the test Hayek's (1934: 393) assertion that 'during the last sixty years the Austrian School has occupied an almost *unique position* in the development of economic science' (emphasis added). Furthermore, while acknowledging a 'potential danger' of reading 'modern Austrian notions into earlier Austrian contributions', Lavoie (1985: 22, 26) made an important beginning by distinguishing between Austrian 'rivalrous competitive process' and the 'neoclassical notion of non-rivalrous, static competitive equilibrium'. Our task will be to subject the early Austrian foundations to closer scrutiny. Foreshadowing one of our results, the Austrian conceptions of competition expounded in this chapter and the one which follows, seem to have been developed as part of the internal logic of Austrian economics set in motion by Menger's *Principles*. By contrast, Morgan (1993: 597–600) noticed that contemporary American conceptions were mostly suggested by economists' observations of existing industrial circumstances. Austrian conceptions were formulated in an intellectual tradition which, while not completely insulated from advances in Marshallian and Walrasian market-theoretical frameworks, produced some unique insights later rehabilitated and developed by Hayek.

COMPETITION IN MENGER'S *PRINCIPLES*: BEHAVIOURAL ASPECTS

Exchange

Patterns of human behaviour elucidated in the *Principles* (Menger [1871] 1950) may be associated with the verb 'to compete' (*Konkurrieren*). Here we follow Hayek (1948: 96) and McNulty

(1968: 640–1, 644) in distinguishing between competitive behaviour or activity in markets, from competition which is formalized by the idea of a market-structure. According to McNulty, 'the "perfection" of the concept of competition, that is, the emergence of the idea of competition as itself a market structure, was a distinguishing contribution of neoclassical economics' (ibid.: 644).

Menger began with what he called the 'simplest case' of isolated exchange, where two traders – bilateral monopolists – are involved in 'economizing' *activity* (*Wirtschaftend*, Menger [1871] 1950: 48 n. 4 – translator's note). The scene is a spatially isolated spot-market where individual trades take place and where 'atomistic' competition prevails. Later Menger ([1883] 1985: 93, 94) made no apology for beginning all his economic theorizing by reducing the 'complicated phenomena' of markets to their simplest 'elements'. In Menger's view it was desirable to proceed by reducing 'the more complicated phenomena of national economy', including presumably the phenomenon of the market, to the 'singular phenomena of human economy'. The atomistic orientation of pure economic theory was, for Menger, a virtue, but this is not to say that he regarded atomistic competitive behaviour as necessarily virtuous or desirable. Atomism was a preferred analytical starting-point for Menger's theorizing.[7]

In Menger's spot market there are no artificial barriers to exchange, although there are some constraints, as we shall see anon. First, exchange is contemplated by both traders because it has the potential to satisfy their needs or, alternatively stated, to fulfil their plans.[8] Menger's economizers make plans to trade *ex ante*; they 'carefully consider every exchange in advance' (Menger [1871] 1950: 117). Second, the traders will only be motivated to exchange if they have 'command' over goods which they are able and willing to dispose of in return for other goods which they value more highly (ibid.: 180). The 'command' condition on its own is trivial; it is a necessary but not a sufficient condition for exchange. Third, for beneficial exchange to be effected Menger specified a knowledge or information condition: the two traders must 'recognise the situation' (ibid.: 179). This condition does not mean that they must have equal abilities to consider the situation and to perceive an opportunity for trade in advance. It requires only given abilities. Menger's subsequent elaboration on the knowledge condition allowed for the possibility that the 'full gains from...trade are sometimes *not immediately forthcoming*...[if] knowledge of trading opportunities' is incomplete (ibid.: 188; emphasis added). Implications for the meaning of competition in exchange are profound: if the traders are *equally* limited by imperfect knowledge or information-processing abilities in understanding all the potential trading possibilities, then no one could act as a predator in the situation. Menger's argument is open-ended on this point, and we shall elaborate on the other implications of imperfect information separately below. The fourth condition for successful exchange requires that economizers have 'the power actually to perform the exchange of goods'. Here power (*Macht*) is used not in the sense of power over the other trader. For Menger, power relates to the ability to trade in the face of given, essentially non-human, impediments: transport difficulties, time, inadequate communication facilities (ibid.: 185, 188–9). Menger implicitly presumed that these impediments operate with uniform effect on both traders. Altogether, Menger's numerical examples of bilateral exchange are founded on his four conditions for mutually beneficial outcomes – planning, command, knowledge and power – being satisfied for 'any given point in time' (ibid.: 187). Trading takes place in a time vacuum. Finally, trading ceases when the economizers mutually and simultaneously calculate that the marginal gains from further trading do not exceed marginal costs, subjectively estimated (see Moss 1978: 23).

Menger's knowledge condition for successful exchange, in conjunction with the planning requirement, deserves elaboration. While economizers' trading plans may be consistent *ex ante*, competition between them may not be perfect in the sense that all opportunities for gain would not instantly be exploited. According to Menger, the 'first trading contacts of economising individuals are usually the most advantageous economically. It is usually *only later* that opportunities for trade that promise smaller economic gains are exploited' (ibid.: 188; emphasis added). Furthermore, evaluation of goods offered in exchange is 'generally...observed to be subject to constant fluctuations' (ibid.: 188). Ongoing production is continuously making available additional quantities of tradeable goods. Consequently, 'the foundations for economic exchanges are constantly changing, and we therefore observe the phenomenon of a perpetual succession of exchange transactions' (ibid). In this process of successive exchange, changes in knowledge and learning can take place; it takes time for all the mutually beneficial opportunities to be revealed and exploited. Whether the process may be conceived as an iterative trial-and-error sequence remains opaque in Menger's text. It is clear, however, that Menger's analysis reasoned towards equilibrium in exchange: that is, 'points of rest at particular times, for particular persons and with particular kinds of goods' (ibid). Notwithstanding this tendency, it is accurate to report that 'Menger stressed all those aspects which make attainment of point equilibria unlikely' (Streissler 1990b: 59). And the knowledge inequalities and imperfections among market participants which Menger alludes to in the chapters on exchange and price imply that his analysis is concentrated on situations in which point-equilibria have *not* been achieved. Thus Menger must not be counted among those economists who 'usually ascribe the order which competition produces as an equilibrium – a somewhat unfortunate term, because an equilibrium presupposes that the facts have already been discovered and competition therefore has ceased' (Hayek 1978: 184). The competitive market 'order' for Menger was one in which knowledge acquisition was made possible, not one where learning had ceased. Knowledge must be viewed as a consequence as much as a precondition for Mengerian competition.[9]

So far we have identified knowledge imperfections and time delays as crucial factors constraining the gains from isolated exchange. Indeed, Menger proceeded as if the time structure of exchange was of the utmost importance; the equilibrium case was a limiting one in which 'no exchange takes place' (Menger [1871] 1950: 188) and in which, *ipso facto*, competitive behaviour is absent. The precise content and consequences of competitive behaviour in Menger's text become clear when he considers how prices are formed in exchange.

Price formation

In the chapter on 'The Theory of Price' (Menger [1871] 1950: 191–225) we might at first gather from section headings that Menger was interested in analysing those factors which influenced price (presented as ratios in exchange) in the case of isolated bilateral exchange, monopoly and types of 'competition' with varying numbers of buyers and one seller, and large numbers of buyers facing more than one seller. We have considered in an earlier chapter Menger's theory of price formation and demonstrated that there were significant differences between Mengerian market pricing and the Walrasian *tâtonnement* process, Edgeworth's concept of recontracting and Marshallian models of monopoly price discrimination.

However, we ignored the behavioural determinants of 'competition' between market participants. It would be misleading to neglect all except section 3 of Menger's chapter on price simply because that section expressly treats competition. Menger used the term 'competition' sparingly in the first two sections of that chapter, but this does not mean that the equivalent conceptual content of the verb 'to compete' (*Konkurrieren*) or connotations of the noun 'competition' (*die Konkurrenz*) are necessarily lacking in some of his illustrations of price formation.

The foundations of isolated exchange in section 1 of the chapter on price include allowances for 'bargaining' ([1871] 1950: 195). Thus:

> Each of the two bargainers will attempt to acquire as large a portion as possible of the economic gain that he derived from the exploitation of the exchange opportunity, and even if he were to try to obtain but a fair share of the gain, he will be inclined to demand higher prices *the less he knows* of the economic condition of the other bargainer and *the less he knows* the extreme limit to which the other is prepared to go.
> (ibid.: 195; emphasis added)

The imperfect knowledge condition upon which isolated exchange is based is prominent in this passage. The outcome of the 'price war' (*Preiskampf*, ibid.: 195) which ensues between the traders will strongly be influenced by the knowledge each has of the situation of the other player both *ab initio* and as it evolves in the exchange process. The general case may be one in which neither one nor the other trader has a knowledge advantage or an 'overwhelming economic talent' (ibid.: 196) to process given information, but in that case the traders would be no more than bargainers *manqué*. In any particular case Menger therefore conceded that the exchange 'will prove sometimes more favourable to one and sometimes more favorable to the other of the two bargainers' (ibid.: 195). In commonly observable cases of exchange, such as the one Menger alluded to in the preceding passage, each bargainer is confronted with a rival whose actions are not fully predictable in advance; the result is an exchange ratio which is highly personalized.[10] In short, the traders do not behave as if they were involved in a 'mutually paralysing' (ibid.: 196) or perfectly competitive situation. Only perfect knowledge or foresight for all traders would have a 'paralysing' effect as Morgenstern (1935) and Hayek were later to explain.[11] For example, Hayek (1948: 95) claimed that the assumption of perfect knowledge had a 'paralysing effect...on all action'. The competitive activity enunciated by Menger involved each trader using an aggressive price leadership strategy during the course of any price war, especially in the usual situation where knowledge was incomplete. Situations of isolated exchange are said to be 'most common in the early stages of the development of civilization'. However, isolated exchange may be 'observed in highly developed economies wherever an exchange of goods that have value only to two economising individuals takes place, or where other special circumstances economically isolate two persons' (Menger [1871] 1950: 177; emphasis added). Going by his earlier remarks, uppermost in Menger's mind here in respect of 'special circumstances' were information asymmetries, and problems of knowledge. The different states of knowledge and their development during the price war are not followed through in Menger's account of pricing, although there are game-theoretic implications here. The Mengerian price war implies conflict, manoeuvre and bluff. Price making behaviour in the *Principles* is highly personalized; it implies that buyers and sellers can practise a market strategy. As a corollary, the implicit notion of competition which is part of the context of pricing, is not of the Walras–Pareto type. Morgenstern was to characterize the Walras–Pareto vision of competition 'as a situation in which no one has any influence on anything, where there is *ni gain, ni perte*, where everyone faces *fixed conditions, given prices*, and has only to adapt himself to them so as to attain an individual maximum' (1972: 1171; his emphasis). Evidence presented from Menger's work up to this point indicates that he held an entirely different conception of competition.

The behaviour of market participants in Menger's well-known horse auction also deserves consideration in a bargaining context ([1871] 1950: 204–8). In the auction there is 'competition' among buyers for horses offered by a single seller. The seller is presumed to 'choose an auction where he must sell...a monopolized good completely within a limited period of time' (ibid.: 208). There is no price discrimination in the first case outlined by Menger. Individual traders are eliminated from the bidding as those with higher valuations use their material buying power as a screening device. For Menger 'competitive strength' is rendered by ability to pay and, coupled with 'eagerness', that strength keeps buyers involved in a price war. As some buyers are eliminated, those remaining may recognize a 'common interest' and by negotiation 'agree to a price' (ibid.: 206) or bid which is just high enough to exclude marginal buyers. It is notable that again Menger allowed for bargaining, initially by way of simultaneous bids first amongst buyers and then between remaining keenest buyers and the seller, before a final transaction price was established. The bargaining protocol in which a final price is found is not given sufficient discussion in the *Principles*, but this should not detract from the broad notion of competition which is implied. First, buyers' competition in Menger's illustrations does not rest easily with what Morgenstern (1972: 1172) labelled 'free competition', which 'cannot take care of the phenomenon of bargaining which pervades all economic life'. Moreover, continued Morgenstern, bargaining 'always takes place where the object sold or bought involves a significant part of one's patrimony or income. At a given level we do not bother to bargain, e.g., for a loaf of bread, but we do bargain when buying a car or a house.' Now Menger's focus was precisely on bargaining over indivisibles – barrels of wine and horses. As well, the buying opportunities in Menger's illustrations were limited in number – buyers could not purchase an unlimited number of horses at a given price; nor were they able or willing to do so. A second dimension to Mengerian competition (which is related to bargaining over budget-significant indivisibles) concerned the finitely small number of buyers in his horse auction. Each buyer constituted a large share of total demand. Consequently, buyers behaved in the belief that other buyers would feel the tangible effects of their bidding activity; they were conscious of potential effects on, and reactions of, other buyers.

That Menger's buyers were rival-conscious raises the issue of knowledge and plan complexity once again. The plans of individuals in isolated exchange would not need to be so complex and so demanding of information as those involving the interlocking actions of several competing buyers in a horse-auction. Menger presumed that each market participant on the demand side must develop increasingly elaborate plans which incorporate responses to the actions of others. The information requirements may be so demanding, and the consequences of insufficient information so devastating to any individual participant, that they may resort to collusion. When Menger considered 'competition in supply' he agreed that '[s]harp competition is usually disadvantageous' to suppliers ([1871] 1950: 221 n. 8). Therefore, in the case of two competitors on the supply side producing a homogeneous good, initially they may be 'hostile to each other, [but] generally [they] come to a quick understanding'. If possible these suppliers may 'enter into a mutual understanding to exploit consumers' (ibid.: 221). Nevertheless, Menger equivocated here. The outcome in this case depends fundamentally on knowledge conditions or, in Menger's words, on whether the two suppliers can generate a 'common understanding'. Consistent with his general methodological outlook on organically created institutions ([1883] 1985: 158), the two suppliers may conceivably generate a spontaneous order by acting 'without an express understanding but "in their mutual well-understood interest"'. In the event, they will continue to pursue 'a monopoly policy toward their customers' ([1871] 1950: 221).

By acting 'independently', two or more market participants on either the demand or the supply side, or on both, can produce 'real competition' (ibid.: 221) or 'true competition' (ibid.: 223), but there is nothing to suggest slavish price taking behaviour in these remarks. There are several behavioural results of Mengerian 'real' competition. First, economizers in competitive situations will be moved to place all their goods on the market rather than withhold or destroy supplies. The 'malpractice' of destroying or underemploying factors of production is also terminated in competitive markets; in the long run more goods will be brought to market (ibid.: 223). Second, 'real' competition for Menger meant that 'even the smallest' profit opportunities were exploited (ibid.: 225). Third, in a final comment on the effects on human behaviour of independent, competitive selling activity, Menger was adamant that sellers cannot act as mere automata in accepting a market price or in being uncritical of existing methods of production. While sellers in a competitive process do not have 'the power to regulate...price or the quantity of goods traded', they must consider their market as changing and changeable. Competition for Menger had the tendency to drive out '*unthinking* continuation of business according to old-established methods' (ibid.: 225; emphasis added). Menger broadened the ambit of competition to include inducing innovations in methods of business organization and production, but surprisingly he says little about product innovation. However primitive, this is still unmistakably a process analysis which advanced beyond competition conceived as a profit-seeking activity involving exploitation of *price* differentials by producers.

To be sure, a full-fledged conception of competition as a dynamic process would allow for the generation of new goods and services, for qualitative changes in existing goods and services and, most emphatically, for rivalry over these innovations. In defence of Menger, he allowed for non-price rivalry in so far as he saw producers struggling to make their products known to market participants who were, *en masse*, uninformed and unsophisticated consumers. Rivalry between producers turned on the provision of knowledge to consumers – and it was this knowledge problem that preoccupied Menger. As he explained:

> Commodities that are little known ['articles that have not been introduced'] have very small clienteles, simply because they are not known. Producers are therefore accustomed to make their commodities 'known' often at great economic sacrifice, in order to increase the number of persons to whom they are saleable. This accounts for the importance of...advertisements, publicity etc.
>
> (ibid.: 242 n. 9)

Advertising was therefore an important dimension of Mengerian competitive activity: it affected the knowledge-content of decisions taken in rivalrous situations. In his article on 'The Meaning of Competition', Hayek reiterated this point, without, however, citing Menger:

> the knowledge [consumers] are supposed to possess...cannot be legitimately assumed to be at their command *before the process of competition starts*. Their knowledge of the alternatives before them is the result of what happens on the market, of such activities as advertising, etc; and the whole organization of the market serves mainly the need of spreading the information on which the buyer is to act.
>
> (1948: 96; emphasis added)

In appreciating that non-price rivalry through advertising was a part of the process of competition broadly conceived, rather than a substitute for price competition, Menger began what was to be a distinctive Austrian approach to non-price rivalry which culminated in the work of Israel Kirzner (1973; 1982).[12] The Kirznerian entrepreneur seeks to bring buying opportunities to the attention of consumers in a process called 'demand discovery'. The process of competition, for Kirzner, is set in motion by market ignorance among market participants. Menger and Hayek provided precursory theoretical foundations for this modern Austrian perspective.

COMPETITION IN MENGER'S *PRINCIPLES*: THE THEORY OF MARKET STRUCTURES

When we attempt to classify the institutional structures within which competitive behaviour takes place in the *Principles*, we are led to consider Menger's theories of markets and of commodities in chapter 7. When the first English translation of the *Principles* became available, it was reviewed by John Hicks (1951: 353), who remarked that 'Menger never assumes a perfect market'.[13] We have already had occasion to reflect briefly on the market structures Menger had in mind in his examples of exchange and price formation: in stating the number of buyers and sellers, this was tantamount to adumbrating a microeconomic structure in which traders behaved. In Menger's horse auction examples, made much of in chapter 5 of the *Principles*, there are at least two buyers and a single seller. The 'competition' among buyers in this auction is a case of oligopsony. Oligopsony is a competitive structure where 'buyers are conscious of the effects on rivals' reactions of their bidding policies' (Machlup 1952: 129). In addition, according to Machlup, oligopsony 'may be unorganised – with buyers engaging in guessing games, bluffing games, or even price wars – or cooperative, with understandings among the allegedly competing buyers' (152). We demonstrated in the previous section that both unorganized and cooperative strategies combined at different stages of the Mengerian bidding process to generate transaction prices.

Competition for Menger originated in monopoly-type arrangements (Menger [1871] 1950: 217). In the preface to the *Principles* Menger promised what later in the Austrian tradition was to be termed a 'genetic-causal' analysis (Mayer [1932] 1994: 57). According to Mayer, genetic-causal analysis explains 'the formation of prices...through knowledge of the laws of their genesis'. Menger did not wish to offer a 'functional' theory of competition and price formation. A functional theory is one 'which by precisely determining the conditions of equilibrium aim[s] to describe the relation of correspondence between *already existing prices in the equilibrium situation*' (Mayer [1932] 1994: 57; emphasis added). By investigating the 'causal connections between economic phenomena', Menger intended to ascertain how 'the more complex phenomena evolve from their elements' ([1871] 1950: 47, 48). Thus the causes of competition were first traced back to their origins in simple isolated exchange activities – bilateral monopolies. These monopolies often called into being oligopsonies where the emphasis was on the volitional actions of more than two individual traders. In any market structure such as oligopsony the precise relationship between buyers' competition and price must be founded on ultimate generative causes residing in the plans economizers make for their needs-satisfaction. So when Menger wrote of a competitor in oligopsony who 'economically excludes' another from an exchange transaction, he denied that the remaining competitor or competitors were still active in the price formation process merely by dint of a 'power physically and legally' to acquire the seller's goods (ibid.: 220 n. 2). The power to purchase fades into the background once the originating cause for an exchange relation and price is located in the filter of the trader's mind, which ranks an individual's needs according to a subjective order of importance.[14]

Geographical isolation and temporal divisions in exchange give rise to considerable price dispersion for the same good (ibid.: 216–17, 252–3). Structures within which competition takes place are described exceedingly broadly as those arrangements which organize 'trading relationships' in special 'markets, fairs, exchanges and [other] points of concentration of trade'. For the economist as an observer the process of competition becomes a 'more complex' one with the advent of these structures (ibid.: 218–19 n. 7). Menger averred cryptically 'the need for competition calls forth competition' (ibid.: 217), thereby implying that no one trader determined the structure within which competition is effected. The complexity of competitive relationships is compounded by the development of 'speculation', formal markets, fairs and exchanges as well as by the varying degree of marketability of commodities (ibid.: 219, 242). Despite the existence of requisite institutions for exchange, a host of factors, including legal or physical impediments to trade, insufficient knowledge on the demand side, and seasonal variations in supply, can all limit both marketability and the nature of rivalrous behaviour over the tradeable goods concerned (ibid.: 242, 247).

With the growth of markets, fairs and specialized exchanges, competitive behaviour becomes organized in time and space. Arbitragers or 'speculators' may be able to smooth out price fluctuations over time. To the extent that potential competitors are easily able 'to find' (ibid.: 249) one another, the subsequent spatial concentration of traders will result in a highly competitive but analytically complex process. There is nothing in the *Principles* to suggest that this process is harmonious; from the point of view of individual competitors, price wars will have the effect of changing their preconceived demand or supply prices. Whether each trader is able to keep any trading plan completely intact during the competitive process is unlikely, although Menger recognized that plan maintenance depended on whether traders were large sellers or buyers, or small traders 'whose scale of operation [is] too insignificant to have any appreciable effect on prices' (ibid.: 250). Market depth is critical. The quantitative limits on amounts that may be sold 'is sometimes wider, and sometimes narrower' (ibid.: 252); if the limits are narrower, price variance may be so great as to subvert stable, consistent 'economic prices' with all that this implies for the revision or ruination of traders' plans.[15] Menger identified markets for financial securities and raw materials as highly 'organised' and 'continuous' (in the sense that they had depth). By way of contrast, less rivalrous interaction amongst traders will take place in markets for specialized, differentiated consumer goods such as 'telescopes, meerschaum ornaments and potted plants' (ibid.: 253). To be sure, Menger entered no judgement that competition for the latter was weak or imperfect or that the dynamic process of competition would be any less conflict-ridden as compared with activity in highly organized markets for (say) financial securities. All that he predicted was that competition in less organized markets led to greater price variance. Overall, Menger did not proceed to the point of analysing highly organized competitive arrangements: that is, competition in atomistic terms where large numbers of small traders predominate and prices are parametric. As we saw earlier, he reserved atomistic trading to less well-organized, more transparent trading situations with small numbers of traders in highly personalized structures such as bilateral monopoly and oligopsony.

On stock and grain exchanges parcels of the same security or of grain respectively may 'change hands ten times in a few hours' (ibid.: 255). Prices will doubtless move about or be dispersed in fairly narrow ranges in real-time trading. Prices in these highly organized exchanges move against one another in an interactive process paralleling the intensive, rivalrous struggle of opposing plans which traders are attempting to implement. Many things are not as easily or frequently traded as stocks and grain, but competition is still active. Menger gives the example of farms and factories: these are 'entirely unsuited to rapid circulation' because they are usually highly indivisible and traders need to take time over assessing their value (ibid.: 255). Greater price variance is the specific manifestation of competition for these goods, since each is unique and traded less frequently than stocks or grain. All this is but a short step to Hayek's path-breaking analysis of competition as a process, especially his insight that 'it takes a *long time* [for market-participants] to find out about the relevant merits of available alternatives [and] where the need for a whole class of goods or services occurs only discontinuously at *irregular intervals*, the adjustment must be slow *even if competition is strong and active*' (1948: 103; emphasis added).

In his theory of markets, Menger minimized discussion of average price outcomes and of single price equilibria as centres of gravity. His concentration on variances was consistent with an interest in dynamic competition. It was Streissler who first correctly interpreted and articulated in the English-speaking literature Menger's perspective on so-called dynamic competitive pricing and who first coined the term 'price variance' to capture Menger's meaning:

> In Menger's vision prices for the same physical commodities are thus *not numbers but stochastic variables*, variables obeying a distribution over space, over time, and – a fact usually not taken into account, but stressed by Menger – a distribution over persons, different social categories of persons commanding different prices. Price distributions for physically identical or very similar commodities thus have a *variance*, which is large in markets where isolated exchange prevails and diminishes with the degree of competition achieved; it diminishes, but in practice never vanishes.
>
> (1973: 171; emphasis in original)

Even in highly organized markets where changes in average prices are usually small, Menger was aware of the importance, in real competitive bidding, of price variance. Thus, when

> a hundredweight of wool of given quantity is sold in a particular transaction on a wool market for 103 florins, it is often found that transactions are taking place at higher and at lower prices *on the same markets and at the same time*, at 104, $103\frac{1}{2}$, and at 102 and $102\frac{1}{2}$, florins.
>
> ([1871] 1950: 273; emphasis added)

The exchange value of wool in *the* market for wool is an aggregative, average measure which is not the same as the individual's valuation. Here Menger emphasized the subjectivism of prices quoted in monetary terms because it is 'the intention of the person making the estimate' (ibid.: 274) of the value of a good that is both the ultimate measure of value and the cause of price variance in highly organized markets. According to Menger, estimating a good's value involved making an allowance for 'the special situation that the good or quantity of goods, whose equivalent (in the subjective sense of the term) is under consideration, occupies in the economy of the economizing individual' (ibid.: 275). Menger's emphasis is on price differences arising from subjective variations in value, presumably in space rather than in time. We could take this matter further and read Mises into Menger:

> The market is not a place, a thing or a collective entity. The market is a process, actuated by the interplay of the actions of the various individuals.... The forces determining the – continually changing – state of the market are the value judgements of these individuals and their actions as directed by these value judgements.
>
> (Mises 1949: 258)

It would be too anachronistic to suggest that Menger's disquisition on the wool market comes close to Mises's concept of the market. But Menger certainly appreciated that the market is not a single place and that market competition is founded on individual valuations. While Menger's wool market is said to be organized, it must not be well organized in space. Price variations observed 'at the same time' imply that the 'same market' for Menger is in fact spatially extended (even within a single auction hall). As a result, there would be more than one auctioneer or seller offering a wool stock.[16] The subsequent knowledge problem for buyers is to understand what is being quoted in different parts of the market so that considerable price dispersion may be observed by the economist even 'at the same time' if buyers' understanding is imperfect or incomplete. In short, information dispersion in space is enough to generate price dispersion in Menger's case of the wool market. The implication for competition is that 'to compete' means merely testing one's information (or plans) as buyer or seller in interaction with other participants. And, as we demonstrated in the chapter on Menger's theory of price formation (Chapter 5 above), transactions *will* be effected even if the trading price is not consistent with some general Walrasian economic equilibrium.

MENGER ON COMPETITION

All Menger's examples of trading institutions within which competition proceeded explored acts of striving to buy or sell by market participants. The trading arrangements were diverse; they exhibited more complexity in so far as they went beyond simple isolated exchange settings and price homogeneity in equilibrium. Menger focused on a variety of possible outcomes and on the variance of prices resulting from competition understood as an activity in all the market forms that he considered. As we shall see, the notion of competition as an activity is carried over into the work of Wieser and Böhm-Bawerk. We shall reserve final assessment of Menger on competition until the last section of the next chapter. For we are about to embark on a study of Wieser's and Böhm-Bawerk's treatment of competition. There are important differences between the founding Austrians on this subject. Whether or not these differences are significant in the sense of being sufficient to signal fundamental intellectual discontinuities in founding Austrian economics is something that we shall address in the next chapter.

8

THE PROCESS OF COMPETITION IN FOUNDING AUSTRIAN ECONOMIC THEORY: II; WIESER AND BÖHM-BAWERK

WIESER ON COMPETITION AS SOCIAL CONFLICT

Hans Mayer ([1932] 1994: 58) maintained that Wieser (and Böhm-Bawerk) 'consistently stuck' to genetic-causal theorizing, following the foundations established by Menger.[1] Like Menger, Wieser began with processes of exchange and price formation for atomistic, isolated, bilateral arrangements; he then proceeded to account for competition and price formation in more complex structures by using what he called the method of 'decreasing abstraction' (Wieser [1914] 1927: 178).[2]

In *Natural Value*, Wieser ([1889] 1930) referred to the Mengerian price war in a section on the 'inter-competition' of buyers for one or more goods offered by a single seller. There is a 'competition of prices' on the buyers' side of the market (ibid.: 41). In the market as a whole the bidding process leads to a price for the goods offered that is determined by the 'marginal buyer' (ibid.: 46). There may not be a single price outcome, since a single seller may price-discriminate by 'find[ing] out those among all the buyers who can pay most and...drive them...to the margin of their purchasing power' (ibid.: 46). If there is more than one seller, the 'inter-competition' among them, coupled with buyers' competition, leads to all buyers 'paying for the same article the same price as is paid by everyone else'. Under 'really free competition', sellers' market power is reduced, supply is augmented, and these factors 'press prices far on the down grade of exchange value' towards a unique market price (ibid.: 55, 56). Wieser mentioned repeatedly the 'struggle of competition' (ibid.: 46) and the 'war of competition' (ibid.:

57). Moreover, the competition which was of interest to him was a 'conflict of price' along Mengerian lines (also Wieser 1891: 119). Wieser's expressions connote ongoing conflicts of interest, of rivalrousness as a source of change; they did not describe frictionless equilibrium conditions. There is also a sense in which competition has social selection effects. Buyers with sufficient purchasing power have a greater chance of survival when they enter the competitive battle for a wide range of goods. According to Wieser:

> The rich have not only the advantage over the poor of possessing more means wherewith to purchase goods; they have the further advantage of being for the most part in a more favourable position to utilise their means...[in] the battle of price.'
>
> ([1889] 1930: 58).

Since the price of bread, for instance, is largely adapted to the valuations of the poorest buyers, those with greater purchasing power pay well 'under their personal valuations' and are thereby able to enter other markets and use their consumer surpluses to compete for a wider range of goods. Wieser developed this elementary insight in his later work.

In Wieser's *Social Economics* ([1914] 1927), at least in the first section, treating the idealized 'simple' or 'natural' economy, the analysis is defined as 'static': here the theory of value and price is 'presented with the assumption of a static economy, showing neither progress or retrogression' ([1914] 1927: 13). The simple economy is 'entirely detached from exchange' (ibid.: 49); competition as it was discussed in *Natural Value* was therefore redundant.[3] Lavoie (1985: 81) rightly argued that 'Wieser's simple or natural economy abstracts from rivalry'. However, the abstraction referred to is not made with any explicitness or conviction in *Natural Value* or in the bulk of *Social Economics*. In the latter the 'social economy' takes up most of the text, and its vital constituents are exchange and rivalry in various market contexts.

When we enter Wieser's 'social economy' the level of abstraction is lowered and the 'social process of acquisition and exchange' ([1914] 1927: 149) is a pre-eminent consideration. Individual market participants 'meet from all directions. Indeed they clash with great force' (ibid.: 151); the consequences of such a clash for price formation will be different depending on both the degree of market organization and the nature of the goods traded. Readers of *Social*

Economics first encounter competition defined as 'rivalry in trade' in the context of an 'auction sale' in which buyers have in their minds a 'demand-index' or 'demand-series' much like a Marshallian demand schedule (ibid.: 174, 181, 182, 184). The demanders as bidders in the auction do not wish to pay their valuations (as imagined in their mental experiments which construct demand-series). Instead they 'will endeavour to make their acquisition with the lowest bid...[and] only gradually will they raise their bids to the upper limit as they become convinced that their end cannot be reached otherwise' (ibid.: 182). Knowledge of market conditions is not presumed to be complete in advance of the auction, at least on the demand side. Once the quantity offered in a closed auction is known, exchanges are effected simultaneously, and normally at a price which is uniform for every unit sold. As Wieser insisted: 'No purchaser will pay a higher price, while someone at his elbow pays less.' Formally,

> the price is regularly fixed between the maximum offer of the lowest demand-series that must still be admitted to trade in order that the entire quantity offered may be sold and the highest offer of the next succeeding demand series, which must be over-bid in order that the higher series may be protected against their competitors.
>
> (ibid.: 183)

It is notable that Wieser simplified the auction by assuming fixed supplies which *must* be sold. Ostensibly the suppliers in Wieser's example do not form supply-series; they merely offer all their goods to the highest bidders. The 'price war' takes place exclusively between buyers who are, in this case, the sole 'vehicles of values' (ibid.: 183). Suppliers in this auction have an entirely passive role; evidently they bring their goods to market in the expectation of receiving a price which at least covers their 'utility value' from the suppliers' standpoint. As Wieser explained, 'we assumed that the consumption wares to be sold have no utility value for the vendor personally.' Otherwise, if the goods have utility value for the vendor, he 'will not be satisfied with anything less than a money-price whose use in exchange still promises a gain over and above the utility value' (ibid.: 185, 186).

In predicting the outcome of competition in terms of price variance, Menger's claim that the characteristics of the goods traded was a vital consideration also found expression in Wieser's example of 'scarcity-commodities' such as antiques, works of art and other luxuries (Wieser [1914] 1927: 183–4). The analysis proceeds in terms of the familiar founding Austrian notion of price bounds or price limits:

> The limits within which the formation of prices takes place, are frequently far apart in the case of scarcity commodities. A comparatively small number of wealthy individuals constitute the effective demand for costly antiques. The outcome of the price-war between these parties for an ardently desired work of art can hardly be anticipated. The prices here realized, vary in amount from sale to sale by considerable sums.... The prices which are realized may be called fortuitous prices.
> (ibid.: 183)

The limits of price formation are wide when the 'whim of the moment', even on the part of a single competitor, moves prices. By comparison, individuals cannot have a significant price influence when competing for mass-produced goods, goods offered in large quantities to a multitude of buyers, and subsistence goods. Price variation is minimized, and demand for these goods becomes 'stratified':

> The series of demand are here formed not by individual persons, but by classes of the people whose stratifications are shaded into one another. These series are interwoven into a network of narrowest meshes, leaving to the formation of prices a scarcely perceptible latitude of movement.
> (ibid.)

In short, the 'struggle of competition' generally confirms the law of one price.

Single-price outcomes of competition are, for Wieser, 'just or equitable' (ibid.: 185).[4] In the markets for mass-produced goods price is 'a social institution' that is 'a result of a social contest for the possession of the offered supply' – a contest between individuals with varying appreciation for the goods on offer and with varying powers of demand (ibid.: 189).[5] The maximum offer of the marginal stratum is decisive. Therefore 'price does not take its standard form from the marginal utility but from the stratified marginal utility' (ibid.: 188–9). The formation of a 'just' competitive price is causally connected not to individual trades ('single combats') but to the 'struggle' which is 'fought group to group and class to class' (ibid.: 185). The social law of one price is derived from 'socially controlled egoism', which produces a form of competition unlike that which is forthcoming from 'a conflict of unbridled personal egoism'. Somewhat paradoxically, while the individual still competes in the sense of making bids and offers in interaction with other market participants, the bid–offer process assumes a co-operative function:

> The individual, cooperating in the establishment in the market of this [just] price by looking out for his individual interest, protects at the same time the social interest; he fulfils a personal and a social duty; he contributes his share to the establishment of the market [bid–offer] series.
>
> (ibid.: 184)

As a consequence, Wieser continued, the nature of competition changes: 'the struggle of price competition will be purged of objectionable elements and will cease to be a struggle at all at the height of social progress'. Supply and demand behaviour will become a co-operative endeavour. Each buying class, for instance, will know its place, having been 'fully educated to social egoism', and classes then co-exist under conditions which are 'morally and legally correct'. Nevertheless prices will not necessarily remain constant, since social competition is a process which may bring about secular price changes. The influence of changes in needs and of changes in income distribution 'may transform the entire system of prices' (ibid.: 192, 195).

Unbridled competition deriving from 'personal egoism' is made the subject of Wieser's obloquy on two grounds. First, competition which leads to 'unheard of prices...for luxuries' is declared 'immoral' because it creates social disruption over income and wealth distribution. Second, in a market that is scattered spatially or temporally, vent can sometimes be given to competition among market participants which is likened to 'panic' and which takes the form of 'the fiercest struggles' on the demand and supply sides (ibid.: 195). Furthermore, in these conditions market 'powers unthought of before' are abused at will (ibid.: 185). In the intense struggle, competition becomes destructive. For example, selling at 'mad prices' may be observed, as may untrammelled monopoly price-discrimination which upsets the 'social judgements' of traders previously accustomed to stable bases for planning to satisfy their needs. In the event, the appropriate marginal offer determined in a stable, stratified market will not be ascertained. That the resulting 'chance prices' would not strictly clear markets (in the Walrasian sense) was not within Wieser's purview. His principal concern was that prices transmitted accurate information to market participants. In 'disorderly' markets, price information was incorrect or insufficient to determine a result which preserved the social *status quo*. For example, putative 'inter-competition' among those with low purchasing power or weak selling power could produce 'over-excited fear'. Thus, 'the competition of the weak is aroused, not so much by the desire of advancement, as by the apprehension of defeat...such competition easily loses all restraint and becomes disorganized super-competition' (ibid.: 208). In Wieser's labour-market illustrations, the price war, if one-sided among large numbers of labourers, would produce 'over-competition' (ibid.: 373) and 'proletarian misery' (ibid.: 381). Labourers would end up not being paid the full value of their marginal products when there was too much competition on one side of the market. In the event just described, inequalities in the distribution of incomes become 'excessive', such that commodity-price stratification becomes 'much too great'; the resulting price structure is 'socially unjustified'. Prices are then deemed to be 'unstable' – in other words, they are an unreliable basis for computation of long-term relative value by market participants. Resource-allocative inefficiencies become inevitable in these conditions (ibid.: 381). Similarly, competition among manufacturers over 'new methods, new territories, new points of departure' may initially take the form of 'friendly rivalry'. It may at any time explode into 'a deadly contest, ending...in ruin and desolation'. Here 'the dangers of competition' become manifest in 'excessive production' (ibid.: 209). Again, we have another illustration of Wieser's notion of 'over-competition'. Competition which leads to over-production and economic and social crises is, for Wieser, perverse, since it renders unreliable the price signals upon which market participants make their calculations.[6] The demand–supply mechanism does not operate efficiently when there is significant economic and social dislocation. In summary, there are social limits to competition in Wieser's system.

The degree of competition need not be perfect to attract Wieser's approval. Indeed, what would now be regarded as imperfectly competitive arrangements, far from being treated as exceptions, were regarded as part of the normal course of things in a growing social economy. Competition promoted *change*. Competition as a state was not dilated upon at length in *Social Economics*. Wieser maintained that, on the supply side in particular, those 'who have the ability will strive to advance beyond the general ruck and will ever be eager to gain headway against their rivals, [so as] to wrest from them in the commercial conflict increasing sales'. Wieser's version of dynamic competition involved sellers mutually underselling one another until cost prices had been reached (ibid.: 205–6). Precisely what 'cost' price is intended here is unclear, although it would be reasonable to surmise that he meant average cost. According to Wieser:

> By the pressure of competition, manufacturers are compelled actually to produce the entire quantity of wares which market conditions allow. Producers will not stop manufacturing until the marginal bid, determined by the receptivity of the demand, coincides with the cost price. Not until this condition of prices has been reached, will an equilibrium have been established in which the cost elements in all their productive combinations are paid for at the same price.
>
> (ibid.: 205)

In some social economies merger activity may be rife; 'competitive conflict' is part of the merger process and is potentially unifying rather than destructive (ibid.: 237). In addition, the aggregation of capital, especially creation of large-scale cartels and trusts, may 'obviate the injuries of over-competition' (ibid.: 224), provided that a tendency towards cost price is preserved. Wieser's argument turned on the need to encourage active competitive process on the supply side among cartels, trusts and combines at the technical and managerial level at one remove from price competition. Rivalry between business organizations took place over technical innovations (which resulted in a larger scale of production) and over leadership (including financial and managerial) skills, both of which impacted on the position each business could take in the price conflict with consumers. As for innovations, competitors 'will feel compelled to adopt technical advances in the service of the market demand, when to do otherwise would mean that [they] might be left behind by [their] competitors, and deprived of the advantage [of their] sales' (ibid.: 204–5). Under the influence of Wieser, Schumpeter ([1911] 1934) outlined 'an entrepreneurial kind of leadership' which created positive economic profits and which attracted competitors who attempt to 'reduce and then annihilate' those profits (ibid.: 89). The profit incentive generated a 'competitive struggle' (ibid.: 131) in which the leader–entrepreneur eventually 'perish[ed] in the vortex of the competition' (ibid.: 134). However, unlike Schumpeter's leader–entrepreneur, Wieser's leadership function did not 'perish', since the factors giving rise to competition as a process are always recreated in a progressing social economy. The overall outcome is not single-price monopoly, but 'monopoloidal' competition, because 'the elements of monopoly one finds in them are interspersed with those of competition' (Wieser [1914] 1927: 237; also 221, 225). This is the closest any of the founding Austrians come to anticipating the Robinson–Chamberlin concept of monopolistic competition developed in the 1930s.

Wieser's discussion of the institutional aspects of competition as a species of social conflict, with social outcomes, distinguishes his contribution sharply from Menger's. While competition selects which traders will be rewarded, the prices paid will be the result of the use of power on both sides of the market. Power is not simply vanquished by some perfectly competitive process in Wieser's system; it remains ever-present and a perennial influence on market outcomes. On the demand side, 'stratified marginal utility' affects commodity pricing. On the supply side, technical or production innovations and leadership 'decide the competitive conflict' (ibid.: 237). Product innovations and associated product differentiation were not explicitly mentioned by Wieser (Streissler 1986: 93). In this respect his discussion paralleled Menger's. Wieser's penchant to personalize competition conceived as a type of behaviour, regardless of the market structure, also had much in common with Menger. Wieser's summary judgement on this matter deserves to be quoted at length:

> competition... exercises so great an effect... under modern conditions, [as] to entitle it to be classed among the most important social economic forces. In the strata of laborers and subordinate employees it is more limited. It asserts itself there only for a smaller number of ambitious individuals; but among the independent owners it affects all. Within each of these groups, it performs... the functions of personal selection; peasant against peasant, master-mechanic against master-mechanic, large entrepreneur against large entrepreneur, each is weighed and measured, approved or condemned in the fierce struggle of competitive conflict.
>
> ([1914] 1927: 210)

For Wieser, this striving for supremacy, as he so often called it, is the essence of competition as a behavioural phenomenon. The motivation for competitive behaviour is related to the desire for some maximand – 'love of ostentation', 'honor', 'material prosperity' (ibid.: 210–11). On a personal level, achievement of one or other of these goals implies victory in the competitive conflict. At the societal level, victory in competition will not necessarily result in anything like 'perfect' competition in the senses that market power will be abolished or that the competitive process will automatically select, in one instant, the most deserving consumers or the ablest business leaders.

COMPETITION AS A BARGAINING PROCESS: BÖHM-BAWERK'S VERSION

Böhm-Bawerk's remarks on competition bore the stamp of their Austrian pedigree. For the most part, competition for Böhm-Bawerk was entirely bound up with behavioural patterns motivated by market participants' mental evaluations of tradeable goods. The interaction of subjective valuations in the trading process involves competition. We must perforce be concerned not with the 'economy of a Crusoe' but with 'the laws according to which we pursue our interests when they are entangled with the interests of others' in exchange (Böhm-Bawerk [1896] 1962: 20). An explanation of human behaviour which leads to price formation in exchange (but not necessarily to some competitive equilibrium price) will also of necessity be an explanation of competition.

Formally, competition 'is a sort of collective name for all the psychical motives and impulses which determine the actions of the dealers in the market, and which thus influence the fixing of prices' (ibid.: 278). The active interplay of these motives on both sides of the market have their superficial, overt referents in bid and offer prices. 'Egoistic price waves' are the consequence of the intensity of the bid–offer duel in which a 'single motive' viz., self-interested gain-seeking is predominant (Böhm-Bawerk 1959b: 212, 214). More fundamentally, subjective marginal-utility valuations give economizing traders the impulse to maximize their utility; they endeavour to exchange goods at a price less than the marginal utility which they confer on those goods. In 'extremely highly organised conditions of exchange', Böhm-Bawerk asserted, economizers make global marginal utility estimates: 'we almost never estimate the value of goods which are indispensable to us according to their direct utility, but in nearly all cases according to the 'substitution utility' of unrelated categories of goods' (ibid.: 152). Like Wieser, Böhm-Bawerk considered prices as signals to act. For example, entrepreneurs observe consumers' bids and may be induced thereby to expand or contract production (ibid.: 112).

The 'free competition' of prices may be modified by the intervention of non-egoistic motives such as habit, custom, pride, national enmity, prejudice and power in general (ibid.: 212). In one of his later essays, Böhm-Bawerk ([1914] 1962) distinguished between purely economic, egoistic motives which if universally applied led to free competition, and non-economic motives which change both the form of competition and subsequent price outcomes:

> Whoever is moved by non-economic, outside considerations like friendship or humanitarian impulses to make a gift to the other party of the bargain, may as a buyer consent to a price which will exceed his subjective valuation and as a seller be content with a price far below his own valuation.
>
> (ibid: 156)

There is presumably 'competition' of a different nature in these circumstances. *Any* motives determining the actions of bargainers are relevant considerations when the form of competition is of interest.

Böhm-Bawerk's horse-auction market was set in a bargaining context (ibid.: 220ff.). In its full-fledged form the auction exhibited competition between bargainers on both sides of the market and it contained rudimentary game-theoretic elements (simultaneous offer bargaining) which have been explored elsewhere (Schotter 1992: 98; Chapter 6 above). Buyers' competition forces price upwards, and sellers' competition drives price downwards. The horse-auction examples in *Positive Theory of Capital* move beyond mere isolated exchange and atomistic arrangements: large numbers of traders become attached to the auction. To be sure, some are 'excluded' as the bid–offer duel proceeds (Böhm-Bawerk 1959b: 228 ff.), but those excluded play an *active* role in determining the final transaction price. The auction price outcome 'virtually shrinks to a point' consistent with the valuations of the 'marginal pairs', provided only that there is a large number of buyers and many suppliers (ibid.: 240, 248). The market is analysed as a process, except in the limit where a hypothetical 'momentary market situation' is imagined in which supply is fixed and buyers' competition produces a single transaction price. As 'time goes on' supplies are considered variable, provided there is ease of entry into horse production and there is 'brisk competition among suppliers' (ibid.: 249; Böhm-Bawerk [1914] 1962: 280). Böhm-Bawerk's entrepreneurs will notice any deviation between trading price and marginal cost and then take advantage of 'unexploited opportunities' (1959b: 254–5). These entrepreneurs act much like their modern Kirznerian counterparts (Kirzner 1979). The entrepreneurs in Böhm-Bawerk's market seize upon opportunities in a spirit of rivalry; they exploit opportunities which are potentially 'infinite in number' generated by the bid–offer bargaining process. There is 'no moment of time... which could boast a complete absence' of profit opportunities (1959b: 256). These opportunities 'are the inexhaustible source from which flows the constant stream of entrepreneurs' profits – and of entrepreneurs' losses as well' (ibid.). Here Böhm-Bawerk turned away from an analysis of equilibrium states in which all profit-seeking, competitive activity had been exhausted.[7]

As a market structure, 'free and perfect competition' is considered with reference to wage determination. In *Positive Theory* the price of labour was said to be the 'object of bargaining' (ibid.: 308). When there is 'effective competition on both sides' of the labour market, Böhm-Bawerk predicted that wages will be determined by the marginal product of labour ([1914] 1962: 162–3). Labour markets were interconnected: 'outside competition' was permitted in that 'employers in all branches of industry' determined wages in any one branch (ibid.: 164). Böhm-Bawerk was chary of committing himself to an analysis of competition and price formation in a general competitive equilibrium sense.[8] His theoretical 'superstructure' was 'built up on a host of communicating partial markets'. Böhm-Bawerk introduced the concept of intertemporal exchange by incorporating the phenomenon of interest, and the problem of exchange of present for future goods, into the 'fully developed competitive market'. However, for the economist, 'to attempt to depict... the whole profusion of influences whose complex interaction constitutes the *activity* of that market [would be] a task of great, nay, of insuperable difficulties' (1959b: 312, and 351; emphasis added). Accordingly he turned his attention to competitive activity in partial, market-by-market contexts.

Market participants have only *partial* knowledge; they take a partial but not a single market perspective when involved in the bid–offer process. They will imagine the potential threat of 'outside competition' or the creation of 'new competition' or new markets in response to their own actions. For instance, employer 'monopolists' in a labour market would have to take into account the potential effects of their attempts to fix the price of labour on the behaviour of employers in other industries. They would have to 'conjecture' on the 'probability of outside competition' for labour. Competitive relationships may arise amongst employers who formerly were not competing with one another. The supposed 'monopoly' control over wages in any one market would be thwarted by uncertainty, for

> just as in ordinary market competition for prices, when negotiations are carried on with covered cards, traders less experienced or less shrewd commit errors in sizing up...market situations, so that actual prices are caused to fluctuate over a wide range.
>
> ([1914] 1962: 166–7)

Coalitions of employers will not be omniscient; they must act without knowing with certainty whether or not outsiders will appear who can 'pierce a hole through the dominant phalanx of entrepreneurs'. In short, the sources of potential competition are difficult to predict in practice. Similarly, on the supply side organized labour may attempt to set wages above the marginal product of labour, but this prompts the appearance of a 'steady stream of competitors' (ibid: 179–80). Workers' coalitions must constantly manoeuvre to stave off potential competitors. In any case, Böhm-Bawerk was supremely confident that 'economic law' would prevail in the conflict of competition. In respect of the subjective nature of competitive interrelationships, Böhm-Bawerk ([1896] 1962) remarked in his essay on the Marxian system that, whereas competition is assumed to be always operative, Marx in fact neglects the motive forces 'causing' competition. These forces are highly individualistic in origin; they are 'psychical impulses' (ibid.: 270) which are 'economico-psychological' (ibid.: 287) in nature. Böhm-Bawerk noted that competition is the result of active 'subjective' factors governing bargaining relations (ibid.: 299). That is, the subjective motive forces making for free competition are rooted in the individual desire for gain; this desire will work within and through coalitions and monopoly elements in labour markets so that the final effect is a price of labour consistent with the level of its marginal product. The latter is an ultimate result of competition; the activities, interrelationships and subjective causes which bring this result about, were of interest to all the founding Austrians, and Böhm-Bawerk was no exception.

Subjective personal desire – that is, the motive for individual gain – counteracts forces making for the concentration of economic power. The motive for gain, which is manifested by arbitrage activity in labour markets, is *the* economic 'power' which defeats monopsony, monopoly or some degree of monopoly. To be sure, the Böhm-Bawerkian market is always reduced for analytical purposes to atomistic or individualistic-competitive interrelationships between participants on either side of the market. There are always actually or potentially maverick traders who are called forth to counteract the strategies of any dominant participant or group of participants. (ibid: 178, 179, 186). Now this theoretical orientation has been criticized because it contains errors of omission:

> He could, furthermore, have pointed out that if employers in an industry have a collective monopoly of the demand for labor, this is generally but a reply to a collective monopoly of labor supply. Assuming, however, a unilateral collective monopoly of demand for labor, without local limitation, there would be no counteracting forces of a 'purely economic nature', for, whilst the employer can react to a rise in wages by adopting different methods of production, the worker possesses no means of evading the effects of a fall in wages. Therefore a wage rate *lower* than the marginal product could be maintained for much longer than a wage rate *higher* than the marginal product.
> (Preiser [1959] 1971: 124; emphasis in original)

In Preiser's argument it is not obvious that every form of monopoly power automatically stimulates latent competitive behaviour. On the other hand, for Böhm-Bawerk it was inconceivable that the individual desire for gain could ever be successfully or indefinitely quelled. As long as markets remain in process – rather than in a state of rest or equilibrium – employers of labour, for instance, can well hold their breath longer in a wage struggle, but they must still act with incomplete knowledge. This is precisely Böhm-Bawerk's point: a collective monopoly of labour demand *without limitation*, to paraphrase Preiser, entails certain knowledge that potential competitors will not appear, which seems to be a strong assumption as long as markets are constantly changing or out of equilibrium.

By paying attention to the problem of power in factor markets, especially in the labour markets, Böhm-Bawerk was driven to consider the nature of competition as ongoing bargaining or contingent negotiational relationships between various socio-economic classes which act as factor market participants. According to Rothschild (1973: 217), 'Menger... carried the process of purifying the economics of distribution from all historical and sociological elements further than his immediate successors.' If this passage means by 'pure' economics a doctrine which was distanced from an analysis of power relations (or strategic, negotiational relations) in the competition which takes place in factor markets, then it is substantially correct. Rothschild proceeded to credit Böhm-Bawerk for anticipating 'many later developments in wage and distribution theory, like monopsony and other "disturbances" of competitive equilibrium' (ibid.: 217). However, it cannot be maintained, following Rothschild's view, that Böhm-Bawerk regarded the process of competition in the 'disturbance' phase as merely ephemeral and therefore not a matter of *general* interest to the economist. To give attention exclusively to Böhm-Bawerk's so-called 'pure' distribution theory – his concept of derived demand for labour, and the associated notion of marginal productivity *in* equilibrium situations – would be to accept a Clarkian, Marshallian or Walrasian neoclassical focus. As far as the 'impure' or 'disturbing' competitive aspects of distribution theory were concerned, and particularly in Böhm-Bawerk's theory of wage-bargaining and wage-fixing, his work had much more to offer compared with other neoclassical distribution theories because it approached the problem by not concentrating excessively on the equilibrium state. Rothschild's expression of a 'competitive equilibrium' would have been disputed by Böhm-Bawerk on the grounds that an equilibrium in the labour market implied the absence of competitive activity. For all the founding Austrians, the epithet 'competitive' was redundant in an equilibrium context.

By the close of his article on 'Distributive Aspects of the Austrian Theory', by contrast with his earlier attempts to single out Böhm-Bawerk's pure distribution theory, Rothschild was full of praise for Böhm-Bawerk's analysis of competition (or bargaining): 'Böhm-Bawerk cleared the way for a fuller consideration of institutional and bargaining elements in the distribution process of a world which is anything but transparent, flexible, and perfectly competitive' (ibid.: 224). The bargaining behaviour which Böhm-

Bawerk discussed does not appear in his work simply to function as the activity which pre-reconciles imagined market disturbances so as to rationalize, or attain in principle, a determinate equilibrium. Bargaining activity is a response to imperfect knowledge or, alternatively conceived, to plan divergence between market participants. This Böhm-Bawerk recognized. So long as bargaining is to some degree personalized – as it was in Böhm-Bawerk's examples – then the concrete circumstances in which the participants find themselves will affect the outcome. Their decision to trade at particular prices is, for Böhm-Bawerk, based on negotiations: to abstract from the specific information content of these decisions would, in effect, amount to denying that such negotiations took place. As we saw in Chapter 6, Böhm-Bawerk was not prepared to theorize exclusively in general terms; the 'second part' of his theory of price formation included variations in concrete institutions, such as property rights and the knowledge content of economic decisions. Accordingly, in analysing competition in labour markets, he did not simplify the analysis by reasoning at a high level of abstraction, since that would have removed competitive processes altogether.

All the ingredients for a market process perspective of competition are made available in Böhm-Bawerk's work. The most striking confirmation of this perspective comes in his implicit acceptance of Menger's theorem of non-equivalence. Menger ([1871] 1950: 192) insisted that exchange involved genuine choice. Traders made decisions to exchange and hence *to compete* over goods which were regarded as being exchanged for other goods of non-equivalent value in a subjective sense. The observed irreversibility of exchanges was proof for Menger that individuals exchanged goods of unequal subjective value. Menger gave the example of trader A exchanging a house for B's farm. Now if 'these goods had become equivalents in the objective sense of the term as a result of the transaction...there is no reason why the two participants should not be willing to reverse the trade immediately' (ibid.: 193). Similarly, Böhm-Bawerk (1959b: 214) apprehended exchange as a 'personal quest for advantage'. Bargaining over goods pointed to 'the existence of some inequality'. An exchange involved a change of ownership whereas equivalence in exchange from the standpoint of the individual trader implied that 'exact equilibrium' obtains and 'no change is likely to occur to disturb the balance' ([1896] 1962: 260). Like Menger, Böhm-Bawerk (as well as Hayek, Schumpeter and Kirzner later in the Austrian tradition) wished to focus on the competitive process which led to the equilibrium situation.[9] Böhm-Bawerk's bargainers considered price as a variable rather than as a parameter; otherwise exchange and competition would have ceased. Böhm-Bawerkian competition is conceived generally as the bargaining actions of traders in markets which generate prices but not necessarily an equilibrium price. Here competition effected changes in a key market condition: that is, price. This orientation meant that he was moving towards a genetic–causal theory of price formation. Austrian economics between the wars, particularly in the Mayer Circle, attempted further to develop a genetic-causal theory, although it remained largely a promise (Boehm 1992: 21).

CONCLUSION: THE 'HAYEKIAN' FLAVOUR OF FOUNDING AUSTRIAN CONCEPTIONS OF COMPETITION

When Hayek (1948) expanded on the distinction between perfect competition as a final end-state, and genuine competition as a process, his contribution acted as a conduit for transmission of some earlier Austrian insights. While we may readily acknowledge that 'Hayek's views on competition...represent a rediscovery and also an expansion and further development of the notion of competition put forward by Adam Smith and his predecessors' (Veit 1990: 105), the more immediate influences on Hayek's ideas surely hailed from Austrian sources. Hayek contended that competition involved the acquisition of 'new knowledge'; it was 'essentially a process of the formation of opinion' (1948: 94, 106). The context of Hayekian competition, like that in the work of Menger, Wieser and Böhm-Bawerk, was one in which market participants had imperfect knowledge. Hayek referred to

> the absurdity of the usual procedure of starting the analysis [of competition] with a situation in which all the facts are supposed to be known. This is a state of affairs which economic theory curiously calls 'perfect competition'. It leaves no room whatever for the activity called competition, which is presumed to have already done its task.
>
> (1978: 182)

When the founding Austrians personalized the notion of competition and related it to the concrete bargaining situations faced by competitors, they were essentially replacing the perfect knowledge assumption (or the more modern optimally imperfect information assumption based on probabilistic reasoning) of perfectly competitive analysis, with the assumption of subjectively held and dispersed knowledge. Hayek carried forward the mantle of subjectivism, with respect to the process of competitive behaviour in markets, which was bestowed on him by the founding Austrians.

Given that the dispersal of knowledge among competitors' minds was a precondition for competitive behaviour, Hayek (1948: 96–7) noticed that competition then functioned to 'teach' participants about the available alternative goods for buying or selling and about the patterns of responses to be expected from other traders with whom they had 'contacts' in the market. (This insight was later to form the basis of his article on 'Competition as a Discovery Procedure' (1978: 179–90.) Indeed, Hayek insisted that an adequate explanation of competition must outline the 'personal relationships existing between [trading] partners' (1948: 96, 97). Just because it might take 'a long time' for market participants to adapt to the variety of tradeable goods in the market or to the behaviour of rivals, this did not warrant application of the epithets 'weak' or 'imperfect' to any competition which took place in the interim (ibid.: 103). As analysts of competition, economists have

> to deal not only with several separate sets of data of the different [competitors] but also – and this is even more important – with a process which necessarily involves continuous changes in the data for the different individuals.... [And] the causal factor enters here in the form of the acquisition of new knowledge by the different individuals or of changes in their data brought about by the contacts between them.
> (Hayek 1948: 94)

Concern with the changing knowledge content of economic decisions was not only the preserve of Hayek. His Austrian predecessors, especially Menger and Böhm-Bawerk, demonstrated awareness of the problem of knowledge-dispersion and acquisition in markets. Wieser was more interested in the results of competitive processes; the information content of prices emerging from Wieserian competition was critical for market participants who were planning or calculating subsequent competitive activity. In comparison, competition in the Hayekian sense played an information co-ordinating role where prices were instruments of decision-making or of competitive action. Wieser came close to appreciating the benefits of competition understood in this manner; for Wieser, competition enabled accurate calculation for the purposes of economizing (Streissler 1983: 361, 364 n. 35). However, the founding Austrians did not singly, or as a group, expressly recognize competitive activity as a form of behaviour which resolved the multi-market or general equilibrium problem of co-ordination; that was Hayek's most celebrated achievement.[10] (Product innovation was also conspicuously absent from their discussions, as it was in other early branches of neoclassical economics before 1914.)

None the less, many Hayekian ideas were in keeping with the ideas of the early Austrians, except that the latter freely added the term 'conflict' to describe the competitive process, while Hayek favoured 'rivalry'. Menger, Wieser and Böhm-Bawerk, much like Hayek, were unencumbered in their theorizing on competition by the contemporary neoclassical distinctions between perfect competition and monopoly or between perfect competition and imperfect competition (later in the neoclassical orthodoxy). The early Austrians were not moved to construct a formal taxonomy of market structures or to analyse the properties of equilibrium states. They were driven by the internal logic of Menger's original analysis of exchange, price formation and markets to envisage the essential character of competition as a conflict over prices. At one remove from prices, Menger, and more so Wieser, considered competition over non-price factors – production and managerial techniques – on the supply side. And Wieser's institutional analysis of competition as a profoundly *social* process in markets where participants were endowed with substantially different buying power was highly original. Only Wieser reflected on the destructive, discoordinating impacts of 'over-competition', leaving some hints for Schumpeter, who later, perhaps under the influence of Wieser, took this idea further.[11]

For Menger, Wieser and Böhm-Bawerk taken together, competition and the prices which were generated therefrom could not be sundered from bargaining. In the early Austrian vision of the market, bargaining behaviour was regarded as omnipresent and acted as a source of change in markets. Another common thread in their respective conceptions of competition was the stress on price-making activity by individuals (and in Wieser's work also by large firms) who set prices and then altered them in the interactive bid–offer process as they gathered additional knowledge of the market and as they adapted their plans in response to the actual or expected actions of others. Error and ignorance may, of course, have affected plan-adaptation.[12] The intellectual linkages amongst the founding Austrians on competition were strong, even though we have demonstrated divergent emphases and differences in detail between them. Continuities in their economic thought on competition are best illustrated by the space all three founders devoted to describing and exploring the interlocking actions of competitors in conditions where information or knowledge problems prevailed. They also conceived competition as a behavioural process rather than as a static state. Finally, they had in common a desire to *understand* the nature of bargaining behaviour in a wide variety of specific circumstances in which individual market participants found themselves. Market outcomes which ensued were usually traced back to individual bargains rather than to formal, deterministic market structures. It is disappointing that these early Austrian orientations were completely swamped by the dominance of, in particular, the Walrasian general equilibrium paradigm in economic theory through a long period of the twentieth century. The founding Austrians offered the building blocks for a more satisfactory theory of competitive conduct than the contributions of Walras, Pareto and their intellectual successors in the twentieth century.[13]

In eschewing exceedingly formal expression of market structures – and even Menger's expressions were very open-ended – the founding Austrians promoted a style of reasoning still evident in modern Austrian economics. Thus a modern Austrian treatment of competition stated:

> Competition has nothing whatsoever to do with 'market structures', so competition and monopoly are not extremes on a continuum. It is inconceivable that a monopolist, defined as a single seller of a particular product – if one can be found in a particular area – has no competition, either actual or potential, to influence its activities. The conventional view, which rests upon a concern that the system produce a satisfactory outcome, is that barriers to competition are bad. Yet it is often in the nature of rivalry that each of the rivals erects barriers *in order to compete*, to try to ensure his own success. Competition means preventing others from being successful.
> (Addleson 1994: 101; his emphasis)

Now we find parallels to the sentiments expressed in this passage throughout the work of Menger, Wieser and Böhm-Bawerk. Recall, for example, from Chapter 7 that Menger explored the notion of competition by beginning with monopoly-type arrangements which were highly personalized and embodied the potential for ongoing strategic rivalry. In Chapter 8 we illustrated how Wieser understood that competition as strategy involving the use of non-price variables was observed among cartels and so-called monopolies. In addition, Böhm-Bawerk's study of factor pricing in 'monopolized' labour markets allowed for the emergence of potential competitors; existing bargaining agents in these markets always had this potentiality to contend with. In short, the Austrians, both old and new, have in common the conceptualization of competition as strategy.

It may have been the case that 'much of what was genuinely Menger's tradition got lost' (Streissler 1972: 430) when Wieser and Böhm-Bawerk came to dominate Austrian economic thought in the early twentieth century. Wieser and Böhm-Bawerk may have imbibed some Marshallian and Walrasian ideas respectively, but these influences were weak and diffuse, especially as regards conceptions of competition. Our results cannot sustain Max Alter's (1990a: 14) claim that 'the predominance of perfect competition in Wieser's and Böhm-Bawerk's theories... served to assimilate the Austrian strand of neoclassical economics into the strands issuing from Jevons and Walras'. The Austrian conception of competition, broadly conceived as a dynamic and faltering human process of rivalry and bargaining, was not borrowed from, or for that matter assimilated by, other traditions in economic thought; it was preserved as a coherent theme in the work of the three leading first-generation Austrian economists before Hayek. Intellectual discontinuities have been noticed in the Austrian tradition on other matters: for example between Menger and Hayek on the concept of institutions (Garrouste 1994).[14] We shall examine one important discontinuity in founding Austrian microeconomics in the next chapter. However, on their understanding of competition, the founding Austrians taken as a group were fitting precursors of the Hayekian and more modern Kirznerian developments in the Austrian tradition.

9

CAPITAL IN FOUNDING AUSTRIAN ECONOMIC THEORY: MENGER VERSUS BÖHM-BAWERK

INTRODUCTION: BACKGROUND TO THE DEBATE

The purpose of the present chapter is to consider theoretical points of separation between Menger and Böhm-Bawerk on an important aspect of microeconomics, *looking back* from the roots of Böhm-Bawerk's ideas towards Menger's *Principles* with particular reference to their divergent views on the theory of goods. Their respective theories of goods embody concepts of capital and of capital goods. This chapter reinforces a speculative conclusion provided by Streissler and Weber (1973: 232): 'One wonders...if...the roots of the disagreement with Böhm-Bawerk [were that] Böhm was too objective for his master.'

The disagreement between Menger and Böhm-Bawerk, encapsulated in Schumpeter's recollection of a comment made to him by Menger, has been noted by many historians of economic thought. As Schumpeter (1954: 847 n. 8) recalled, Menger told him that the 'time will come when people will realise that Böhm-Bawerk's theory [of capital and interest] is one of the greatest errors ever committed'. Spann's (1930: 269) recollection of 'traditional talk in Vienna' appears to confirm Schumpeter's story.[1] It has been investigated in *ad hoc* fashion by Streissler (1972: 430–6), who commented in passing on Menger's apparent dislike for Böhm-Bawerk's objectivism; his one-dimensional and excessively technical capital theory, as well as his neglect of commercial goodwill.[2] However, the fundamental presuppositions underlying Böhm-Bawerk's central economic concepts, and the scope of his economics (compared with Menger's) implied therein, are not considered by Streissler. This is because Streissler approaches the problem largely from

Menger's standpoint and by reviewing and speculating on Menger's occasional utterances about Böhm-Bawerk's work. Böhm-Bawerk's first publication was entitled *Rechte und Verhältnisse vom Standpunkte der Volkswirtschaftlichen Güterlehre* ([1881] 1962).[3] It was only mentioned by Streissler in connection with an incipient theory of certainty equivalents that it contains, yet that publication is dedicated to laying the foundations for a theory of capital and interest which conflicts with Menger's theory.[4] In particular, the present chapter locates the very basis of later differences between Menger and Böhm-Bawerk in the more generous scope of Menger's theory of goods that Böhm-Bawerk exposes in the *Rechte* (hereafter *Rights*). Böhm-Bawerk emphasized the material side of goods, while Menger insisted on a much more subjective understanding of goods by individuals than Böhm-Bawerk was prepared to concede. Only Menger was therefore able to provide the building-blocks for a truly subjectivist theory of a 'capital-using economy' (Garrison 1985: 161) later developed in the Austrian tradition by Ludwig von Mises ([1934] 1981; 1949) and Ludwig Lachmann (1956; 1978; 1986: 59–82).

There is no doubt that Böhm-Bawerk intended the *Rights* to be both a first approximation, differentiating his ideas from his predecessors' and contemporaries', and a springboard for much of his future work in economic theory. His aim is 'to shed light upon some general, basic and fundamental tenet of economic theory' which would become a vantage-point from which a revision of economic theory might be undertaken (Böhm-Bawerk [1881] 1962: 30).[5] In general the *Rights* is a counterpart to chapter 1, 'The General Theory of the Good', and chapter 2, 'Economy and Economic Goods', of Menger's *Principles*.[6] In some parts of the *Rights*, Böhm-Bawerk pays tribute to Menger, and this makes his differences with Menger seem merely apparent when in fact they are real and fundamental.[7]

ON THE DEFINITION OF GOODS: MENGER AND BÖHM-BAWERK

Böhm-Bawerk departed immediately from Menger when defining goods. In Böhm-Bawerk's view, the five necessary and jointly sufficient 'subjective economic conditions' for a thing to become a good are: (1) there must be a human need the thing can serve; (2) the thing must possess useful properties able to satisfy a need; (3) individuals must be aware of the capacity of these properties to satisfy a need (knowing that); (4) individuals must have the knowledge how to utilize that useful thing's properties (*Gebrauchskunst*) to satisfy a need (knowing how); and (5) individuals must have power of disposal (*Verfügungsmacht*) over the thing ([1881] 1962: 41–2). In reflecting on these previously described 'subjective' conditions, Böhm-Bawerk was driven to add some important caveats:

> The existence of want, the awareness of usefulness and of 'usability' are matters which are completely subjective, and availability and disposability are partly so (in that they exist or do not exist, according to the situation of the economic subject). The possession of useful qualities is the sole purely objective requirement to be fulfilled by the thing itself
> (ibid.: 42)

By contrast, in his four conditions for goods-character (*Güterqualität*) Menger did not distinguish between knowledge of a causal connection between the existence of a useful property and need satisfaction, and knowledge of how to use that property (Menger [1871] 1950: 52). Böhm-Bawerk surmised that Menger placed the latter under the power of disposal condition. However, Menger's fourth condition can be translated unambiguously as 'command of a thing sufficient to direct it to the satisfaction of the need', which subsumes 'knowing how' (Menger [1871] 1950: 52; 1923: 17). Indeed, in Menger's subjectivist schema it would be difficult to understand why command is worthwhile if there is insufficient knowledge either in the 'knowing how' sense or in the 'knowing that' sense.[8] Böhm-Bawerk's stated reason for splitting this condition is to distinguish between the putatively objective, 'purely external factor' of command and the 'purely subjective factor' of 'knowing how' to use a good's properties:

> 'Ability or knowledge of how to use' is lacking in Menger's enumeration of the conditions requisite for goods-quality. I felt that it was necessary to list it as a requirement independent of and different from the factor that Menger lists next under the name of 'power of disposal'. My reason for this is that the latter is a purely external factor while 'ability to use' (or knowledge of how to use) is a purely subjective factor. Furthermore, if one were disposed to regard it as something that is included under power of disposal, the result would be, it seems to me, to assign to the latter factor too large an area to cover.
> ([1881] 1962: 42 n. 2)

By 'external factor' in this passage, Böhm-Bawerk was implying that an external observer could ascertain whether or not an individual possessed the *practical* skills to use a good to satisfy needs. This is a fine point which has no theoretical significance if, following Menger, we consistently take the economizing subject's perspective. For there would be no point in economizers conferring goods-status on a thing if they had no idea how to use it!

A related departure from Menger is Böhm-Bawerk's interpretation of condition (2). For Menger, who was a thoroughgoing subjectivist, goods-character was 'nothing inherent in goods and not a property of goods, but merely a relationship between certain things and men' (Menger [1871] 1950: 52 n. 4, 58). Individuals sought to consume subjective images of those things. On the other hand, Böhm-Bawerk understood the possession of a useful property as an inherent, purely objective requirement to be fulfilled by the thing itself. In other words, 'steel must have hardness; glass must possess resistivity and transparency; ink must exhibit adhesion and colour-fastness' – almost as if these properties existed independently of an interpreting, purposeful economic subject ([1881] 1962: 41–2). Böhm-Bawerk drew back from an all-embracing objectivist conclusion by conceding 'that the goods-quality of a thing is never a purely objective matter' (ibid.: 43), but the damage to Menger's conditions had already been done; the implication of an independent objective property in things remained. In introducing a distinction between command over a thing and 'knowing how', and in stressing the objective nature of useful properties of things, Böhm-Bawerk moved away from taking the individual economizer's perspective and he allowed an element of objectivism into the definition of goods. It had the consequence of establishing important points of contention with Menger on other, related theoretical issues, as we shall see below.

CATEGORIZING ECONOMIC GOODS

In categorizing economic goods – that is, scarce goods in relation to human requirements for them – Böhm-Bawerk distinguished three divisions. The first group of economic goods was corporeal or material goods which serve as a means to well-being (but not their renditions of service, yields or revenues as such, which serve as ends or aims). The second group is personal services which serve as means (but not necessarily personal abilities or 'human capital' as such).

Third, there is a less definitive group of 'goods' constituting legal rights and relationships (*Verhältnisse*).[9] Böhm-Bawerk was not as content as Menger to divide goods into two classes: corporeal goods and useful human actions (Menger [1871] 1950: 55). The latter, in particular, left a decision as to what constitutes a good to an individual's subjective judgement. A useful human action for Menger was one that was beneficial to the individual who perceived it as such. Böhm-Bawerk's position was more discriminating. He was not satisfied, *from the point of view of the analyst*, to leave the definition of a good up to an individual's judgement in particular cases and contexts, as Menger assuredly was (Menger [1871] 1950: 58). For instance, when discussing personal services as goods, Böhm-Bawerk deliberated over listing either individuals themselves as goods, or their talents, qualities and powers, or the physical renditions of service that ultimately emanate from individuals. He would not include all these phenomena, since 'it would be a patent pleonasm or duplication to seek to list as goods not only the useful things and also their useful qualities but, *in addition*, their renditions of service' (Böhm-Bawerk [1881] 1962: 51; his emphasis). He decided that useful services that become available through individuals are the true goods because 'these alone... can function as *independent* entities in economic life and become the object of consumption, of exchange [and] of rental' (ibid.: 51; emphasis added).

Menger insisted that the world be viewed not through the eyes of the economic analyst but through the eyes of the individual subject, that is, the person who determined goals and acted accordingly.[10] Menger therefore included not only personal services rendered as goods but also decisions of forbearance taken to withdraw such services. He gave the example of a doctor (Dr A) who ceases practising medicine in a small town in which there is only one other doctor (Dr B) giving rise to a benefit (a good) to the remaining doctor, who thereby becomes a monopolist (Menger [1871] 1950: 55). At the back of Menger's categorization was a simple subjectivist reference point – something that benefits an individual from that individual's viewpoint, despite its possible harm to others, must be considered a good. Böhm-Bawerk dismissed Menger's more general view, concluding that:

> pure forbearances can never find an equal place beside true goods and positive renditions of service in an inventory of things that promote human well-being. For a so-called useful

forbearance is, strictly speaking, not the cause of an economic advantage, but only the *cause of the absence of any economic disadvantage*. If we wanted to count as an economic good every absence of any cause of an economic disadvantage, we could easily go too far in this respect.

([1881] 1962: 129; his emphasis)

Here Böhm-Bawerk missed Menger's point; any human action which created a good from some given situation could legitimately be regarded as a good by an individual. A deliberate decision to act or not act by one economizer could have goods-character for another – this is Menger's point. Böhm-Bawerk predetermined an individual's judgement of goods-character in spite of Menger's warning that the causal relation between a good and well-being depended 'upon the nature of this relation in *particular* cases' (Menger [1871] 1950: 58, emphasis added; also 69–70). Hence in Böhm-Bawerk's predetermination it is a matter of course that Dr A's 'forbearing to practice is economically important, but it would also be of equal or at least similar importance for him if Dr B in a neighboring town also forbore to practice in Dr D's town and also if Professor C in the capital city... forbore to practice there' ([1881] 1962: 130). As if Dr D had contemplated such other possible forbearances! In Menger's original example, his particular case, these possibilities do not figure at all, since the example is designed from the unique point of view of Dr A. Moreover, Menger's economic subjects are shown to have limited perception and regularly to act in error, at least in concrete cases to which all empirical-theoretical work referred.[11]

Since the intangibles in Böhm-Bawerk's third category of economic goods are potentially infinite, he considered it pertinent to analyse this category further with a view to avoiding double classification. In concentrating on one aspect of this problem – namely, the economic significance of two groups of intangibles, legal rights and relationships – Böhm-Bawerk noted how a condition precedent for goods-character was command of the goods in question. Legal claims upon material things will signify physical possession or at least provide good prospect that possession can be obtained. Legally conferred command over a material good would be useless if it did not also connote actual or prospective 'natural, physical control over it' (ibid.: 59). The crux of Böhm-Bawerk's case was that these property rights in themselves did not merit the status of goods.

Thus, '[l]egal title to a thing, like the physical possession of it... simply helps make the thing a good in the first place' (ibid.: 62).

Consider his example on legal rights of ownership:

> Let us think... of a house – just any house at all. Then second [think]... of the house as my house, that is to say, let us think of my right of ownership of the house as an additional concept.... Does our first cover one good, and are there subsequently two? By no means. Rather it is true that in the earlier instance there was for me no good in existence at all. The house did not become a good for me until it became my property. The thousands of other houses in the city to which I have no title, are just as certainly not goods for me as the millionaire's wealth is not a good for the beggar.
>
> (ibid.: 62)

A lacuna in this analysis of ownership rights to anyone familiar with the early part of Menger's *Principles* is any consideration of the causal nexus between goods.[12] Each 'good' for Menger can enhance well-being and can achieve true goods-status 'not by itself, but only in combination with other goods' ([1871] 1950: 75). Thus complementarity or mutual dependence between things 'produces' full goods-status. While the textual evidence is inconclusive, ownership rights for Menger may have the function of higher-order goods (producing an ability to command other goods) linked ultimately to needs satisfaction. Following Böhm-Bawerk's illustration, the beggar may have a need for the millionaire's wealth but lacks command of it to satisfy his needs. The millionaire's wealth is therefore not a good for the beggar, but if the millionaire voluntarily presented some of his wealth to the beggar or was legally compelled to part with his wealth by way of wealth taxes, then that wealth might well attain goods-character for the beggar. Conceivably, the institution of charity in the first instance, and the institution of law in the second, are consequences of useful human actions in Menger's sense that they could have higher-order goods-status in producing a lower-order good from the beggar's viewpoint. In the relevant passage, Menger (ibid.: 55) pointed out that friendship, love, religious fellowship and the like constitute 'beneficial actions' to individuals who enjoy them. He then argued that, in so far as there are property rights in them, they can be considered goods. In any case, Böhm-Bawerk omitted from his examples the factor of complementarity between goods of various orders, and their mutual dependence in satisfying needs. In his view, then, property rights did not help produce final, consumption goods; rather, property rights defined the conditions precedent of production. He subsequently denied the existence of a *separate* category of intangibles that could be labelled 'rights' and valued as goods. In these categories we would include patents, copyrights, trademarks, commercial goodwill, and payment claims.

WEALTH AND ITS COMPUTATION

Böhm-Bawerk followed Menger almost to the word in defining wealth as the totality of economic goods at the disposal of an individual (Böhm-Bawerk [1881] 1962: 86; Menger [1871] 1950: 109). He proceeded to enumerate forms of wealth that constitute alternatives to *materials* of wealth in the computation of wealth. He then sketched his own operational or computable wealth concept that included material goods which had a prospective flow of future yields, and excluded payment claims that confer a right to an anticipated yield on goods not yet materialized. Those economists who did not deny goods and hence wealth-status to payment claims, evidently including Menger, were said to indulge 'in fictive anticipation of that which is *not yet in existence*' (Böhm-Bawerk [1881] 1962: 96; his emphasis). Here Böhm-Bawerk's objectivism is fully revealed. Payment claims are anticipations of 'goods expected to materialize in the future' and, unlike material producers' goods, do not correspond to a 'factual supply of goods' at present (ibid.: 87, 89). To include these intangible claims as goods would conflict with 'the objective state of things' (ibid.: 96).

Böhm-Bawerk's operational wealth concept included the possession of (1) material goods of direct but deferred utility (ice-skates in summertime); (2) durable goods of lasting utility (houses); and (3) material producers' goods (goods of higher order) (ibid.: 99–108). This inventory would then be subject to valuation. Contracted labour services, and payment claims due in future, are not easily computable or valued as wealth, since the person of the labourer or debtor is not at the complete command of the employer or creditor respectively, barring slavery. In both cases the contract or credit pertains to goods not yet in existence. Böhm-Bawerk was led uneasily to the conclusion that (4) for the purpose of acquisition and transfer these phenomena should be listed in terms of a future good which had not yet materialized, and not in terms of a right to a future utility as an object of valuation and wealth (ibid.: 110–11). Modern 'derivatives' products such as futures and options contracts spring readily to mind. And, in fact, Böhm-Bawerk came close to stating a simple options contract, but he failed to attribute goods-status and hence value to that contract in the interim: that is, at any point in the period between the contract's purchase and physical delivery. His example ran as follows:

> I posses a payment claim (a right) covering the return to me within the next three months of a hundredweight of hay... there is involved a *hundredweight of hay which will be at my disposal in three months' time*. That is the one single good to which I am looking and to which I must look, if I am to justify at all the inclusion of this item of wealth in my balance sheet as of today.
>
> (ibid.: 113; his emphasis).

Now in this illustration Böhm-Bawerk could not see any separate present financial value in the right to enforce a claim over the hay in future. To be sure, markets in such claims may not have been in existence when he wrote the *Rights*, but rights to enforce a delivery of physical goods in future at a specific price are now regarded as a separately valuable, if variable, component of an *individual's* wealth. Böhm-Bawerk implicitly assumed in his example that the hay for future delivery would not vary in value at all; there was no uncertainty, so the 'options contract' entered into was in itself valueless. This, of course, begs the question as to why the 'payment claim', as Böhm-Bawerk called it, had to be made in the first place. Only under the restrictive condition of perfect foresight or no uncertainty would we now be able to agree with Böhm-Bawerk 'that wherever we encounter rights purporting to be objects of wealth, they can never signify an augmentation of wealth or of true goods, but at all times signify only a form under the guise of which men have a predilection for thinking and of representing other goods' (ibid.: 116; his emphasis). As we shall see presently, Menger's later reference to the importance of financial rights (*Forderungsrechte*) in a capitalist exchange economy based on monetary computation in conditions of uncertainty represented a path-breaking treatment of this matter.

In his suggestions for operationalizing wealth, Böhm-Bawerk purged all intangibles from the scope of the computation, just as he purged them from the goods concept. Personal services could be included because they have ultimate observable referents. Intangibles, including warrants, patents, goodwill, trade secrets, and copyrights, 'exist only in our imagination, even though we treat them like present factual things for purposes of acquisition and transfer' (ibid.: 111). He was aware that when computing the value of their assets individuals in practice capitalize the value of various intangible claims and business connections. However, these phenomena pertain to 'corporeal objects' somewhere down the line. If there were no objects, in Böhm-Bawerk's view, then these rights and connections would be non-existent. The right to a good, for instance, constitutes the good's *alter ego* and cannot be classed or computed as wealth. Indeed, rights and business connections can never augment wealth (ibid.: 115–16); their microeconomic significance is therefore impugned. This proposition was crucial to Böhm-Bawerk's divergence from Menger on capital and interest and therefore deserves more detailed examination.

The *Rights* is essentially a theory of barter (Rogin 1956: 500). Credit in the *Rights* is a neutral economic mediator and has no current goods-character. Rogin's point is well taken and deserves full quotation:

> obviously, the distinction between claims to goods and relations (such as good will), which have a capitalized value in the market place, and consumer goods and means of production is fundamental. The difficulty is that Böhm-Bawerk, following the anti-mercantilist tradition, does not merely distinguish but purges the former from the precincts of economic theory. The theory which ensues, then, is essentially a theory of barter, mediated by money and capitalized claims and relations – with both of these 'neutral'; the implications of money, of other economic claims, and of relations are left unanalyzed. The upshot of the liberal substitution of material welfare for the private acquisitive criterion of mercantilism is thus a technique of analysis which in principle cannot cope with the consequences of the purely acquisitive financial and speculative aspects of the economy.
>
> (1956: 500)

Moreover, while credit is later mentioned in *Positive Theory*, it indeed has what Rogin called 'neutral' connotations so far as its economic significance is concerned. There is also an implication of 'Say's Law': that is, all savings are automatically invested:

an economically advanced nation does not engage in hoarding, but invests its savings. It buys securities, it deposits its money at interest... puts it out on loan, etc. In this way, it is added to the nation's productive credit, increases the producer's purchasing power for productive purposes, and so becomes the cause of an increase in demand for production goods.

(Böhm-Bawerk 1959b: 113)

By way of comparison, Menger did not hold that capitalized claims, commercial relationship goods and credit were in any way 'neutral' mediators in economic affairs. For example, credit in Menger's *Principles* could be a useful forbearance by the creditor (hence a good from the debtor's viewpoint) who decides not to use (say) a higher-order good in any other way. However, as already discussed, Böhm-Bawerk ruled out the goods-character of forbearances. Second, and more substantively, credit claims for Menger increase the quantity of capital at the disposal of recipients. 'The productive activity of people', argued Menger, 'is greatly promoted by credit'; 'production... is very often only possible through credit' (Menger [1871] 1950: 159). From the point of view of an individual, loans add to the means of recipients and subtract from those of creditors. The ability of an owner of higher-order goods to transfer them to a third person 'on credit' is a useful human action. Thus it is possible for Menger, but not Böhm-Bawerk, to allow within the ambit of his economic analysis the phenomena of credit, monetary and financial-cum-speculative aspects of the economy, especially those orientated towards the uncertain future.[13] When credit is absent, in Menger's view the result is often a reduction of wealth – 'a pernicious stoppage and curtailment of productive activity' (ibid.: 172). If, then, we follow Böhm-Bawerk and quibble over the goods-character of rights that are not immediately vested in concrete things, the boundaries of economic analysis will be drawn more narrowly than originally intended by Menger. We would find ourselves equipped only to theorize about wealth computation in a barter economy devoid of uncertainty.

A second phenomenon that has financial-cum-speculative overtones is the business relation called goodwill. Böhm-Bawerk ([1881] 1962: 116 n. 14] was surprised that Menger should see fit to include goodwill in the category of economic goods. In surveying the literature from Aristotle to Roscher on the status of various relations as goods, Menger adopted, *inter alios*, A. E. F. Schäffle's perspective on goodwill as enunciated at length in *Theorie der ausschließenden Absatzverhältnisse* (1867) (Menger [1871] 1950: 54 n. 7, 286–8). In his obituary of Böhm-Bawerk, Menger ([1915] 1935: 300–1) argued that Böhm-Bawerk's view on commercial goodwill lacked relevance for empirical-theoretical work.[14] He added a vital insight in a footnote to the effect that relations such as commercial goodwill and rights with a financial aspect, or capable of being valued financially as they are in real cases (*Forderungsrechte*), do not net out, at least from an individual's point of view. On the other hand, these rights may net out in the aggregate, but that should not preclude them from being computed as part of an individual's wealth in the Mengerian sense (Menger [1915] 1935: 301n.). Böhm-Bawerk's alternative position may be represented as follows: assume that one individual had been able to sell a particular good for 150 because of loyalty or reputation with customers, while other sellers without this loyalty or reputation had been able to get only 140 for the 'same' good. If the customers suddenly discovered that there was really no difference in product-quality, the goodwill component as calculated by the previously reputable seller would disappear. From an aggregate economic standpoint, however, no loss would be incurred. What the first seller lost would have been obtained by her customers in the form of a lower price. So far the difference in theoretical orientation between Menger and Böhm-Bawerk reduces to the former holding a more consistently microeconomic position; Böhm-Bawerk held a macroeconomic perspective on wealth computation. He went further, however. Instead of granting some force to microeconomic explanations of wealth computation, he found no merit whatsoever in allowing everyday modes of wealth classification and calculation to enter his formal economic analysis.

Consider the case of customers' goodwill (*Kundschaft*), which in Böhm-Bawerk's view resulted from buyers' habits of regularly seeking goods from a particular vendor. He supposed that such habits may originate from a variety of factors including trade brands, patents, convenient geographical location of the vendor, product reliability, vendor reputation and trustworthiness, or the existence of few, if any, competitors. In all cases goodwill may seem to be a source of future profit, if in some situations a very uncertain profit given that many factors affecting goodwill are dependent on changeable consumer desires. Goodwill can be capitalized on the transfer of business assets or when computing the value of such assets on the basis of their probable future yields. The essential difference between goodwill and other assets that give prospective future returns is that the prospective 'assuring' elements in the present in respect of goodwill are more uncertain. Present material producers' goods give concrete 'assurance' of future returns, and in the case of present contracted labour services and payment claims, the medium of 'assurance' in practice is 'a person bound by a legal obligation' ([1881] 1962: 121), whereas the basis upon which goodwill is capitalized is *prima facie* more tenuous. Searching for overt evidence of goodwill, Böhm-Bawerk arrived at 'customers' acts of purchasing' (ibid.: 122). He found that these beneficial acts ultimately produce net profit on sales of concrete goods or renditions of service, but not profit on the relation of goodwill as such. Certainly when transferred, goodwill appears to have value in an exchange relationship. Again, consistently with his objectivist outlook, Böhm-Bawerk was quick to locate criteria external to the exchange process for evaluating the value attributed to goodwill. Customer patronage, like any other social custom, is merely an appellation for the 'true objects of wealth' that it designates. This includes material goods and/or services flowing from material goods, and/or observable personal services available now or in the future. Co-extensive with these objective phenomena are physical returns of, for instance, wages for personal services, and eventual profits on the sale of material goods. Locational goodwill is a factor in the market value of a piece of concrete property. Goodwill in general does not augment wealth; it is only a name for a value that is already or prospectively in concrete goods and services. Goodwill is therefore imaginary and must be '[r]uled out of the list of genuine goods' (ibid.: 127). In the case of customers' goodwill – a specific relationship 'good' – Böhm-Bawerk was adamant that a person's power of disposal over the so-called asset labelled goodwill rested on a 'tenuous foundation'. The economic advantages deriving from such an asset

> are individually too indefinite, too difficult to observe and, above all,...their contact with any relationship to the vendor's advantage is all too tenuous and incomplete. *Minima non curat praetor* (the magistrate has no regard for trifles) is a maxim which we will do well to apply...in the field of economics.
> (ibid.: 125)

MENGER VERSUS BÖHM-BAWERK ON CAPITAL

Indubitably, Menger's ([1871] 1950: 54) charge that too many contemporary economists had become victim of the 'unconscious working of the material bias of our time which regards only materials and forces (tangible objects and labour services)...as goods' would have applied with equal force to Böhm-Bawerk in this instance.

Böhm-Bawerk turned next to legally compelled relations of patronage in the economy, such as patent rights and copyrights. Again he found that such rights should not be valued since only the material goods and material conditions of service flowing from them should enter into the wealth calculation. He considered copyrights in some detail. Intellectual property is described as 'a fiction' ([1881] 1962: 128 n. 4). This 'protection against interference affords an opportunity for the entrepreneurial activity of an author (or his authorized publisher) to engage unimpeded in lucrative reproduction and distribution in quantity of his intellectual product' (ibid.: 128). The totality of profits emerging from purchases of that product is what counts. The 'entrepreneurial activities' stimulated by the copyright, should, according to Böhm-Bawerk, also be considered a valuable good – a labour service created by a law prohibiting all competitive activity. These material goods and services emanating from copyright 'leave no room anywhere for any independent "relationship good"' (ibid.: 128) deserving separate classification and computation in an individual's wealth-holding.

Böhm-Bawerk's analysis of wealth computation was devoid of any appreciation of the goods-character of rights and relations, not for the fully informed Crusoe but for many imperfectly informed interacting traders in facilitating stability in market exchange where monetary calculation was the norm. For Menger, the distinctiveness of rights and relations as economic goods rested on their inherently psychic, unintended value in securing and stabilizing the market process. Menger followed Aristotle, who wrote that to every viable community there corresponds a kind of stock of common attitudes, beliefs, expectations or information sources among its members which manifests itself in reciprocity (*antipepenthos*).[15] This was not, for Menger, established on the basis of deliberate design but was the unintended result of individual decisions.[16] This perspective can be applied to the role of social and legal institutions in Menger's economics. It carries with it an implication that the 'economic progress of civilization' through an 'organized market' exchange process is dependent on the development, *pari passu*, of knowledge-bearing, non-material assets.[17] Also, this is tantamount to requiring legal and trading institutions which give order to the market process. These institutions ensure stability in the buyer–seller relationship. Goodwill is one of those institutions. To command goodwill (as a good) is to have at one's disposal a valuable, but not perfect, informational reservoir. For example, the concept of a retailer's customers' goodwill is implicit in Menger's discussion of the problem of planning lower-order goods requirements in a developed market exchange context. He pointed out that 'experience teaches us' that, despite uncertainty as to future needs, sellers attempt to predict changes in demands 'within feasible limits' and 'sufficient for their practical affairs' (Menger [1871] 1950: 82, 84, 89). Similarly, sellers of intermediate goods will be able, with producers' goodwill at their command, to rely on selling appropriate inputs to *known* buyers rather than to an anonymous market.[18] The idea of producers' goodwill underlies Menger's outline of the problem of producer-planning for future requirements on the basis of goods in the possession of other industrialists 'with whom they maintain trading connections' (ibid.: 90; emphasis added; also 86–9 passim). Goodwill is not fully captured by calculating the aggregate market-value of physical goods or observable services; it has a non-material, psychic quality. It is a 'knowing' or 'perceiving' by parties to exchange and can only be commanded in an entirely subjective sense. Later in the Austrian tradition, Hayek deplored exclusion of relationships from the analysis of markets. He proceeded in Mengerian spirit to demonstrate how commercial goodwill relationships were a source of necessary information for traders in circumstances where knowledge was imperfect:

> Especially remarkable...is the... complete exclusion from the theory of perfect competition of all personal relationships between the parties. In actual life the fact that our inadequate knowledge of the available commodities or services is made up for by our experience with the persons or firms supplying them – that competition is in a large measure competition for reputation or goodwill – is one of the most important facts which helps us to solve our daily problems.
>
> (Hayek 1948: 97)

Furthermore, Ludwig von Mises (1949: 376) argued cogently that 'it does not matter whether goodwill is based on real achievements and merits or whether it is only a product of imagination and fallacious ideas. What counts in human action is not truth as it may appear to an omniscient being, but the opinions of people liable to error.' Goodwill in Mises's view can sometimes have the character of an 'imaginary good' (ibid.: 381). Menger ([1871] 1950: 53), following Aristotle, also explicitly admitted 'imaginary goods' into economic theory but did not state that commercial goodwill belonged in this category.

Apart from Menger's command condition, were other conditions for the goods–character of relations such as goodwill satisfied? There is, first, definitely a human need for various trading connections. As Menger ([1883] 1985: 157) elaborated in the *Investigations*, 'trade customs etc. are nothing but institutions...[which are] the result of efforts serving individual interest'. Second, individuals are able to use trading connections for needs-satisfaction because of their existence as self-interested economizers in a market of exchanging individuals. Possible command over these goods is co-extensive with living and participating in an organized market but it is not costless. They are economic goods since they require continuous maintenance via active participation in exchange, searching and checking by both buyers and sellers.[19] Creating, procuring and maintaining goodwill, in Menger's theory, can involve extensive advertising. He writes that producers of commodities with initially small clienteles are 'accustomed to make their commodities "known" at great economic sacrifice' in order to increase customer loyalty (Menger [1871] 1950: 242n. 243ff.). Goodwill is therefore just as much a created good as anything material that may be obtained with the same sacrifice. Finally, the very fact that individuals desire to procure trading connections attests to their recognition, however imperfect, of causal links between such connections and needs–satisfaction (Menger's third condition for goods-character: see Chapters 2 and 3 above).

Trading connections for Menger involve command of a significant cognitive element at the micro-level. Individuals will come to have command over differential ways or degrees of 'knowing' about the loyalty of those with whom they are connected in exchange. Their varied methods and experiences in interacting with other market participants presents them, in turn, with differential market advantages. At the societal level the institutions that result will have grown 'organically' with the progress of the community. Menger means by this that commercial institutions and relations are the unintended result of innumerable efforts of self-interested economizers, and, by helping to organize markets, institutions simultaneously serve 'the interests of the common good' (Menger [1883] 1985: 147, 157–9).

This discussion therefore substantiates Streissler's (1972: 432) claim, made without elaboration, that Menger understood the creation of goodwill (and similar trading connections) as increasing not only private wealth but also, with a caveat, national wealth. Menger's caveat, not mentioned by Streissler, refers to problems arising when an attempt is made to aggregate individuals' wealth into 'national wealth' in the presence of externalities (Menger [1871] 1950: 113). As purveyors of scarce economic knowledge, these phenomena are distinct economic goods. And above all, unlike Böhm-Bawerk, it is not necessary for Menger that relationship goods such as goodwill have objective counterparts in the market process.

COMPETING CONCEPTS OF CAPITAL

The divergence between Menger and Böhm-Bawerk on the goods-character of rights and relations extends correspondingly to their competing concepts of capital. Böhm-Bawerk developed a capital concept that stressed materiality. Many scholars came to oppose some or all aspects of his conceptualization, including John Bates Clark, Frank A. Fetter and Irving Fisher. It is less well known that within the first generation of Austrian economists, Menger, both before and after Böhm-Bawerk's contributions on capital, is to be counted in the opposition as well.

Böhm-Bawerk's 'capital' consisted in concrete goods, and he opposed any attempt to make something intangible the essence of capital. First, he believed that capital is a collection of goods, so that the Clarkian distinction between capital as a permanent fund and capital as material goods is repudiated. Following J. B. Clark's criticism in the 1890s, Böhm-Bawerk (1895: 121) argued defiantly: 'I know no capital other than the concrete goods which constitute it; and I believe the world of facts knows no other.' Capital is 'common material goods called mills, looms, ploughs, locomotives'. It is these and not any incorporeal sum of value that 'can grind corn or spin yarn, or plough up land or carry a load' (Böhm-Bawerk [1889] 1923: 58). In his taxonomy of the contents of general ('private') capital he included that 'group of products which serve as a means to the acquisition of goods' (ibid.: 38). The fact that capital goods are products implies that other factors, nature and labour, are more original (ibid.: 76). Capital is an intermediate product of nature and labour. Böhm-Bawerk distinguished 'social capital' as a subset of general ('private') capital (ibid.: 63–4). Social capital is a 'natural store' of productive instruments independent of considerations such as historico-legal claims to ownership. It is an aggregate of all intermediate goods in the economy exclusive of non-warehoused, durable consumption goods advanced or rented out by their owners. The latter are not productive goods but are included in more general, private capital. The essence of the category 'private capital' is not the presence of a right to ownership founded on history and law (which he grants is implicit) but the presence of another distinct 'natural store of goods': namely, durable consumption goods. Thenceforth, through successive editions of *Positive Theory*, Böhm-Bawerk restricted his analysis to social capital, that is, capital as instruments of production (1959b: 74). This followed from his definition of capital as 'a complex of produced means' in his earlier history and critique of capital and interest theories ([1884] 1932: 6). Excluded from capital are

> 'incorporeal' capitals, such as debts and other claims, 'good will', the 'state', etc. These things do not belong to capital because they are not true goods at all. They are, as I have shown elsewhere, nothing but verbal symbols or collective terms for some sum or other of genuine goods. These genuine goods may or may not be capitals. If they are, then they are already contained in the categories that were listed above. If they are not, then again there is no necessity for establishing a special capital category for them. In either case such an addition is superfluous. Many economists include here certain rights and relations such as patents, customer-relationships, legal claims. Naturally I reject them at this point on principle, and for the same reasons as apply to my refusal to create for them an independent category of capital.
>
> (1959b: 74)

Böhm-Bawerk's position here was perfectly defensible so long as he reasoned at the level of social aggregates: the double counting involved in regarding as economic goods both the goods themselves and claims to them, or relations associated with their delivery, would have to be avoided when calculating social capital.

Böhm-Bawerk's ideas on both the function of capital in production and the formation of capital, for the most part in a growing economy context, warrant consideration before we draw comparisons with Menger's alternative vision. Up until the early 1980s, Böhm-Bawerk's contribution to the study of the concept, functions and formation of capital had become synonymous with the Austrian approach to capital theory.[20] If we follow the chapter sequence of the fourth and last edition of *Positive Theory* closely, the standard Böhm-Bawerkian approach is revealed by the author meticulously, if repetitively and at great length. He dealt first with the function of capital.

Capital promoted more productive roundabout methods; his well-known opening example related to individuals using 'boats and nets to catch fish' (the roundabout method), 'instead of scooping them up by hand in shallow pools' (1959b: 95). Nevertheless the capital used here is not the real cause of the productivity of the boats, nets, etc. The 'originary productive forces' reside in nature and are merely transmitted, through human intervention and the boats, nets, etc., to produce a great quantity of consumption goods:

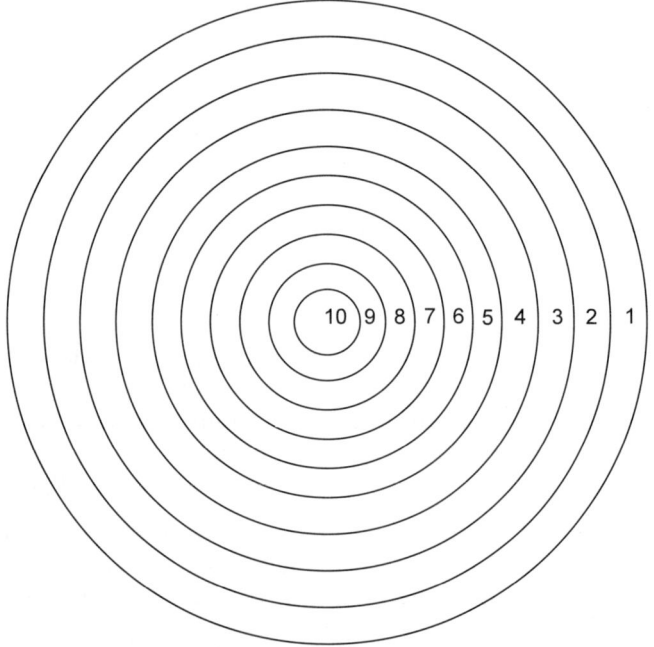

Source: Böhm-Bawerk 1959b:106.

Figure 4 Böhm-Bawerk's representation of the time structure of production

namely, fish. Capital is therefore merely a 'tool of production' (ibid.: 95–6) but it cannot act independently as a factor of production. Capital is 'indirectly productive' only in the restricted sense that it makes possible the adoption of new and fruitful roundabout methods of production' (ibid.: 101).

The Robinson Crusoe parables which adorn Böhm-Bawerk's chapter on the theory of capital formation have the following central themes. First, capital is created by saving out of current consumption. Second, capital is then produced as a 'mass of intermediate products' which eventually 'mature' by producing consumption goods. Third, there is a time profile or structure in the production process which is represented by concentric circles (see Figure 4 above).

At point 10 in the core of these concentric circles, Böhm-Bawerk depicted a production process in its infancy: the capital in this process is at its lowest maturity. Only at point 1 is capital on the brink of being converted into consumption goods; points in between 1 and 10 represent various intermediate stages in the roundabout, time-consuming production process. This is all very reminiscent of Menger's ([1871] 1950: 149–60) distinction between orders of goods – first-order goods being consumables, and higher-order goods (second- and third-order goods etc.) denoting those goods used to produce consumables.

In a revealing comment explaining his concentric circles, Böhm-Bawerk's understanding of the function of capital diverged from Menger's:

> The outermost of the concentric circles has the greatest area, and the areas of the succeeding rings diminish gradually. In exactly the same way the greatest proportion of the total capital of the community will at all times consist of the first maturity class, the goods that are at a point in the production process closest to completion. Similarly, the increasingly remote maturity classes will represent a progressively diminishing proportion of the community's capital.
>
> (1959b: 107)

Now Böhm-Bawerk gave two reasons for these observations on Figure 4. First, roundabout production methods vary in length 'by reason of their varying *technical* nature' (ibid.: 107; emphasis added). The longest production processes, represented initially at 10, are presumed to have capital engaged throughout the 'maturity class'-range from 10 through 1. Shorter production processes have intermediate capital goods formed over fewer classes. Thus 'the quantity of intermediate products becomes greater as progress is made toward the first maturity class' at 1 in Figure 4 (ibid.: 108). The second reason why the outermost rings in Figure 4 have the greatest area relates to the fact that new labour is added to capital goods at each stage. According to Böhm-Bawerk's illustration, at 'one stage, the intermediate product wool is transformed by the addition of labor into [the production of] yarn; in a later stage labor is again added to transform it into the intermediate product cloth, and so on' (ibid.: 108). By this argument, within each production area capital formation increases, so that it reaches a maximum in the highest maturity stage at 1. In this schema there is obviously no place for employing rights, claims and relationship goods as capital, productive forces, intermediate goods, or instruments of production. What is particularly alien to the Mengerian vision of production and capital formation is Böhm-Bawerk's emphasis on the natural, technical aspects to the neglect of subjective phenomena, such as entrepreneurial activities and knowledge requirements (innovations, inventions, assessment of consumers' requirements, prospective relative prices for inputs and outputs, market conditions in general). These subjective considerations are part and parcel of decisions taken at the micro-level to form capital. Garrison (1990: 142) rightly pointed out that 'Böhm-Bawerk was not always careful to stress the subjective element in his capital theory'. Böhm-Bawerk's passing mention of the entrepreneur in this section of *Positive Theory* gives us no confidence that he considered these phenomena important (1959b: 112). To be sure, Böhm-Bawerk followed Menger in conceiving of production as a time-consuming, sequential process in which higher-order goods are transformed into consumption goods. But Böhm-Bawerk gave the clear impression in his discussion of the concentric circles that the temporal relations in production are objective, being determined by the given technical nature of known methods of relating inputs to outputs.[21] Böhm-Bawerk essentially analysed the structure of physical capital; he stipulated that each production process in that structure had a definite starting- and finishing-point, and physically identifiable inputs and outputs, and took place over an elapse of calendar time.[22] As Lewin (1994: 212) commented, this scenario 'is only possible in a world where unexpected change is absent, where all production techniques are known...[and where] all production plans are consistent with one another'. Plan coordination problems in production could not easily be dismissed in what Böhm-Bawerk recognized as 'the existing economic organization which is predominantly individualist in character' (1959b: 111). Menger had already referred to these problems in connection with his reflections on the entrepreneurial role, the problem of knowledge, and related difficulties of calculation in a monetary economy. We turn now to consider these matters from the perspective of Menger.

In Menger's work, the traditional classical tripartite classification of factors of production into land, labour and capital is jettisoned from the beginning in favour of a simple elastic division between higher-order and lower-order goods. As with his other fundamental concepts, Menger ([1871] 1950: 304) defined capital more broadly than Böhm-Bawerk, as 'a *combination* of economic goods of higher order (i.e. complementary quantities of these goods) whose services also have economic character and therefore yield income' (his emphasis). Two conditions must be met for goods to be classed as capital. First, command over these goods must extend over a sufficiently long time-period to allow an individual's production plan to proceed to conclusion. Second, the amounts and types of these goods must be such that, through them, direct or indirect command of other necessary complementary goods of higher order is possible so that goods of lower order may be produced (ibid.: 155–7, 303–4). Stigler (1941: 156) argued that this is a 'vague and unsatisfactory definition' even though in another place he admitted that Menger's caution was 'almost clairvoyant' in developing fundamental concepts (Stigler 1937: 250). Careful reading of section 3 of chapter 3, and Appendix E, of the *Principles* reveals that Menger was deliberate in his intention to construct an open-ended capital concept, the form and content of which could vary depending on prevailing historico-legal conditions of production and on individual plans. Following a strictly microeconomic and subjectivist standpoint in these parts of the *Principles* he concentrated on a private, acquisitive notion of capital. Social capital in Böhm-Bawerk's sense was not afforded theoretical articulation. Menger refrained from pre-empting the individual economizer's decision as to what types of good (material or immaterial) to classify as 'capital'. In addition he expressly wanted to separate 'items of wealth' (capital goods or assets) standing on their own and yielding an income (land, buildings, etc.) from capital which was a production process-specific combination of heterogeneous capital goods ([1871] 1950: 304–5).[23] This distinction between itemized assets and capital as a specific combination or 'stock' of assets was reiterated in Menger's early lectures of 1876.[24] It reached a mature formulation in the *Principles*, where Menger wrote that capital 'is not just the technical means of production... [it] includes all goods that can be used for the satisfaction of human needs *only by being combined* with other goods of higher order (ibid.: 157 n. 18; emphasis added). Capital is therefore more than the sum of its constituent items of wealth, since what binds these items into a complex whole called 'capital' are: (1) various entrepreneurial activities, the most important of which is obtaining knowledge of relevant market conditions; (2) command over necessary higher-order goods for a time period conducive to the production process that the individual has in mind; and (3) property in capital goods. The very ability of an individual to participate in reaping the advantages of combining higher-order goods in a production process 'is dependent... on disposal in the present over quantities of goods of higher order for the coming period of time or, in other words, on possessing *capital*' (ibid.: 55; his emphasis). Here a property right or title to capital goods enables its holder to claim returns from the useful action of combining them into capital. As Menger argued, 'command [itself]... is a means to the better and more complete satisfaction of their [individuals'] needs, and (is) therefore a good' (ibid.: 156).

Menger's capital concept is elaborated in his much-neglected 1888 article 'Zur Theorie des Kapitals'.[25] Böhm-Bawerk ([1889] 1923: xxvii) lamented that it was published 'too late for me to make full use of it'. Indeed it is doubtful whether Böhm-Bawerk could have used Menger's article for substantive support. The Böhm-Bawerkian approach to 'original' factors of production was reproved by Menger for confusing technical with economic considerations. The technical proposition that capital goods originate as a product of nature and labour was, for Menger, economically irrelevant (Menger [1888] 1935: 171–2; [1871] 1950: 165–7). There are no given generic factors of production; all capital goods are heterogeneous and directly or indirectly instruments of production. In its economic characterization capital is simply a multi-dimensional combination of goods of higher order.[26] All factors of production are similar only in respect of their fundamental scarcity. So-called original factors would not even be economic goods but for the existence of other higher-order goods employed in conjunction with them. Depending on the decisions and production intentions of the entrepreneur (*Unternehmer*), economic goods of any kind might be considered as capital.

A second theme in Menger's article of 1888 expounded a view contrary to Böhm-Bawerk's preoccupation with social capital and its measurement. Menger's 'capital' is conceived in an individual, financial, ownership sense. The physical heterogeneity and the likely intangible aspects of various capital combinations in the economy prohibited the application of a natural unit of measurement which could be imposed by some scientific observer. Menger therefore resorted to a commonsense, popular unit of measurement which was meaningful to entrepreneurs in their everyday economizing activities. He foreshadowed such a concept of measurement in the *Principles*, where it was maintained that 'under developed trading conditions capital is usually reckoned in terms of money' ([1871] 1950: 304). These comments related unambiguously to institutional conditions of the modern exchange economy (*Verkehrswirtschaft*), where there was widespread private property, market exchange, monetary calculation and business enterprise. In his 1888 article Menger embarked on an attempt to outline the standard accounting view of capital as the money value of property devoted to acquisitive purposes, as opposed to the Böhm-Bawerkian (English classical and Jevonian) emphasis on social capital: that is, produced instruments of production. Capital included 'the productive property, whatever technical nature it may have, so far as its money value is the subject of economic calculation, that is, if it appears in our accounting as a productive sum of money'.[27] The mercantilist origin of this practical, everyday notion is recognized in the *Principles* (ibid.: 304). From an accounting perspective, capital is a fund embodied in business assets. The fund pertains to an anticipated value of saleable goods produced by these assets as they are combined in a particular business. Menger's entrepreneurs create capital in the present on the basis of an *expected* value of the output to be forthcoming at a future date (ibid.: 157–8, 161). From the entrepreneur's point of view, capital is an accounting concept – a fund of prospective values which can be estimated in the present.[28]

As Menger warned, this fund is not obviously determinate, since the present market values of lower-order consumption goods may not be a satisfactory guide to the current value of capital (higher-order goods) intended for use in their production:

> The prospective value of goods of lower order is often – and this must be carefully observed – very different from the value

that similar goods have in the present. For this reason, the value of the goods of higher order by means of which we shall have command of goods of lower order at some future time...is by no means measured by the current value of similar goods of lower order, but rather by the prospective value of the goods of lower order in whose production they serve.

(ibid.: 150)

Menger's 1888 article took for granted what was said in the *Principles* about the role of the entrepreneur. Entrepreneurship as an economizing activity was a higher-order good – a vital part of any capital combination. Entrepreneurial activity involved gathering information about market conditions; economic calculation (such as monetary computation of the 'value' of the capital combinations used in the actual or intended production process); the 'act of will' which combines complementary capital goods into a specific production process; and the supervision of the production plan over time ([1871] 1950: 160).[29] Far from having aggregation as an objective in theorizing about capital, Menger's discussion of 1888 proceeded in terms of the capital of the individual entrepreneur or, at the very most, of the single business enterprise. We can now understand why he so readily accepted that capital was a 'fund' in the financial, acquisitive sense, not a list of items constituting possible instruments of production. Capital was described in terms of the money value (*Geldwert*) of the present worth of business assets productively combined in a specific process aimed at producing exchangeable goods for an income. The filter of the entrepreneur's mind was critical for turning mere assets into actual productive, income-generating capital. The technical nature of assets was inconsequential. Capital could therefore include various legal claims, intangibles, and especially goodwill and 'business connections'.[30]

In the posthumous edition of the *Principles*, published in 1923, Menger elaborated on the important distinction between technical aspects of capital and production, and the economic aspects – a distinction which cries out for substantiation in his earlier 1888 article on capital theory. In a section entitled 'The Two Basic Directions of Human Economy' he explained:

I call these two directions that the human economy can take – the technical and the economizing – basic [*elementar*], though these appear as a rule, indeed, almost always linked with each other, they *nevertheless spring from causes that are essentially different and independent from one another*, and in some branches of the economy actually make their appearance alone.... The technical direction of the human economy is neither necessarily dependent upon the economizing one, nor is it necessarily linked with it.

(1923: 77; his emphasis)[31]

In relation to the subject of this chapter, human requirements for consumption goods necessitate capital formation. Production is in one sense an engineering problem; methods of production are largely technical or engineering data, necessitating a given relationship between inputs and outputs, and a given time dimension for production. The imaginative actions of the entrepreneur are motivated by the problem of insufficient resources available for satisfying human needs. It is at this point that the creative filter of the entrepreneur's economizing mind comes into its own, driven by the prospective, but not certain, demand for final consumption goods. While particular resources may be logically linked with a definite roundabout production scheme and a specific stream of outputs in an engineering or technical sense, they are not necessarily associated with this scheme or these outputs. It all depends on the allocative decisions emerging from the economizing behaviour of entrepreneurs ('the economizing direction of human economy', as Menger stated it in the 1923 edition of the *Principles*). Capital formation must, in this view, always be linked to individuals engaged in economizing activity who assign (and, where necessary, reassign) specific roles to resources available. And that activity is openended. The Böhm-Bawerkian capital concept in Menger's view was thus too technical also because it entailed negligible direction by economizing entrepreneurs; their decisions were tightly constrained, if not predetermined, even though the maturation of capital into final consumption goods takes time.

In summary, just as in their respective treatments of the goodscharacter of goodwill, Menger's sympathy for the everyday practices of economic agents and Böhm-Bawerk's lack of concern for them are evident in their competing capital concepts.[32] Menger's respect for the lessons of 'experience' (a word he used tirelessly) led him to restrict capital to its actual role as diverse possessions which generate private incomes in a monetary economy (capital in the acquisitive sense).[33] Böhm-Bawerk recognized the dual meaning of capital – that is to say, capital in the acquisitive sense, and capital in the technical sense – as an instrument of production. However, the centrality of the technical element in his choice of social capital as a guiding conception did not lead him beyond capital as an aggregate of produced goods with a durable foundation. He sought a universal notion, whereas Menger developed a view as to the content of capital historically specific to private ownership and entrepreneurial economizing in a monetary economy. In such an economy, entrepreneurial behaviour was not merely perfunctory or secondary to the technical dictates of the so-called Böhm-Bawerkian 'instruments of production'. Menger's theories of capital and money had microeconomic foundations: uncertain needs were served by holding cash balances, including speculative balances. The use of money cannot be precisely scheduled; it acts as a stock against the disappointment of individuals' plans in uncertain conditions. Indeed, 'Menger again and again stresses that demand is fickle, that it changes in unpredictable ways and that such changes bring about economic frictions' (Streissler 1973: 167).[34] It is precisely in these conditions of uncertainty generated through demand fluctuations that the concept of capital in the acquisitive sense is formed in the minds of Menger's entrepreneurs.[35]

Finally, Böhm-Bawerk's choice of capital in the technical sense was underwritten by a desire to abstract from historico-legal relations of production. We have it from Preiser ([1959] 1971: 119) that Böhm-Bawerk saw historico-legal elements as either having transitory economic effects or having influence within and through economic laws. How, then, did Menger deal with vestigial historico-legal elements in his conception of capital as diverse possessions combined in a certain way to produce money income? In Menger's ([1871] 1950: 173–4) estimation, the distinction between ethical justifications for the distribution of authority over capital goods was not to be confused with positive questions about the effects of an existing, undisturbed distribution of possessions. Hence he felt free to expatiate on theoretical advantages of accepting popular conceptions of capital without implying that they are socially just.

THE MEANING OF INTEREST FOR MENGER AND BÖHM-BAWERK

A related topic of theoretical divergence in microeconomics between Menger and Böhm-Bawerk concerned the meaning and source of interest income. In Böhm-Bawerk's history and critique of interest theories ([1884] 1932: 261) it was maintained that

Menger came into 'collision with truth' on these matters. The origins of Menger's and Böhm-Bawerk's differences on interest can be traced to their opposing views on the goods-character of legal rights and relationships. Menger's interest concept was already contained in his notion of capital, which followed from his theory of goods. It was probably for this reason that Menger did not answer Böhm-Bawerk's specific criticism of his 'use theory' of interest.[36] We shall first point out the salient features of Menger's theory; Böhm-Bawerk found most of these objectionable.

Menger's interest theory was founded on the assumption that the disposal of capital goods can be separated from the substance, capital itself (a specific combination of complementary capital goods). Interest represented a payment by individuals who, with the institutionally appropriate rights of disposal, effectively locked scarce capital goods into a production process over a definite period of historical time. This payment, moreover, 'will be more certainly obtained the more developed the legal system of a people' (Menger [1871] 1950: 173–4). In a system of private ownership, disposal rights are traded and will take the form of capital goods claims mediated by money. The lender of the claim exchanges an economic good with a subjectively estimated monetary value equal to the borrower's perceived advantage of disposal plus a risk premium. For Menger, disposal rights cannot be sold without transferring capital goods. The resulting risk for their lender must be compensated by a premium (ibid.: 172 n. 35). Lenders exchange one economic good for another without sacrifice. Abstinence is not therefore a good and cannot give rise to interest (ibid.: 156). The borrower requires money to finance new capital goods and plans to use those goods in a specific combination (ibid.: 155–61, 172–3).

In his correspondence with Böhm-Bawerk during 1884–5, Menger argued that borrowers confer subjective value on disposability (*Verfügung*) over capital goods because the intangible thing – use of capital – offers a chance to make profits. Menger's concept of 'the chance of economic activity' (*Erwerbsgelegenheit*) captured the situation in which entrepreneurs are confronted with the potential for gains in changing economic circumstances and these changes were not estimable either with any certainty or with uniformity amongst entrepreneurs in advance (Yagi 1983: 8; Tomo 1995: 131). Therefore, the subjectively anticipated market value of consumer goods was, *inter alia*, a value for disposal of capital goods in addition to repayment of the substance of capital used up in the production process (the latter providing gross savings for eventual replenishment of the substance). It is notable that time figured in the explanation of interest, but it lurked in the background; disposal rights were pre-eminent in the *Principles*. By contrast to Böhm-Bawerk, Menger ([1888] 1935: 181) recognized both the diverse nature of capital goods, and the individual agent's subjective viewpoint in a money economy, when he insisted against over-generalizing and aggregating the interest concept. Rather, interest should apply to the return on loanable funds (*Leihsummen*) and not be confused with an all-embracing yield on property (*Vermögensertrag*) which disguises the diversity of economic phenomena, in particular the heterogeneity of capital and the widely varying estimates of the chance of making profits among the users of capital.

As a founding Austrian contribution to the theory of interest, Menger's rather fragmentary remarks had the merit of taking a microeconomic perspective on interest. He certainly rejected any macroeconomic theory purporting to explain the rate of interest (Streissler and Weber 1973: 232). From a twentieth-century Austrian point of view, his analysis was incomplete. He made an important start, in the first edition of the *Principles*, by suggesting that time-preference was an underlying reason for interest: 'All experience teaches us that a present enjoyment or one in the future usually appears more important...than one of equal intensity at a more remote time in the future' ([1871] 1950: 153–4). This suggestion was deleted from the *Principles* when it was published in a second, posthumous edition in 1923, to remove any association with Böhm-Bawerk's theory.[37]

Now a more complete, subjectivist approach to interest has been accepted in the modern Austrian tradition, following early work by F. W. Fetter, M. Rothbard and L. von Mises (Pellengahr 1986: 70–2, 82–9). According to this approach, interest is synonymous with the rate of time-discount contained in the structure of prices of all higher-order goods – capital and all other inputs. In short, impatience is the sole reason for a positive real rate of interest. The following account encapsulates very neatly the modern Austrian perspective towards which Menger made a tentative approach:

> market participants are not indifferent about time considerations: they do have time preferences. Whether it is taken as a preference for 'sooner' rather than 'later', the future is systematically discounted. As a consequence, the sum of the equili-

brium values of (present) inputs falls short of the anticipated value of (future) output by the extent of the time discount. In a classical model this value differential would be taken to indicate that the inputs are 'productive.' Austrian theorists have consistently rejected this inference. In their view the difference between the value of the inputs and the value of the output is fully attributed to the time preferences of market participants. A systematic discounting of the future is both necessary and sufficient to give rise to the market phenomena that superficially may be seen as value productivity.

(Garrison 1985: 169)

In stating that 'Austrian theorists' rejected productivity explanations for interest, this passage implicitly excluded Böhm-Bawerk from the Austrian tradition. Doubtless, Menger's interest theory (like the modern Austrian perspective as outlined above) is seriously incomplete from a Böhm-Bawerkian standpoint (e.g. Wicksell 1958: 188, 196–7). For Böhm-Bawerk provided an extensive explanation of the reasons for positive real interest rates. He definitely admitted time preference as a 'cause', but productivity considerations were also regarded as crucial 'causes'. The productivity of capital took the form of a general expectation that more goods are to be made available in the future compared with the present (Böhm-Bawerk 1959b: 265–7); productivity was also justified on the ground of the superiority (in terms of output growth) of roundabout methods of production (ibid.: 273–89).[38] It is widely acknowledged that Böhm-Bawerk (1959a) gave Menger's theory of interest harsh, dismissive treatment (Stigler 1941: 196; Blaug 1978: 597). Böhm-Bawerk's preconception, following the logic of his *Rights*, was that a business right or commercial relation cannot increase the prospective value of output. Thus, to attach value to a 'right of disposal' over capital was 'the product of a fiction' (Böhm-Bawerk [1884] 1932: 214). Again, Böhm-Bawerk's objectivism rose to the occasion. He saw no disposal rights independent of the instruments of production.

At this juncture the general contrast in outlook between Menger (along with modern, subjectivist Austrians) and Böhm-Bawerk may be brought into sharper focus. The notion of 'original stores of goods' or original factors of production is objectionable because it makes no reference to entrepreneurs' production plans. Those plans aim to produce consumption goods and they involve the use of a wide range of inputs, including capital combinations which employ intangibles such as 'business connections'. And it is the entrepreneur who is the sole judge of the economic significance of the various inputs used (Garrison 1985: 184). By locating the economic significance of inputs in the individual decisions and plans of entrepreneurs, Menger and his modern patrons do not admit of some historically given, original factors of production. Furthermore, no good is a capital good by virtue of its original, natural, objective form. So, in conclusion, the interest return on capital is best related to the mental process by which goods are subjectively assigned a function in capital goods combinations in the context of the forward-looking production plans of entrepreneurs. At least by the modern, subjectivist Austrian account, which seems to be entirely consistent with Menger's embryonic insights on these matters, interest is therefore best explained in purely subjective terms as well. Hence the modern Austrian predilection for accepting subjective time preference as the cause of interest (Garrison 1985: 177–81; Rothbard 1987).

CONCLUSIONS

The Austrian theory of capital and interest was, for a long period in the twentieth century, associated almost exclusively with Böhm-Bawerk (Hicks 1973, Dobb 1973: 197; Blaug 1978: 498–569). However, Böhm-Bawerk's ideas on this subject have remained controversial within the Austrian tradition (Rothbard 1962: 142; Lachmann 1977: 127, 253, 261–2; Garrison 1990; Lewin 1994). Most of the Austrian critics of Böhm-Bawerk's ideas have been informed and inspired by Menger's insights on capital and interest. In this chapter we have demonstrated that sharp differences between Menger's and Böhm-Bawerk's concepts of capital and interest were symptoms of deeper theoretical points of separation apparent in Böhm-Bawerk's first publication. Böhm-Bawerk had no desire to depart from Menger (Böhm-Bawerk [1884] 1932: 213). Filial respect notwithstanding, his theory of goods was narrower in scope than Menger's. In not attributing goods-status to property rights and commercial relations, Böhm-Bawerk's fundamental concepts clearly derived from more objectivist foundations than Menger's. The *Rights* established differences with Menger which later surfaced in Böhm-Bawerk's capital theory. For Menger these differences were profound enough to warrant his charge, reported by Schumpeter, that Böhm-Bawerk's theory was 'one of the greatest errors ever committed'.

Menger's alternative approach to capital and interest clearly lived on in Lachmann's study of *Capital and its Structure* (1956). In that work we are treated to a disquisition on such familiar Mengerian notions as 'the plan structure' of the economy and two types of complementarity: '*plan complementarity*, the complementarity of capital goods within the framework of one plan, and *structural complementarity*, the overall complementarity of capital goods within the economic system' (ibid.: 54; his emphasis). Lachmann explained these concepts by reducing the level of analysis to entrepreneurial actions: that is, the making and ongoing revision of individual production plans (ibid.: 13). In a manner reminiscent of Menger, Lachmann critically evaluated Böhm-Bawerk's notion of capital as produced instruments of production: 'But to us the question which matters is not which resources are man-made but which are man-used. Historical origin is no concern of ours. Our interest lies in the use to which a resource is put' (ibid.: 11).

Lachmann's early work eventually provided the impetus for a resurgent Austro-American, subjectivist view focusing on a theory of the 'capital-using economy' which is strongly Mengerian in spirit (Garrison 1985). The insights of Mises ([1934] 1981; 1949) in the twentieth century also helped to articulate and extend Menger's ideas, as well as to critique and distil 'Böhm-Bawerk's basic ideas from the non subjective, technical...garb in which they had been presented' (Kirzner 1976b: 54).[39] Notwithstanding the Misesian influence on modern Austro-American capital and interest theory, in his very last discussion of the theory of capital, Lachmann (1986: 59–82) showed how fertile capital theory could be if developed using ideas which belonged originally and wholly to Menger rather than to Böhm-Bawerk. In that discussion Lachmann illustrated the importance for capital formation of the network of entrepreneurial plans based on expectations of uncertain market conditions; the importance for economic analysis of disaggregating macroeconomic notions such as the capital stock; and the fundamental insights to be gained from distinguishing between complementary capital combinations and capital goods. The latter, as Menger had also submitted, lose their capital quality if they cannot be incorporated in a production plan. He concluded that 'the maintenance of capital is always a problematic human activity' (Lachmann 1986: 70) given the uncertainty pervasive in a modern monetary economy.

We shall continue to emphasize the Mengerian approach to capital and interest theory in the following chapter. In reorientating our attention back to the founding Austrians we shall discover that the theoretical divergence or discontinuity between Menger and Böhm-Bawerk on capital theory is not by any means extended or reinforced by Friedrich Wieser. The Wieserian theory of distribution, including capital and interest, exhibited its Mengerian pedigree even though it absorbed some other intellectual influences.

10

MENGERIAN DISTRIBUTION THEORY: WIESER'S CONTRIBUTION

INTRODUCTION

In the previous chapter we established that fundamental theoretical points of divergence separated the founder of the Austrian economics tradition, Carl Menger, and another leading Austrian economist, Eugen von Böhm-Bawerk. Böhm-Bawerk's capital and interest theory, in particular, stressed a degree of classical materiality and adopted a level of aggregation sharply in conflict with the basis of Menger's contribution. As Streissler and Weber (1973: 231) speculated, 'Böhm-Bawerk's Menger cannot be the whole Menger.' Menger's successor in the chair of economics in Vienna was Friedrich Wieser.[1]

We shall now assess whether, and to what extent, the economic-theoretic legacy of Carl Menger endured in Wieser's distribution theory. Standard renditions of early Austrian economics in history of economic thought textbooks usually suggest that Wieser's work can be placed squarely in the Menger tradition.[2] Indeed, going on Wieser's (1923) biographical account of Menger and from Wieser's (1891) survey of Austrian value theory, we should not be led to suspect otherwise.[3] However, Wieser's place in furthering the tradition of economic theory begun by Menger is impugned in Streissler's revealing analysis of Menger's contribution. Streissler (1972: 429, 430) suggested that Menger's followers in the Austrian tradition, including Wieser, progressively 'escaped' their master over time and 'assimilated other traditions' with the consequence that 'much of what was genuinely Menger's tradition got lost'. An example, as Streissler and Weber (1973: 227 n. 4) explained, is Menger's monetary theory, for which Wieser, when re-writing Menger's article on 'Money' for the *Handwörterbuch der Staatswissenschaften* substituted an entirely different version. It has been said of Wieser that he 'occupies a position of indisputable importance in the history of economics' and that he 'presented one of the best theories of capital which had emerged' in his time (Stigler 1941: 158, 177).[4] Yet Wieser's ([1889] 1930) theory of capital and interest (which is later enunciated and extended in Wieser 1891; [1914] 1927) is mostly still unappreciated in the literature.[5] Instead, there has been extensive analysis of the putative apotheosis of 'Austrian' capital and interest theory provided originally by Böhm-Bawerk in 1888 and later refined by Wicksell (e.g. Kregel 1976: 28–33; Blaug 1978: 498–569; Brems 1988; Negishi 1985; Niehans 1990). As well, Streissler (1972: 434–6) concentrated exclusively on those elements in Böhm-Bawerk's capital and interest theory that possibly displeased Menger. To anticipate one of our conclusions in this chapter, Streissler omitted to give an account of Menger's attitude to Wieser's formulations of the capital and interest problem, and we suspect, from the evidence presented here, that Menger would have sympathized with many of Wieser's ideas.[6]

Accordingly, in this chapter we give special consideration to Wieser's much-neglected capital and interest theory in order to assess its origins and composition, and ultimately to estimate the extent of Wieser's departure from the Menger tradition. We compare, as and where the detail of our exposition demands, Wieser's theory of capital and interest with other contemporary Austrian and non-Austrian treatments of that subject. Our attention will also be focused on the relations between Wieser's theory and the broad directions given by Menger for the construction of an adequate theory of capital and interest – a theory which we analysed in Chapter 9. As far as interest theory was concerned, Menger's ideas were very much inchoate. Among the other founding Austrians, Wieser offered an alternative to Böhm-Bawerk's contribution on this subject.

WIESER'S CONCEPT OF CAPITAL

The protean nature of the term 'capital', in both economic theory and everyday use, necessitates extended discussion of the term in Wieser's work. As we saw in Chapter 9, Menger ([1888] 1935) insisted that economists should take cognizance of the popular, everyday concept of capital as a pecuniary magnitude; capital in this view is, for the *individual*, a fund of purchasing power which consists of money and productive assets calculated in terms of money.[7] Wieser ([1889] 1930: 125 n. 1) complains, in deference to Menger's concept, that the popular concept is too broad because it encapsulates 'all the parent wealth of an acquisitive economy existing in or calculated in money, without respect to the technical nature of the instruments of acquisition'. Wieser searched for a universal capital concept applicable in a communistic state as well as a private, acquisitive economy. He reasoned that all

> references ... to the nature of capital must be such as will meet the approval not only of the supporters of the existing order but also the most radical apostles of socialistic views. To accomplish this, it is necessary to eliminate from the current, practical concept every reference to the pecuniary form of capital and private property.
>
> (Ibid.: 62)

Thus, 'to take note of those forms of capital which serve in the formation of income outside of production', as loosely implied in Menger's concept, is 'too closely connect[ed] with the specific condition of the existing economic order of things' (ibid.: 125 n. 1).[8] Wieser rejected identification, *à la* Jevons and Böhm-Bawerk, of the subsistence fund with capital. The subsistence fund exists to maintain labour, whereas capital must be associated with things upon which labourers employ their labour power. Therefore, the form of capital – 'natural' or 'productive' capital as Wieser termed it – is confined to 'perishable or ... movable means of production': in other words, to producers' technical means of production. Computations of the value of such capital may be made in monetary units. The implication is that Menger was led astray in identifying the monetary valuation of capital as substantially identical to the enduring content of productive or natural capital as Wieser ([1914] 1927: 296–8) understood it. Wicksell (1958: 104–5) concurred with Wieser's view and adopted Wieser's definition in his own work.[9] Hayek (1941: 46) also finds Wieser's definition useful (see Figure 5 below).

Chronologically speaking, as far as concepts are concerned, Wieser, Wicksell, and Hayek restricted the form and content of capital to **b** and **d** in Figure 5. Restricting the capital concept to non-permanent resources enabled Wieser to state, and to attempt to solve, the 'capital problem' under a specific set of stationary economy conditions.

Kinds of Resources	Permanent (non-consumable)	Non-permanent (consumable)
Non-producible ('original')	a	b
Producible ('augmentable')	c	d

Source: Hayek (1941: 58 n. 2).

Figure 5 Hayek's delineation of alternative types of capital

CAPITAL AND THE IMPUTATION PROCESS IN A STATIONARY ECONOMY

For Wieser, 'one of the most important and difficult problems of economic theory [is]...to explain the fact that capital yields a net return' ([1889] 1930: 124). Three sets of economic circumstances are distinguished. First, he conjectured that there was a period in economic history where there was 'almost no capital', zero property in capital and therefore 'zero of return from capital'. Second, and more pertinent to the economic system under consideration in *Natural Value*, there was the stationary economy case defined by a constant, positive net return to capital, a positive, 'prevailing' or natural rate of interest, neutral time preference, and zero capital accumulation (ibid.: 149–50). Third, a 'progressing' or growing economy case is distinguished where there is a positive, possibly increasing, net return to capital, a positive but fluctuating rate of interest which depends on the rate of technical change; and net capital accumulation (ibid.: 50; [1914] 1927: 134, 348).[10]

Following Hayek's terminology in Figure 5, capital for Wieser is a stock of non-permanent resources which are periodically consumed and reproduced. Capital is designated 'productive' or 'natural' if it yields a net return (*Reinertrag*). Productive capital may permit production in a progressing economy to be maintained at a permanently higher level than would be possible without it. In a stationary economy, where there is no net capital accumulation (after reproduction and maintenance), the net return of capital is transformed into consumption goods ([1914] 1927: 71, 134). In a stationary economy 'capital is used only to bring forth consumption goods. In a progressing society it is also used to bring about an increase of productive commodities' (ibid.: 71).

Capital productivity may have either a physical or a value basis. Both physical and value productivity relate to Wieser's concept of the net return:

> Physical productivity exists where the *amount* of goods which form the gross return is greater than the amount of capital goods destroyed... Value productivity exists where the value of the gross return is greater than the value of the capital consumed.
>
> ([1889] 1930: 126; his emphasis)

Proof of physical productivity is a necessary precondition for proof of value productivity. To resolve the capital problem the economist's ultimate task is to show that capital has value productivity.

In formulating the capital problem for the stationary economy Wieser postulated (implicitly) that all capital is completely consumed in the hypothetical production interval. The production process is repetitive but not statical – in the sense that production takes place in a time interval, and in the sense that there is not strict simultaneity between the use of inputs and the production of outputs. All output arrives at the end of the production process: that is to say, at the end of the life of the capital goods. In short, we have a point input–point output theory of production. The amount of capital in use, both in terms of volume and of quality, is fixed for the purpose of simplification; there are fixed production co-efficients, and diminishing returns are inadmissible (ibid.: 125–44). It was as if Wieser believed that the conditions of capital supply were fixed by nature. This observation may be compared with Stigler's (1941: 174) rather imprecise interpretation that 'the total supply of capital' is assumed fixed in Wieser's theory. It should be emphasized that Wieser did not assume the amounts of capital in use to be variable in a stationary economy; there was no given supply schedule of capital (in the sense of a range of quantities associated with a list of capital 'prices') in Wieser's stationary economy model. Only Robbins (1930: 208) offered an explanation consistent with our view, when he stated that Wieser was 'assuming fixity of supply', by which was meant a fixed volume and quality of capital in use. No allowance was made by Wieser for flexible supplies along a given capital supply schedule; instead he reasoned in a pre-Marshallian manner by conceiving of single-point price–quantity relations.

Output prices at the beginning of the production interval are expected to be constant, and in conditions of perfect certainty in the stationary economy such expectations cannot be disappointed. In one of his early publications Wieser ([1876] 1994: 219) made this strong assumption: 'let us assume for the time being that changes in the economic situation which would lead to variations in...value do *not* occur' (emphasis added). It is upon this assumption that Wieser attempted to solve the problem of imputation (*Zurechnung*): that is, the problem of assigning value to each higher-order good used in the production of a consumer good. Once the value of the output or consumer good was known and given, and the supplies of higher-order goods used also given, the economist's task was to value the contribution of each higher-order good. We would now call this contribution the marginal productive value of inputs. In the case of capital inputs used in production, one consequence of the given and constant output prices assumption is that the physical and value productivity of capital must be proportional. Wieser's theory of imputation was developed as early as 1876, and it asserted that a portion of output must be assigned to capital inputs. Following Thünen, he asserted that capital had a given net physical productivity; otherwise there would be no reason for using it (Wieser 1884: 139–41; [1889] 1930: 126, 131).[11] Capital produces gross physical product some of which – a physical surplus – is not consumed in production. In value terms the value of capital cannot exceed the value of the gross product. In Wieser's example, the

> 'materials...out of which...bread is produced, cannot possibly be worth more than the bread itself. And those things from which the materials...themselves are produced, and which, consequently, are the producers of bread one stage removed, have, in the prospective gross return – the perishable bread – a maximum limit of value.
>
> ([1889] 1930: 140)

The physical or net return (*Reinertrag*) produced cannot wholly be absorbed by capital reproduction; thus, if 'from the value of 105, 5 are set aside as fruits which may be consumed without preventing the full replacement of capital, only the remainder of 100 can be reckoned as capital value' (ibid.: 140–1).

In commenting up to this point on Wieser's attempt to solve the problem of valuing capital inputs in the production process, Stigler (1941: 177) took a more mainstream neoclassical perspective. He criticized Wieser's assumption of given output values because it 'eliminates the problem of the relation of physical to value productivity, and consequently ignores also the problem of effects of variations of factor supplies on their relative shares of the product'. Now Wieser had come very close to anticipating this criticism in his first seminar paper, which was probably not available to Stigler. According to Wieser, the economizer in fact

> does not carry out the determination of the value of the productive good and the organisation of the related production at the beginning of the period alone, but continuously. The value of the productive good and the organisation of production, provided that its modification is acceptable, will therefore not be established once and for all but will be continuously regulated according to the economic situation. Any change in the latter produces a change in value.
>
> ([1876] 1994: 219).

In the strong-case, stationary-economy case, Wieser abstracted from the problem of 'continuously' valuing, for instance, capital inputs as changes in 'economic conditions' (e.g. demand, consumer needs-valuations) occurred. In any case, even if he had tried to analyse this matter in more detail, it is doubtful whether he would have formulated a solution in Walrasian or Marshallian terms. He would not, in particular, have envisiaged inputs, including capital, along fixed market-supply schedules, with the stationary behaviour of the amounts of the factors actively used in production emerging *pari passu* with the fixity of all the unknowns of a solution as a consequence of a determinate general equilibrium system. This point is missed by Dobb (1973: 195), who, in evaluating Stigler's criticism of Wieser's 'solution', maintained that Wieser may have been aware of the possibility that 'an appropriate equilibrium-condition (e.g. equality of costs and revenue) can be postulated to allow for some *mutual adjustment* of product-prices and output and prices of producers' goods *in the course of reaching equilibrium*' (emphasis added). However, no such simultaneous mutual adjustment or equilibrating process is evident in Wieser's stationary economy. Wieser was simply not equipped to analyse the problem of imputation, factor pricing or distribution in terms of 'mutual adjustment'; his illustrations of 'general imputation' problems established one-way causal sequences, from utility valuations of consumers' goods to factor values, prices or costs. For Wieser, as for Menger and Böhm-Bawerk, utility was the sole cause of factor values.

Let us consider one of Wieser's solutions to the problem of imputation in the three factor, three product case. He used x, y and z to represent the three factors of production or higher-order goods. As already stated, product values were taken as given; they were ultimately reflections of the marginal utility valuations placed on consumer goods. He presented the following three equations, applying to three production processes, with quantities of inputs on the left-hand side, and product values on the right-hand side:

$$x + y = 100$$
$$2x + 3z = 290$$
$$4y + 5z = 590$$

Solving these equations simultaneously, we arrive at values for the factors x, y and z of 40, 60 and 70 respectively. Wieser concluded that the productive contribution of each factor, capital inputs among them, was 'that portion of return in which is contained the work of the individual productive element in the total return of production. The sum of all the productive contributions exactly exhausts the value of the total return' ([1889] 1930: 88). This 'solution' deserves elaboration. Each of Wieser's factor inputs, what he referred to as 'the individual productive element', is unique, distinguishable and possibly indivisible. If these inputs are capital goods in a stationary economy, they are not always readily substitutable with other factors; they exhibit strong degrees of complementarity and indivisibility.[12] Complementarity becomes more pronounced and makes factor substitution more difficult the longer a production process has been in motion during any production period: 'modification of the production already in progress is only possible if the latter is not yet so advanced that the productive goods are tied to one or other category of [consumer] goods' (Wieser [1876] 1994: 221). Smooth and speedy factor substitution was definitely not something Wieser could accept. Wieser's numerical illustration indicated that factors are combined in fixed proportions in each production process, though these proportions vary from one process to the other. The difficulty with this assumption is that the separate productivity of each factor cannot be imputed when production co-efficients are fixed. A factor's marginal product can be isolated if factor proportions are variable and extensive substitution is possible. Wieser's idea that all factor inputs are to a certain extent discrete, manifold and uniquely associated with the production of specific goods assisted him to deflect this objection.

In Wieser's strong-case, stationary economy context he made no allowance for continuous variation (as he well recognized). It was precisely in this context that his capital and interest theory was initially developed. Beyond the strong case, Wieser ([1889] 1930: 89–90), like Menger ([1871] 1950: 162–3), recognized both the diversity of factor combinations and the likelihood that these could outnumber the types of producers' inputs available. Furthermore, when he admitted 'change in the economic situation', he allowed for substitution within and between production processes:

> Whatever form the changes may take, the organisation of production has to be modified along with them. Our examination will be facilitated if we assume at the outset that the new economic situation will in turn be permanent and that any further change is therefore ruled out. It is this probably continuing economic situation which now determines our subject's production schedule. He would have a poor understanding of his interests if he continued to use the same quantities of the productive good as before to produce the individual categories of the first-order goods. For the conditions which justified the former organisation of the production of goods, the probable value of the products and the ensuing value of the productive good, have changed. The probable value of the products, with regard to each quantity of them that is produced, is different; the value of the productive good, determined with regard to the most advantageous production, is different.
>
> (Wieser [1876] 1994: 225–6)

In the above passage he moved from reasoning in terms of an 'economic situation' which was 'calm and not subject to variation' to one which was affected by a one-off set of changes. He outlined changes in available quantities of factors, uniform improvements of production across industries, and changes in human needs (ibid.: 225). Any change was analysed by keeping in view the restoration of stationariness after the change had worked itself through from consumer valuations of outputs to changes in factor proportions and factor-values. Individuals, according to Wieser, 'are caused by their economic interests to restore the equilibrium in value of the higher order and first order goods which has been disturbed by the change in economic situation by restricting production here and expanding it there' (ibid.: 227). His curious 'exception', in which 'restoration of equilibrium has become impossible', applied to the case where production of a specific category of a first-order good was no longer economically justified. Here Wieser referred to the importance of factor substitution based on subjective opportunity cost. For the value of an input determined on the basis of 'other categories of goods may have risen to such an extent that the production of goods of the category in question' from this input is no longer economically acceptable. He apparently used the term 'equilibrium' here in a very restricted sense. It meant stationariness in that there were no changes taking place in the relative values of inputs used in the production of categories of consumer goods. If one category of consumer goods was no longer being produced, then input valuations in that activity would have no purpose.

The equilibrium in relative factor values distilled from Wieser's three-factor, three-consumer-good illustration, was regarded by Stigler (1941: 170) as 'distasteful' because it was 'overdeterminate', and derivation of a 'stable equilibrium' solution was for Stigler not possible, since mutual determination of product and factor values was inadmissible. As well, we would add that Wieser's very recognition of heterogeneity in the sphere of production implied that 'equilibrium' solutions for factor-pricing of the kind desired by Stigler could not capture demonstrably more fluid and more concrete situations where factors, and factor combinations, exhibited extreme diversity. Indeed, argued Wieser ([1889] 1930: 90 n.), 'among all the different kinds of goods employed in production, it would be difficult to find one which... would always be combined with others according to the same unalterably fixed formula'. Moreover, in acknowledging that factor combinations are changing and changeable (ibid.), it was implied that the problem of factor-pricing may only systematically be discussed as an equilibrating, rather than an equilibrium, phenomenon. Collapsing factor valuation and substitution into a one-time, determinate outcome, where the economists' analytical apparatus is concentrated exclusively on the end-state equilibrium, seemed unsatisfactory to Wieser.[13] For example, his very first attempt to discuss factor price formation and factor price variation referred to a situation of economic change and to the details of equilibrating processes which realigned relative factor values with changes in consumers' valuations of outputs. His first publication always referred back to 'people's [economizing] efforts, in production as in their economic affairs, to safeguard their interests as far as possible which they achieve by directing their efforts... toward realising the value of... productive goods in that of the products' ([1876] 1994: 233). Giving details of the equilibrating process meant, for Wieser, tracing the *one-way causal sequence* of valuing outputs to valuing producers' goods used in their production.

We now return to the strict, stationary-economy case, where the same available quantities of diverse types of inputs, including capital inputs, and the same demand conditions recur over 'specific periods of identical length' (ibid.: 218). During any one period of production and consumption the same quantity of diverse inputs is called forth to produce the consumer goods which were ascribed the same marginal utility valuations in previous periods. Therefore, just as in Wieser's numerical illustration of imputed factor values, *no variations* in factor supplies are permitted in a specific production interval or between intervals in the stationary situation. Factor supplies were constant, and each factor had a given use. So, for instance, labour supply could not vary along some given supply schedule subject to the disutility of labour. This notion of stationariness was required in order to make final demands for consumer goods the exclusive causes of factor values.[14] We can now understand why Brems (1986: 11), wrongly characterized founding Austrian distribution theory, including Wieser's, as

> dealing with static general equilibria. In such equilibria, mathematics – even the rudimentary mathematics used by Walras – would have taught them [Menger, Wieser and Böhm-Bawerk] the lesson that a variable is neither the 'cause' nor the 'effect' of any other. All variables are determined on an equal footing and simultaneously, and all are the effects of the only causes found in the model, i.e., its parameters.

Following Menger in spirit and workmanship, the distributive aspects of Wieser's theory attempted in principle to remain consistent with the underlying ultimate or generative causes of economic phenomena, that is, to isolate the simplest elements from the complexity of everything real. This Austrian philosophical position rejected any notion of *strictly mathematical determination* of variables in a static general equilibrium system. As demonstrated in the Menger–Walras correspondence:

> Having been taught by his father to regard universal concomitance and exact proportionality [between *raretés* and prices] as the criteria of causality, Léon Walras felt that his construction of an overall system of simultaneous equations bound together by the marginal utility principle had proved that *rareté* was the cause of value. Menger, on the other hand, thought that the object of economic research was to discover those laws governing market phenomena which can be traced back to their ultimate genetic determinants in man's...nature. Mathematics cannot do this.
>
> (Jaffé 1976: 521–2)

Wieser was also a captive of Menger's philosophic outlook. Wieser's method, like Menger's, was causal-genetic rather than mathematical-functional, and causal relations were sequential for both writers.

In this connection, Stigler's (1941: 170) claim that Wieser's assumption of constant output prices is equivalent in content to assuming that final demands are infinitely elastic along a determinate, continuous, demand function attributed more to Wieser's work than is textually supportable. Demand functions are not evident in Wieser's sketch of the stationary economy; the potential for 'stationary'-like movements along either a fixed-demand or a fixed-supply schedule, as a consequence of an emergent, equilibrium solution is not contemplated by Wieser, since he reduced notions of supply and demand to single-point, price–quantity relations. The economy was already at rest; factors were already optimally arranged as far as Wieser was concerned.[15]

INTEREST ON CAPITAL IN A STATIONARY ECONOMY

The derivation of interest income on capital, while part of the general problem of imputation, deserves special treatment here. Did Wieser follow Menger in this matter or have anything substantially different to contribute from Böhm-Bawerk? How does Wieser explain interest? He believed that interest on capital and profit coincided in the stationary economy. In the dynamic, progressing economy, interest and profit became different income categories, as we shall see in the next section of this chapter.

Now interest expressed some 'definite relation between capital value and net return'. An interest rate is the percentage of net increment to capital employed in a specific production interval. In a stationary economy in a large number of 'connected' cases of production the rate of interest is the general percentage of increment to all capital in the market (Wieser [1889] 1930: 141, 144). Wieser is guarded about generalizing the rate of interest to all diverse forms of property, perhaps heeding Menger's earlier warning (Menger [1888] 1935: 181). Wieser restricted his analysis of interest to producers' capital, although he was reluctant to refer to interest as a single rate on the genus capital as a whole. We should, at this point, recall Wieser's concept of productive or natural capital. It *excluded* durable consumption goods, that is, 'material possessions of service trades and goods rented for use [as well as] loan-capital for lending on these goods' (Wieser [1914] 1927: 297). Natural capital was producers' means of production.

While he avoided generalizing the rate of interest in an economy, Wieser nevertheless alluded in *Natural Value* to possible equalization of interest rates in the strong, stationary-economy case; the equalization of interest on various forms of producers' (natural) capital, and interest on consumption loans; and, on another level, equalization between money market interest rates, and interest rates ruling in markets for different types of producers' capital. Effectively, the demand and supply of money, and the demand and supply of producers' capital, are regarded as identical. In the stationary case, the equalized natural rate of interest is determined independently of monetary factors, and solely by the rate of return on natural capital: that is, on capital invested in producers' goods. The amount and value of capital goods are brought into strict conformity with the costs of producing them, thus regulating the interest rate ([1889] 1930: 145, 155–8).

Time preference is allowed to vary between individuals, but the net societal effect is to value present goods as equal to future goods of like quantity and quality. Time preference is therefore neutral and not apparently relevant in explaining the existence of a positive rate of interest (Wieser [1889] 1930: 16–19; [1914] 1927: 131).

Instead Wieser adopted another ground for explaining interest as if it were a sufficient condition for a positive rate of interest to obtain in a stationary economy as he conceived it: that is, he appealed to the inherent productivity of capital as a cause of the differences in valuation in the present and in the future.[16] Wieser's productivity theory of interest is founded upon the assumption that the net physical productivity of diverse capital goods which cannot directly be observed has been established by imputation, supplemented if necessary by introspection if the logic of his imputation theory is not fully accepted. Wieser's case in favour of capital goods yielding a net return and of interest representing the net increment of capital could, he believed, be clinched by facts gleaned using the method of introspective psychology. In 'testimony to... [the] correctness' of his capital and interest theory Wieser had merely submitted 'axioms which every layman recognises, axioms of ripened experience' ([1889] 1930: 143–4).

A net physical return on capital creates a value discount on the future. For Wieser, present possession of capital was equivalent to having received a net return from the use of that capital in the immediately preceding production interval. In a stationary economy, possession of capital at a future date (the end of the next production interval) guaranteed the same net return but at the end of that interval. That is, 'capital which, in twelve months from the date of possession yields the same gross return (say 105) and the same net return (say 5), is valued at the date of possession at the same amount (say 100). It is, nevertheless, not a matter of indifference whether the capital comes into possession now or only at the end of the twelve months inasmuch as possession now guarantees a return of interest besides' (ibid.: 142–3). Therefore:

> [if]*wants are continuously to find the same satisfaction, equal amounts of return* must continuously be produced. And if equal amounts of return are continuously produced, capital must remain continuously the same in substance. But if capital is actually to remain the same in substance, and so is able to yield continuously *the same returns*, this must find expression in a valuation which ascribes to capital a higher value, the earlier point in time it comes into our possession. For the earlier point of time, the earlier, and consequently the greater, the return that may be expected.
>
> (ibid.: 143; emphasis added)

This passage is hardly unambiguous. Indeed, Wieser might be mistakenly arraigned for introducing dynamic elements into his theory of interest which contradict conditions outlined earlier for production in a stationary economy. The notion of 'continuous' renewal of capital substance is misleading if taken too literally. If it is to remain consistent with his concept of stationariness, we must think of discrete, hypothetical production intervals. Whatever the length of the production interval, the economy 'shows neither progress nor retrogression'. Constant returns in value terms for any particular stationary economy are ultimately determined by 'future need values', which do not change (Wieser [1914] 1927: 71, 141). Capital in Wieser's sense is used up completely in each interval, and, between production intervals, in order for production to recur, interest presumably exists in order to ensure reallocation of the same 'capital substance' to the same uses as in previous intervals. This is to say, also, that a positive net yield on capital is required to ensure capital reproduction and therefore to keep the 'stationary' economy 'stationary' in Wieser's sense. For heuristic purposes it would not matter whether the intervals themselves had different hypothetical production durations; each duration completely depends, correspondingly, on the assumed physical productivity of the diverse capital goods which are used in specific production processes.

We are now in a better position to comprehend the preceding passage quoted from *Natural Value* ([1889] 1930: 143). In that passage, Wieser is implicitly comparing recurring production processes in a stationary context; each process yields the same constant physical product at the end of each production interval, but each is characterized by different production intervals and therefore by different qualities of capital.[17] Wieser suggested, in other words, that capital employed in a shorter production interval and yielding the same physical rate of return in each recurring interval, has a higher value productivity than capital which has the same physical productivity but which takes a longer production interval. This interpretation has two important implications. First, Wieser presupposes a positive interest rate; he does not prove that the interest rate will be positive. Second, a higher opportunity cost of waiting is entailed for the same physical returns arriving at the end of a longer production interval. Interpreted in this way, Wieser's 'explanation' of interest in his model of the stationary economy does not admit diminishing returns. By contrast, in Böhm-Bawerk's well-known explanation of the reason for a positive rate of interest, present capital goods yield a larger physical product than an equal quantity of future capital goods at a future date applied to roundabout production, because of diminishing returns from a lengthening production interval. Parenthetically, there is a 'period of production' notion in Wieser's theory, although *not* one which involves the introduction of more productive time-consuming processes. Wieser's production interval is one characterized by a given production process yielding constant physical returns.

Despite Wieser's attempt to assert neutral time preference, we cannot avoid the implication in his stationary economy that a degree of impatience is involved on the part of producers (entrepreneurs or central planners as the case demands) who have rights of possession over a given volume of capital of the same quality (as opposed to capital of lesser quality) which is merely periodically duplicated. Furthermore, it seems for Wieser that these possessors avowedly desire quicker physical returns, and thence greater value returns, over successive recurring production intervals. In respect of consumers in a stationary economy Wieser was more explicit, but he did not recognize an inconsistency with earlier pronouncements repudiating any significant role for time preference:

> consumption goods are available only as such and are useless for anything else. However, the latter may be turned over into consumption goods *more or less slowly*. The *more rapidly they are despatched*, the sooner will the new production process have to be set on foot.
>
> ([1914] 1927: 132, emphasis added).

His position on the existence of interest in a stationary economy would have been more defensible if he had given time preference a more central role. Instead, the order of his 'explanation' of interest made productivity causal and primary; time discount was merely the resultant. Capital productivity, in other words, had exclusive influence on comparison of present and future gratifications. The burden of Wieser's explanation of interest therefore rested precariously on the existence of a technical net productivity of capital.[18]

CAPITAL AND THE TREND OF INTEREST IN A PROGRESSING ECONOMY

In reading Wieser's work we find that the stationary and the progressing economy form two separate, though not competing, stages of exposition. Fragmentary discussion of the progressing economy is evident at frequent points in *Natural Value*. It is more fully enunciated in *Social Economics*, a work recently dubbed 'the definitive textbook of the Austrian School' for the early decades of the twentieth century (Streissler 1987: 921). In a dynamic 'progressing social economy', discussed extensively in *Social Economics*, capital is both reproduced and augmented (Wieser [1914] 1927: 71). The context for Wieser's discussion of economic progress was a capitalistic, exchange economy where monetary calculation was prevalent.

In outlining the simple stationary economy in *Natural Value* and again in the early sections of *Social Economics* Wieser always appeared to be ready to break out of the strong-case theorizing which was required of him. First, his discussion of the physical productivity of capital showed acute awareness of the *varieties* of capital goods which complicate calculations of a return on the genus capital as a whole, even though such a return may be imagined in principle (Wieser [1889] 1930: 133). Second, competition will assist in generating movement towards a uniform, natural rate of interest across the economy, but institutional impediments often conspire against such an outcome. He exclaims, for example, that

> the individualism of our present economic order distributes production among individual undertakings...yet at how many points do we find great gaps; how many dislocations through excessive accumulation of means of production at the wrong places; how often things go too quickly, how often not fast enough!
>
> (ibid.: 145)

Third, in circumstances of 'private ownership' the money markets and capital goods markets are not always well-synchronized; under a 'communistic regime' the central planner's calculation of a general, uniform interest rate may be easier in the absence of a private commercial money market (ibid.: 144). Private money markets are buffeted by alternating and irregular periods of 'intensive activity' and of 'quiescent business', such that commercial money rates of interest can exhibit a high variance in the short period: that is, 'within a year' (Wieser [1914] 1927: 348). Time horizons and associated contractual obligations in the market for money credit destined for more permanent productive investment are much longer and substantially different from horizons which normally obtain in the market for consumption loans.[19] Wieser was therefore driven to doubt the applicability of his Law of the Equalization of Price, and of interest equalization in particular, in the dynamic, progressing economy. He doubted the existence of a single loan-interest rate which, through the action of strong equilibrating forces, is adjusted into conformity with a common market rate of interest on all forms of income generating assets, broadly conceived. In the case of money and capital markets, '[e]ven with complete security of the loans, the *interests of the different groups are too diverse* as regards the period of the loan and a number of other conditions for a central market to form in which the law of the unity of price might prevail.' (ibid.: 304; emphasis added).

An undeniable implication here is Wieser's leaning towards the Marxian view that interest rates on money capital are determined temporarily and perhaps permanently by causes which are independent of what happens to the rate of interest on producers' capital.[20] As well, Wieser was aware of Menger's view, expounded in 'Zur Theorie des Kapitals' ([1888] 1935), which insisted that the rate of interest on money markets, the yield on industrial or natural capital, and the yield on other categories of income bearing assets 'need separate explanation each according to its nature and its different origins. The problem of the return on property (*Vermögensertrag*) is, 'for practical purposes...in no way synonymous with the problem of interest' (ibid.: 181). Wieser's sympathy towards both the Marxian and the Mengerian view placed his theory of interest, especially in *Social Economics*, outside the typical marginalist tradition in economics which included Jevons and Walras and which recognized, first, that money rates of interest could vary only temporarily from some natural rate, and, second, that the money rate was determined exclusively by the rate of return on various forms of producers' capital. *Per contra*, Wieser decided to leave the way open for the possibility of monetary influences on the latter. No longer may we be sure, after reading relevant sections of *Social Economics*, that a permanent change in the money market interest rate would affect costs of production in the same manner, and would ultimately amount to the same thing as, a permanent, equivalent change in the rate of interest (or profit) on producers' capital.[21]

Wieser's Law of the Equalization of Price (*Gesetz des Priessaus gleiches*) is certainly an important analytical device in the *Ursprung* and in *Natural Value*. Streissler (1972: 438) interpreted the law as 'rather evocative of a process leading to equilibrium, not of equilibrium itself'. The fact that Wieser jettisoned his Law in respect of pricing in money and capital markets in the progressing economy context in *Social Economics* adds further weight to the proposition that he not be classified as a typical, fledgling, equilibrium economist who wished generally to determine equilibrium price and analyse equilibrium positions. His affinity with Menger in this connection is more striking than has been recognized hitherto.[22]

In *Natural Value* there were allusions to 'solitary' instances of rises in interest on a particular form of capital input (perhaps because of a one-off invention, but Wieser was not explicit), while the prevailing rate of interest remains unaltered on other capital goods. Furthermore, alterations in the prevailing rate may result from 'changes in supply, in demand [and] in technique' ([1889] 1930: 147, 150). Universally adopted inventions, for example, 'would cause a general rise in the net return to capital' relative to 'those capitals which had no part in the effects of the invention' (ibid.: 150). In a progressing economy an increase in the amount of capital of the same kind as used before necessarily leads to a decline in the interest rate; a simultaneous increase in new varieties of 'specific capital' will counterbalance this effect ([1914] 1927: 140). Here Wieser showed awareness of the fact that inventions and improvements are not introduced at one fell swoop. Wieser was non-committal about the certainty and regularity of changes in the quality of capital; it is precisely this outlook that lends itself to an open-ended serial-process analysis rather than equilibrium theorizing.[23] Indeed, such a process comes to the fore in Wieser's distinction between interest on capital and entrepreneurial profit – the latter being positive only in the progressing economy (ibid.: 355–6). For Wieser, profit is not to be confused with regular wages of management, although such wages form part of entrepreneurs' income. Economic progress required rare skills. Such skills were necessary for 'a specific command of capital... specific in its unique character or else in its magnitude'. And these skills return a profit so long as they have not become 'common property'. Entrepreneurs also secure a preferred market position of a specific character for their enterprise. In their superior leadership they were originally 'pioneers of unusual ability and training, combining technical knowledge and capacity with market experience and organizing power' (ibid.: 356, 357). Such power, coupled with the 'talent of economic leadership', often gets its return from capital gains on property; from audacious innovations, from promotion of joint-stock companies and from various forms of 'creative speculation' and arbitrage activity which assist in the equilibrating process of price formation (rather than full determination in a mathematical sense) in a progressing economy (ibid.: 357–66).

In the case of diverse types of fixed capital where 'instead of one single future return there are several returns', Wieser maintained that in the ideal stationary-economy case these returns are determined by discounting using the uniform natural rate of interest determined in respect of circulating capital. However, Wieser allowed for expectations and uncertainty. The complications introduced by 'uncertainty [as to] ... whether the returns expected will actually be received at all' made calculation of the value of fixed capital subject to some uniform interest rate, more difficult in the progressing economy. Insurance was mentioned as one way out of the dilemma, although Wieser did not indicate that such a device could be effective in all cases where uncertainty appears ([1889] 1930: 152). In addition, vast aggregations of indivisible items of fixed capital ('mammoth capital') in a dynamic, advanced capitalist economy tend to thwart competitive pressures making for a natural, equilibrium rate of interest on the use of such capital (Wieser [1914] 1927: 209–10).

The process of new capital formation in a progressing economy where there is widespread monetary calculation and exchange is represented in Wieser's work as a complex time-consuming exercise 'distributed over a large number of individuals' (ibid.: 298, 299–303). It involves distinct capitalistic and entrepreneurial activities. In the first place, a supply of new savings has to be forthcoming although the economic mechanism to encourage savings such as an interest rate incentive, is not given much emphasis.[24] Second, 'money capitalists' advance money capital to consumers and to 'speculating' capital-employing entrepreneurs. The latter, in advanced forms of capitalistic economic organization, may also assume the role of money capitalists. Entrepreneurs cannot usually employ productive capital until capital goods are purchased from capital-producing entrepreneurs, who in turn may also require money credit from money capitalists in order to make their enterprises into going concerns. In short, money and credit facilitate the accumulation of productive capital in Wieser's sense. Money and credit could also potentially prove an obstacle to capital accumulation, depending on the conditions – including power relationships and state regulations – of trading on financial markets.

In *Social Economics* Wieser summarized his position on the role of money in the capital-formation process:

> In the money economy...natural capital in the hands of entrepreneurs...requires the supplement of money capital and constant reference to the monetary form. It is only thus that the natural capital forms a unit and may be united with other forms of capital. This homogeneity has always been tacitly assumed...for in asserting the equalizing tendency of interest it presupposes a monetary form of capital in which alone the individual kinds of capital may be compared....The entire importance [of the power of capital] is never appraised in the natural form alone, great as is the productive wealth of the goods involved. The ultimate support of this power is to be found in the unifying monetary form...[which] is the nucleus not only of the practical concept but of the actual power of capital as well.
>
> (ibid.: 298)[25]

Here there are rudiments of a monetary theory of the rate of interest (or profit) on productive capital; it is merely a glimpse made apparent by Wieser's terminology. Finally, only when capital-employing entrepreneurs actually realize a (previously prospective) net gain from the use of productive capital can capital formation be said to have taken place (ibid.: 299).

The long-run movement of the interest rate on capital in the progressing economy is not well charted in Wieser's analysis. Indubitably, he followed English and German classical economists in believing that the rate of interest displayed a clear, downward secular trend.[26] In *Natural Value* he argues that the interest rate 'rises from the beginning' and goes on 'growing so long as the economic world thrives' ([1889] 1930: 151). This is apparently contradicted in *Social Economics*, where it is insisted: 'During *the entire course* of economic development the trend of the rate of productive interest is downward' (emphasis added). Despite all technical progress, continues Wieser, 'the increase of capital reduces its marginal yield' ([1914] 1927: 348).[27] Wieser's meaning is hardly straightforward; the meaning lies between as much as within the lines. Successive increases of capital of the same quality would, it appears, lead to diminishing returns. Is this Wieser's likely meaning: that otherwise technical progress could carry on indefinitely to keep up the trend of interest rates or at least keep the interest rate from falling? Textual interpretation is not assisted by another passing statement Wieser made, implying that there was an intrinsic limit on investment opportunities in a progressing economy – a limit approached as productive capital became more abundant. Thus:

> when the opportunities for capitalistic enterprise have been discovered and seized upon to a great extent, the established enterprise provided with a large capital obtains a supremacy against which the gifts of the newcomer cannot easily prevail.... There has also arisen a new class, a well-trained personnel; schooled in the new methods, they are ready to aid the entrepreneur in his problems of leadership at a wage rate by no means exorbitant. In the end the prospects of profit for even the older established enterprises will become less favorable... The abundance of accumulated capital will ultimately assert itself by crowding all opportunities for business enterprise.
>
> (ibid.: 357)

In addition, nowhere did Wieser suggest, when remarking on the likelihood of a falling rate of interest in a progressing economy, that the interest rate would eventually fall to zero, and the possibility that a zero rate may be approached asymptotically is not broached ([1889] 1930: 151; [1914] 1927: 348). At least partial reconciliation of Wieser's scattered statements on this matter rests on drawing a distinction (as he often did) between isolated 'specific capital' investments incorporating particular inventions on the one hand, and 'universally effective invention' or the most generally adopted technique on the other ([1889] 1930: 150). The former are not sufficient to keep up the general interest rate, although individual entrepreneurs who first adopt a new technique would, for a while, reap the higher net profit return on specific capital investments. Wieser's distinction is probably due to his reading of Marx, to whom tribute is given in Wieser 1884. Streissler (1987: 921) noticed that some of Wieser's 'terminology' owed something to Marx; here we are suggesting that Wieser's general outlook on the long-run microeconomics of development presupposed a law of the falling rate of interest or profit which had classical and, of course, Marxian connotations. Of these connotations Wieser was doubtless aware. He did not exaggerate the differences between his economic-theoretic innovations and those of his classical predecessors.[28] Wieser ([1889] 1930: 200ff.) definitely aimed to refute the labour theory of value and Marxian exploitation theory, although the refutation was nowhere near as successful and uncompromising as Böhm-Bawerk's ([1896] 1962) well-known critique of Marxian theory.

THE PLACE OF WIESER'S THEORY IN THE FOUNDING AUSTRIAN TRADITION

In 1914, on the occasion of writing the third edition of *History and Critique of Interest Theories*, Böhm-Bawerk (1959a: 411), paid obeisance to the 'marked individuality' of Wieser's capital and interest theory although he was not prepared to accept its validity. Wieser ([1914] 1927) appears to have remained impervious to Böhm-Bawerk's earlier criticisms, thus inciting Böhm-Bawerk to provide another critique (1959a: 483, 40 n.). We have already mentioned Wieser's penchant to assume, implicitly, what he proposed to prove in attempting to separate a net return of capital from the net return attributable to other factors. Böhm-Bawerk expressed this problem with Wieser's 'proof' as follows:

> It is true that a *net return of production*...is concededly present when the total gross return yielded by all three collaborating factors exceeds the value of the capital consumed. But a *net return of capital* is not present until the individual aliquot share which is attributed to capital out of the gross return exceeds the capital consumed. And the existence of the first condition, by very reason of the radical difference in the presuppositions, leaves absolutely no ground for inferring the existence of the second.
>
> (1959a: 415; emphasis added)

Böhm-Bawerk granted that Wieser's 'general imputation' theory ascertains the portions contributed by the various factors to gross product. A theory of interest on capital must, by contrast, show the portion of net product contributed by the factor 'capital'. Wieser always maintained by assumption that capital in the stationary economy would not be employed if it did not produce net physical and value productivity. Such an assumption rested, in the final analysis, on introspective knowledge – on adequate understanding of producers' concrete plans, which always included an 'interest' category. Böhm-Bawerk noticed that Wieser often wished to fall back on this ground, viz., the supposition that the economist 'knows as a fact within our experience that the portion of the gross return attributable to capital exceeds the amount of capital consumed' (ibid.: 415). On the demand side Wieser had already given much weight to the economist's casual, introspective knowledge in constructing and evaluating the theory of consumers' wants and diminishing marginal utility. However, in this connection, Böhm-Bawerk (1959b: 430 n. 81) warned that Wieser appeared 'to go somewhat too far' in relying on the methods used by 'psychological laymen'. These methods, according to Böhm-Bawerk, Wieser used as explanatory devices when the powers of pure psychological (*Wissenschaftliche*) and of pure economic theory provide a sounder basis for a proper scientific treatment. Böhm-Bawerk had originally judged that Wieser meant only that the 'training of universal experience' offered 'relatively superficial facts' which economists needed to explain with other methods (ibid.: 195). Now he was no longer so sure of that judgement.

If Wieser's capital and interest theory cannot firmly be located in the Böhm-Bawerkian, 'Austrian' tradition then what were its doctrinal origins? An heirloom from von Thünen – a simple productivity theory of capital – was Wieser's explicit point of departure. Wieser's imputation theory, from which his theory of capital and interest was further developed, was motivated by lacunae in Menger's approach to imputation. Menger ([1871] 1950: 157–65) believed that the correct method for valuing higher-order goods was to withdraw one unit from production and observe the effect on output. The loss in total output is the marginal product of the (variable) higher-order good in question, and the consumer's utility of output forgone establishes its value. The imputed value of the higher-order good is not immediately obtained from the direct loss of (marginal) utility but is equal to a potentially small loss after any remaining complementary inputs have been reassigned by entrepreneurs to their next-best uses in other production processes (if any). This was Menger's 'loss principle' for valuing inputs. Wieser extended and deepened Menger's theory; he did not make use of Menger's method of negative imputation, since the withdrawal of one unit of a higher-order good from production necessarily reduced the productivity of remaining units. He proposed not a loss principle, but a method of positive imputation which measured the product gain by adding units of an input. He achieved this objective by, for example, valuing additional capital units assuming fixed production co-efficients. In his numerical illustration of general imputation discussed earlier in this chapter, he captured important aspects of interdependence between production processes and aspects of factor complementarity.

The contrast between Wieser and Böhm-Bawerk on capital interest and distribution theory in general could not be sharper. For

WIESER'S THEORY OF DISTRIBUTION

Böhm-Bawerk avoided explicit analysis of interdependence between production processes. In the theory of a *stationary* economy, (a) Wieser did not give co-ordinate rank and mutual influence as between technical productivity and time preference; (b) he conceived of the interest problem as connected only with produced means of production, as did German classical economists; and (c) he systematically formulated, by way of an imputation theory, the specific productivity or productive contribution of each factor input – the productivity of capital, in particular, serving to 'explain' both the amount yielded by a group of capital goods, and the rate of yield calculated on the valuation of the principal or capital substance. In respect of (a) he was at one with Menger but inconsistent with Böhm-Bawerk. Wieser's orientation in both (b) and (c) earned the fervid denunciation of F. A. Fetter ([1914] 1977), the Austro-American theorist and contemporary of Wieser who developed interest theory along pure time-preference lines. As for (c), Wieser had many points in common with J. B. Clark (Fetter [1927] 1977: 272). Lastly, in considering the mixed origins and allegiances of Wieser's capital and interest theory, our study would not be complete without investigating F. H. Knight's (1950: 31) tribute to Wieser's theory as being far 'sounder' than other Austrian theories on the subject. First, for Knight, time preference played no role in the determination of the rate of interest – a rate which in his view always remains positive, since, conceptually, a zero limit could not be reached. Second, Knight argued that the ability of capital to yield services – its productivity – becomes the basis for interest, the rate of which is defined as the 'anticipated productivity ratio' (Knight 1916: 298). Third, Knight (1934) also conceived of production as involving a collection of highly specific, complementary capital goods. These three facets of Knight's capital and interest theory had much in common with Wieser's, so it comes as no surprise that Knight liked Wieser's theory.

It remains for us to draw attention to the place of Wieser's capital and interest theory and certain other related components of his economic thought, in the founding Austrian tradition. Noteworthy is Hennings's (1986: 232) authoritative survey, which made a case, first, for distinguishing Wieser and Böhm-Bawerk on the reasoning that Wieser places 'less emphasis' on the temporal nature of production than does Böhm-Bawerk.[29] Following our account of Wieser's theory, this interpretation deserves qualification. Hennings's claim is valid in relation to the stationary economy model;

Wieser's concept of stationariness implicitly excluded consideration of the effects of temporal integration of production processes in the Böhm-Bawerkian sense. In Wieser's stationary economy the Law of the Equalization of Price prevailed and the separation of monetary from real variables was complete. However, close textual study reveals Wieser's impatience with attempts at explaining and refining the logic of the stationary case. He was led perforce to consider at length production in a progressing economy where temporal issues, indeed real historical changes and problems of monetary calculation, were pervasive.

Hennings's (1986: 237) second conclusion was that 'Menger, Böhm-Bawerk and to a lesser extent Wieser, were much more concerned with disequilibrium processes' than early equilibrium economists who dealt with production theory. Again, this is not an accurate portrayal of Wieser's concerns relative to Menger's and Böhm-Bawerk's, especially if his *Social Economics* is given the studious attention it deserves. It should be remembered that *Social Economics* was Wieser's 'last and ripest message on pure theory' (Schumpeter 1951: 300). Our explanation, which includes consideration of *Social Economics*, demonstrates Wieser's concern for ever-changing production plans and uncovers his suggestive hints relating to the strategic influence of monetary factors on these plans in the progressing economy. We have seen how Wieser's capital and interest theory was a special hybrid, composed of mixed doctrinal elements from classical and postclassical or marginalist sources.[30] However, more specifically, in many respects and on many fundamental points his work remained closer to Menger's than to Böhm-Bawerk's ideas. Wieser's avowed intention not to over-generalize the interest concept suggested, like Menger, uneasiness with the notion of interest as a broad macroeconomic category. Very much like Menger, Wieser justified a return to capital from its function as a unique co-operating element in production. Wieser maintained the Mengerian emphasis on the differences among capital goods. While process analysis in the *Ursprung* and in *Natural Value* was diffuse and subdued, Wieser nevertheless made some important digressions on such matters as the diversity of factor combinations; the tendency of factor combinations to change, and the discontinuous nature of production functions. Furthermore, Wieser was not generally inclined to reason in terms of continuous, determinate schedules of demand and supply. In *Social Economics* Wieser's more generous allowance for equilibrating processes *à la* Menger was exemplary.[31]

WIESER'S THEORY OF DISTRIBUTION

It would be misleading to draw the comparisons between Wieser and Menger in such a way that the former might be placed squarely in the Menger tradition. None the less, the existing historical record has neglected points of theoretical convergence between these two leading 'first-generation' Austrians. After all, Menger was not moved to make the charge of a 'great error' in regard to Wieser's construction of a capital and interest theory as he was to do in Böhm-Bawerk's case (Schumpeter 1954: 847 n.). Wieser not only remained loyal to Menger's subjective theory of value; he heeded Menger's fragmentary adumbrations for developing a coherent theory of capital and interest. Above all, right from his first publication in 1876 (Wieser [1876] 1994), Wieser's work had a strong subjectivist quality in keeping in view the forward-looking activities of economizers (entrepreneurs) in using capital goods ultimately to satisfy their needs in consumption. He was, from the outset, less interested in the objects of economizers' activities – the physical properties of inputs such as capital goods. His focus was instead on entrepreneurs' production plans relative to consumption requirements. Wieser subsequently produced a hybrid theory which revealed certain distinguishing characteristics inherited from Menger. These characteristics were particularly discernible, although not exclusively so, in the variant of Wieser's theory which applied to a progressing economy. Wieser's break from the Menger tradition was therefore neither as fundamental nor as decisive as Böhm-Bawerk's.

11

THE FOUNDING AUSTRIAN VERSION OF NEOCLASSICAL MICROECONOMICS: SUMMARY AND CONCLUSIONS

AUSTRIAN ECONOMICS IN THE FORMATIVE YEARS OF NEOCLASSICISM

In the first chapter we cast the problem of interpreting the place of founding Austrian microeconomics in the 'neoclassical' movement from the 1870s in terms of trying to pin down a moving target. The formative years in the development of neoclassical microeconomic theory from the so-called 'marginal revolution' of the 1870s through to advanced twentieth-century refinements in the present always allowed a place for an Austrian branch.

Some elements of the founding Austrian branch were jettisoned in the formative years up to 1930, and other elements were assimilated into mainstream neoclassicism at a later stage. It was therefore submitted in Chapter 1 that the logical structure and completeness of modern neoclassical microeconomics (as evidenced, for example, in a widely used modern textbook such as Kreps 1990) needs to be distinguished from the *history of the development of neoclassical microeconomics*. What has complicated our task in subsequent chapters is a recognition that, just as the neoclassical movement in economic theory from 1870 to the 1920s was not monolithic, there was also nothing uniform about founding Austrian contributions over this period. In fact, at first glance the Walrasian and Marshallian branches of neoclassical economic theory seem to have more identity and homogeneity than the Austrian branch. In reflecting on the historiographical significance of the founding Austrian contributions to microeconomic theory in the history of the development of neoclassical economics, we shall

SUMMARY AND CONCLUSIONS

turn first to a brief survey of some of the recent literature on this subject.

We have Erich Streissler's (1990a: 151) firm conviction that the founding Austrians, Menger, Wieser and Böhm-Bawerk, 'started ...one of the three branches of the marginalist or neoclassical revolution in economics'. Streissler's rather disarming commentary first recounted in very general terms the points of theoretical convergence between all the early neoclassical revolutionaries: a microeconomic approach to economic analysis, an emphasis on individual decision-making and on consumer choice in particular, and extensive use of marginalist concepts. According to Streissler's capsule summary of early developments, 'marginal utility plays a decisive role' in all branches of early neoclassicism, whether Marshallian, Walrasian or Austrian. Wieser was the first to use the felicitous term '*Grenznutzen*' as a substitute for Jevons's 'final degree of utility', and Marshall translated this into the oft-used term, 'marginal utility' (ibid.: 151–2). If there was any sense of competition between the early branches of neoclassicism, on Streissler's reading it soon dissipated: 'they became ever closer as time went by', so that any asserted 'uniqueness' of one branch or other had little of substance for professional economists. By the early twentieth century at the very latest, all leading economists 'were in correspondence with each other; they read each other's works, mostly in the original... and they opened their particular journals to members of the other schools' (ibid.: 152). Now we cannot take issue with this general reading of early developments in neoclassicism and the absorption of Austrian ideas into the main neoclassical movement by the 1920s. However, Streissler's message has since been qualified by several scholars familiar with the history of Austrian economic thought in the 1920s and 1930s.

In the first place, Stephan Boehm (1992: 4) inquired as to whether there was any Austrian school in existence in the interwar period, because he was not clear 'to what extent, if at all, Austrian economists thought of themselves as upholding a tradition setting them apart from other neoclassical streams of thought'. His study revealed a limited 'Austrian self awareness' (ibid.: 22) during the interwar period by comparison with a much stronger identity among Menger, Wieser, Böhm-Bawerk and their followers up to 1914. Second, and reinforcing this view, Karen Vaughn (1994: 8) understood the interwar years as years partly of Austrian assimilation into the mainstream of the academy and partly of Austrian diaspora. Those who assimilated (and they were eminent economists who had left Austria during the 1920's or 1930's, men like Joseph Schumpeter, Fritz Machlup, Oskar Morgenstern, and Gottfried Haberler) carried on inquiry into Austrian theories using accepted neoclassical language and techniques. Those who did not assimilate (Ludwig von Mises...[and] Friedrich Hayek...) existed on the sidelines of academia, marking time and despairing for the future.

As Vaughn's research on the migration of the Austrian tradition to America so well illustrates, this tradition was assimilated into the mainstream. Now this conclusion does not entail that all the innovative doctrines introduced by the founding Austrians up to the 1920s were successfully assimilated. Further, some ideas which were still common currency among Austrians in the Mayer circle were left to languish on the periphery of neoclassicism in the 1930s (Boehm 1992: 22). As Ludwig Lachmann noted in his article 'The Salvage of Ideas' (1982), there was much in founding Austrian economics to rescue and rehabilitate in the post-Second World War years – founding ideas which had not been successfully assimilated into the mainstream of neoclassicism. For example, as we demonstrated in Chapter 9, Lachmann's distinctive treatment of capital in economic theory from the 1940s through to the 1970s, drew heavily on ideas which were ignored in the interwar years. Moreover, in the 'Age of Mises and Hayek', as Kirzner (1994c: viii) called it, between 1940 and 1970 Austrian economics was developed and extended in such a manner that it sharply diverged from the mainstream of neoclassical microeconomics. And we concur with Kirzner that the intellectual roots of this more modern divergence are to be found in the unique insights proffered by the founding Austrian economic theorists.[1]

This is not the place to review the intellectual climate in economics during the interwar years. Nevertheless, that climate produced a rather ironic unintended consequence for our leading, founding Austrian theorists, and for the 'moderns' – Mises and post-1940 Hayek. It emerged that there was 'no continuing basis for emphasizing any uniquely distinctive characteristics of Austrian economic thought' (Kirzner 1994b: xi). In Kirzner's estimation, Robbins (1932) had much to answer for in this connection, since it was a

SUMMARY AND CONCLUSIONS

book which represented to the Anglo-American economics profession everything that was supposedly valid or important in founding Austrian economics up to that time. The evidence presented in Chapters 4 and 5 demonstrated how Robbins in fact misrepresented the Austrians in so far as he was remiss in not producing a faithful and complete rendition of all the important founding Austrian ideas on the nature and scope of economizing behaviour. Robbins's errors of omission and commission were all the more critical given the centrality of hypotheses about choice behaviour in microeconomic theory. Doubtless, Kirzner's (1994b: x) depiction of Austrian economics being 'benignly absorbed circa 1930 into the neoclassical mainstream' raises questions about the sociology of the economics profession at this time, and about the historical significance and relatively weak influence of the Mayer circle on the development of neoclassical microeconomics in the interwar period.[2] Austrian economics in Austria seemed to become more insular in the 1930s and 1940s and most of its prominent theorists had migrated to the USA or the United Kingdom in order to preserve their intellectual freedom.

Kirzner's (1994a: xi) authoritative survey referred to the 'widely held' belief in the economics profession by 1930 that the historical development of neoclassical economic theory had accommodated, absorbed and assimilated all the essential elements of Austrian microeconomics, particularly the notion of opportunity cost, a subjective theory of value and the formal logic-of-choice. Therefore, according to this dominant view, the emergence of founding Austrian economics was a brief episode in the history of economics – an historical curiosity as it were, which was 'benign' in its impact on the advance of microeconomic theory in its Walrasian and Marshallian variants. The problem which must be raised here is that 'benign absorption' by the 1930s implied shedding much of the richness and diversity and many of the unique insights of founding Austrian microeconomics. This implication has not yet been fully appreciated in the literature, perhaps because insufficient attention has been paid to the commonalities (and differences) between the contributions of Menger, Wieser and Böhm-Bawerk – the very subject of this book. It is scarcely surprising that by the early 1950s economists observed the obligation to read founding Austrian treatises more in the breach, usually as part of an antiquarian, 'great man' approach to the history of economic thought. Having surveyed the work of three founding Austrian economists, we can hardly avoid the conclusion that Menger, Wieser and Böhm-Bawerk would have regarded the 'benign absorption' view as at best accurate for only a short episode in the history of economics, and at worst an attempt to efface an intellectual tradition stemming at least from Menger which was doctrinally distinctive in many important respects. To use a metaphor more favourable to the Austrians, it may well have been the case that distinctive founding Austrian contributions to microeconomic theory were in fact excised from mainstream neoclassical theory by 1930 because of their potentially malign influence. That the excising took place in a period of geopolitical upheaval and a great migration of intellectuals, including Austrian economists, might provide a weak explanation; as we suggested in the introduction to Chapter 7, doctrinally biased neglect provides another possible explanation.

It has been our intention throughout this book to subject founding Austrian contributions to detailed analysis with specific reference to microeconomic theory. It is now apposite to sketch some of the Austrian theoretical innovations which have been distilled from our expositions, keeping in mind contemporaneous developments in other branches of neoclassicism.

COMPARING FOUNDING AUSTRIAN MICROECONOMICS WITH ASPECTS OF CONTEMPORARY NEOCLASSICAL ECONOMICS

Historiographical issues

The themes developed in foregoing chapters served as helpful benchmarks against which to compare, as the case demanded, Austrian approaches to specific theoretical problems with alternative approaches adopted by Marshallian or Walrasian branches of the neoclassical movement up to the early 1920s. The year 1923 marked the approximate end-date of our study of special topics in founding Austrian microeconomics – that year marking the publication date of Menger's second posthumous edition of the *Principles*. Wieser's work in microeconomics was completed in 1914 with the publication of *Social Economics*, and Böhm-Bawerk's final (fourth) posthumous edition of *Positive Theory* was completed in 1921. Accordingly, only broad developments in other branches of neoclassicism up to about 1920 would make relevant comparisons with founding Austrian approaches.

SUMMARY AND CONCLUSIONS

The dangers of taking an unqualified, extremely anachronistic perspective on both Austrian economics up to about 1923 and other branches of early neoclassical economics must be faced squarely. To compare founding Austrian microeconomics with, for example, the content and logic of neoclassical economics post-1950 carries with it the danger of neglecting those uniquely Austrian styles of reasoning and the distinctive insights which it had to offer on specific analytic problems of interest to economists both then and now. Many of those insights were not absorbed successfully into the neoclassical mainstream. The danger of obscuring the pioneering, innovatory contributions of Menger, Wieser and Böhm-Bawerk, *in context*, are heightened by historically inaccurate definitions of neoclassical economics. It has been our contention that the founding Austrians were part of a broad postclassical movement in economic theory which had several branches developing in tandem between the 1870s and the 1920s. Therefore the expectation in modern treatments of founding Austrian economics that past theorists such as Menger should have 'put all the pieces together' according to some modern standard of judgement is misplaced. Karen Vaughn offered a prime example of this approach to the historiography of Austrian economics:

> The economic theory that he [Menger] espoused...began with a theory of individual action that was very similar to, but not identical with, neoclassical economics. That he *never completely managed to put all the pieces together* explains many of the conflicts in Menger scholarship.
>
> (1994: 16; emphasis added)

In addition, Kirzner (1994b: xiii) stated a similar view: that 'it was the Mengerian subjectivist legacy, *with all its incompleteness*, which was to inspire...subsequent developments in Austrian economics' (emphasis added). The charges of 'not putting *all* the pieces together' and of 'incompleteness' would apply to all branches of neoclassicism up to the 1920s, not just the Austrian one.[3] That is why it should be insisted that statements or expositions in the history of neoclassical economic theory should be clearly separated from statements which use the logic and so-called completeness of some modern theoretical perspective – Austrian or otherwise. That way two interpretative advantages become evident. First, confusion generated from historical oversimplifications of 'neoclassical' economics may be avoided.[4] Second, from the standpoint of founding

Austrian economics appreciated in context, anachronistic readings from a modern neoclassical viewpoint which eclipse or erase early distinctive insights will be rendered transparent.

Scope and Method of Economics

Early Austrian styles of reasoning paralleled only in some respects the styles of Jevons and Walras: all possessed a desire to develop the purely theoretical branch of political economy, starting with an analysis of consumer choice. There were important differences in the Austrian impulse to focus at the outset on building a means–ends, economizing framework in great detail and to analyse the interplay between humans and their need for goods. In this the Austrians drew upon a rich German classical and historical economics literature – only Alfred Marshall in another early branch of neoclassicism could be said to have been influenced by this German stream of thought, although substantive links between German economic thought and Marshall's *Principles* of 1890 are very indirect and should not be exaggerated. Parenthetically, the Austrians, like Marshall believed that they were building on the work of predecessors (Marshall paid obeisance to English classical economists) in a manner which was hardly revolutionary, whereas Jevons and Walras, rightly or wrongly, held that their contributions marked significant breaks with the past.

One finding in Chapter 2 above bears repeating here: Menger desired to concentrate debate in the *Methodenstreit* on the risks of taking a 'one-sided' attitude to the development of economic science; he was tolerant of all the avenues of inquiry – statistical or historical, theoretical or applied policy-orientated work. Perhaps more might be made of Menger's plea for methodological tolerance or even pluralism, since it closely mirrored Marshall's broad-minded attitude (Coase 1975). Menger's frequent use of what he called empirical-theoretical reasoning, and his employment of conjectural histories (see Chapter 5 above), are good illustrations of his methodology in practice. Böhm-Bawerk's distinction between a general theory of price (along Mengerian exact-theoretical lines) and a more applied theory of price involving variation in concrete market circumstances (see Chapter 6 above) provide a further example of the founding Austrian interest in lowering the level of abstraction of microeconomic theory. Lately, Léon Walras's conception of economics as a social science has been shown to be far closer to

SUMMARY AND CONCLUSIONS

Menger's general position than previously recognized.[5] Walras took for granted that a many-sided economic science would evolve as economists of all persuasions, using a wide variety of reasoning styles, devoted more time to economic research. In 1883, in correspondence with Menger, Walras expressed impatience with Menger's methodological questions: 'For heaven's sake, stop asking how science can best be done – do it any way you like, but do it!'.[6]

In their microeconomics the Austrians did not share Jevons's, Edgeworth's, Walras's or Pareto's enthusiasm for mathematics. The concept of causality implied by the use of Walras-type, functional-mathematical reasoning did not suit the Austrian philosophic bent. A penchant for one-way causal relations rather than mutual causality also explains the Austrian reluctance to use schedular representations of demand and supply, even though they would have been aware of them in German classical economic theory (e.g. in Rau). The concept of genetic causality which we addressed at several points in the foregoing chapters gave rise to Menger's insistence that all economic phenomena must be traced back to their 'true elements' or to their genetic determinants in human nature. This insistence doubtless had biological connotations (Vaughn 1994: 7); but for the economist *qua* economist writing on microeconomic theory, this notion of genetic causality concentrated the analyst's mind on important microfoundations of the economy, viz., individual needs, and acts of choice or decision flowing from those needs.

Choice Theory

Founding Austrian theoretical constructs of choice behaviour and of the individual decision diverged significantly from other neoclassical, logic-of-choice models which were emerging at about the same time. There was no antinomy here between Menger, Wieser and Böhm-Bawerk on the one hand, and (say) Jevons, Walras, Pareto and Wicksteed on the other. Only a broader focus of attention marked the founding Austrian approach to choice. The Austrian perspective included as part of its conceptual tools, the pure logic-of-choice (recall, for example Wieser's proto-logic-of-choice expressions). The pure logic-of-choice was formulated in a fully refined manner only in the 1920s, most notably in the second-generation Austrian tradition by Strigl (1923).

The founding Austrian analysis of choice conceived as economizing behaviour had two dimensions: first, a loose, static logic-of-choice model which did not clearly specify constraints on choice and which merely approached the brink of perceiving choice as a problem of constrained maximization; and, second, a more open-ended, dynamically subjectivist formulation which admitted insights from cognate social science disciplines. The latter deserves more attention in the literature on Menger, Wieser and Böhm-Bawerk, because it defines their broader vision of economizing as compared with other early neoclassicists. The second dimension was supplementary in the case, for example, of Menger, who, as we demonstrated, placed the statically subjectivist model of economizing side by side with a dynamically subjectivist model. Both these models, and the research techniques which are to be employed in each case, reflected perfectly his methodological preconceptions – that is, an asserted harmony between exact-theoretical and empirical-theoretical reasoning respectively. Menger's explanations or models of economizing of both kinds were purveyors of different types of knowledge for the economist.

Among other contemporary neoclassical economists, only Alfred Marshall seems to have recognized that economists could fruitfully analyse economizing behaviour along less static, mechanistic lines (perhaps because of his extensive reading of German literature on the subject). As we have demonstrated elsewhere, Marshall's study of consumer choice did not require elaborate axiomatization of economizing; his discussion of consumers' needs-hierarchies and the growth of needs did not contradict contemporary Austrian treatments. Indeed, like some of the founding Austrians, Marshall introduced a logic-of-choice formulation (in terms of utility maximization) but hastened to move beyond it towards a process conception of economizing ('deliberateness'). He relied on this conception to place the analysis of choice in time. Finally, like the Austrians, Marshall did not forge strong links between static utility maximization and the demand schedule (Endres 1991c).[7]

Increasingly as the founding Austrians developed the economizing concept, they came to understand the value of making further theoretical investigations which proceeded beyond the restrictive logic-of-choice framework. Menger's discussion of the scope of economizing and of the structure and growth of needs in the process of economic development, and Wieser's stress on the ethical ends of economizing, highlighted the early Austrian interest in what we have called the 'second dimension' of choice. As the Austrian branch of neoclassicism unfolded, the concept of marginal utility conceived in a more mathematical sense, as an increment of utility with respect to a change in quantity consumed, became less opaque, especially in the work of Wieser and Böhm-Bawerk. Nevertheless, it is still valid to report that maximization is a mathematical procedure imposed by other branches of neoclassicism on the acting economizer – a procedure that the founding Austrians were loath to follow closely. Wieser seemed to grasp the concept clearly, even if he did not use mathematical terminology *à la* Jevons, Walras or Marshall.

In the founding Austrian economists' reflections on the measurability of utility, there are vestigial elements in Böhm-Bawerk's work suggesting cardinality, which was the hallmark, for instance, of early logic-of-choice models in general and of deterministic formulations in Jevons and Edgeworth. That Böhm-Bawerk was rebuked by Čuhel nicely demonstrated the highly subjectivist, ordinalist approach to utility and its measurement (intrapersonally) by the acting economizer (*not* the analyst) which had been signalled by Menger and supported by Wieser. The dynamically subjectivist dimension in Böhm-Bawerk's work was not swamped, however, because he could not bring himself to deny a significant role for imagination in the human valuation process. Finally, all the founding Austrians may be distinguished from their contemporary neoclassical counterparts on the grounds that the former were united in admitting the internal operation of the human mind into their theoretical investigations. In this they broached a difficult, intractable field of research, which some would maintain is the preserve of social sciences other than economics.

Price Theory

In our review of Austrian price theory, just as in other matters, there are *both* correspondences and dissonances with other contemporary branches of neoclassicism. Stephan Boehm (1992: 13) stated the issue we are concerned with here in a concise manner: 'If Austrian theory is neither partial equilibrium analysis in the Marshallian nor general equilibrium in the Walrasian sense, what is it?' This book has offered several responses to this question for Austrian microeconomics up to the 1920s. A central conclusion has been that Austrian price theory concentrated on equilibrating processes rather than equilibrium end-states. It is undeniable that the notion of equilibrium was an important reference point for early Austrian price theory, but that is just about as far as it goes.[8]

NEOCLASSICAL MICROECONOMIC THEORY

In founding Austrian economics there are superficial parallels with Marshallian and Walrasian approaches which concentrated on equilibrium outcomes of one form or another. For Menger and Böhm-Bawerk, however, the purpose of price theory was to explain the process of equilibration in markets where there are limited numbers of participants, where those participants have limits on their knowledge of relevant data (including the potential effects of their individual actions on other participants) and where the goods traded can exhibit significant degrees of indivisibility. In studying Menger's ideas on price formation, we drew a distinction between equilibrating processes leading to supply constrained price distributions, and equilibrating processes leading to market clearing, equilibrating price outcomes. The latter resemble Walrasian equilibria, but there is no clear mandate from Menger's *Principles* which would permit this comparison to be pressed too hard. Menger did not reflect on instantaneous, multi-market clearing in which all markets are interdependent and price is the only prominent variable. Instead, Menger's illustrations, like Böhm-Bawerk's, were generally of equilibrating tendencies in single-market settings where trading took place without the need to invoke some general economic equilibrium.[9]

In Menger's work there is a clear reluctance to aggregate: that is, to move from an analysis of individual bids and offers in auction market contexts to market demand and supply relations. By contrast, aggregation in this sense was not regarded as problematic for Jevons, Walras, Edgeworth or Marshall. In both Menger's and Böhm-Bawerk's theories of price formation there is no resort to smooth functional-mathematical expressions of demand and supply relations. And, while his theorizing on the individual's mental construction of what he called 'demand series' in an auction context had definite Marshallian connotations (Chapter 8), Wieser did not express this series in schedular terms. In the founding Austrian view, individuals' bid and offer valuations were generated in an entirely subjective, genetic-causal process by the creative imagination; such valuations were heterogeneous and not easily captured by schedular or functional constructs. Functional constructs also relied on the *ceteris paribus* condition not usually employed by the Austrians. The active interaction of these individual valuations in an interpersonal market process generated prices at which goods were actually traded. To most contemporary neoclassicists these prices were the objective facts of the market, but not so to the founding Austrians.

SUMMARY AND CONCLUSIONS

Trading prices were regarded by the Austrians as subjective outcomes in the sense that as 'data' of market outcomes they were readily recomposable by the ultimate generative causes of price: namely, the everyday decisions flowing through the imaginative filter which was the human mind. Moreover, in many cases of price formation considered by Menger and Böhm-Bawerk, individual market participants can make a difference to trading prices by bargaining in conditions of less than uniform information between traders. In Böhm-Bawerk's *Positive Theory of Capital*, there was dispersed information among potential traders at the opening of an auction market, and some 'recontracting' process reminiscent of Edgeworth seems to have been assumed before trading took place. Similarly, in Menger's work an Edgeworth–Bowley rational reconstruction may be applied by the historian at certain points relating to isolated exchange. The reconstruction we attempted in Chapter 5 was imperfect and speculative because neither Menger nor Böhm-Bawerk mentioned Edgeworth. We drew similar conclusions when attempting to locate Menger's ideas on monopoly pricing in a Marshallian price discrimination framework. Böhm-Bawerk's demand–supply equilibrium analysis could be placed in the short-period price determination model of Alfred Marshall, but only, as we noted, in the face of Böhm-Bawerk's expressed protest.

Any standard modern textbook in neoclassical microeconomic theory now includes detailed consideration of the theory of games and bargaining behaviour (e.g. Kreps 1990: 355–576). In this connection we have offered evidence on how the founding Austrians came to understand the crucial importance of bargaining with incomplete information in different market settings, and of strategic behaviour in those settings. Menger's notion of price conflict, and Böhm-Bawerk's ideas on price formation in auction markets, possessed game-theoretic elements. Indeed, the theory of games has intellectual linkages to Menger's and Böhm-Bawerk's auction market constructions. The institutional arrangements and bargaining protocols in those constructions were, however, rather unclear. As we currently understand the content of neoclassical microeconomics, which might be said to include a game-theoretic dimension, the founding Austrian branch of neoclassicism can be regarded as a fitting precursor. And, in so far as modern Austrian economics in its Kirznerian form conceives of the market as a process in which equilibrating forces are predominant, founding Austrian price theorists are also appropriately regarded as precursors because they too stressed the equilibrating features of markets.[10]

Conceptions of competition

The wide compass of founding Austrian ideas on the nature of competition in markets is nicely outlined by Hayek (1948). For, like Menger, Wieser and Böhm-Bawerk, Hayek was firmly opposed to treating knowledge solely as a precondition for competition conceived as a form of human behaviour in markets. Competition for the Austrians involved change in market circumstances prompted by learning on the part of market participants.

In Chapter 7 above, the Mengerian conception of competition is presented as a situation of price conflict among rival-conscious individuals. Sometimes competitors were spatially dispersed, and asymmetric information usually prevailed. Mengerian competition thus often produced price variance or dispersion in markets. Menger's conception was contrasted with the Walras–Pareto vision of competition as a situation where individuals faced fixed conditions, including given prices, and merely adapted uniformly to these conditions to attain maximum returns from exchange. There are no formally established, perfectly competitive structures adumbrated in any founding Austrian treatise, and to this extent they diverged from all the other branches of contemporary neoclassicism, which were grounded in more complete perfectly competitive settings (especially those of Walras, Pareto and Edgeworth). Yet, like Cournot (before them) and Edgeworth, the founding Austrians were inclined to begin their studies of competition in the context of isolated exchange and personalized bargaining in situations of bilateral monopoly; more complex arrangements were analysed later (Streissler and Weber 1973: 230).

Austrian competition was an activity implying the absence of equilibrium in exchange. In Böhm-Bawerk's discussion of wage-fixing, for example, he avoided concentration on what we might regard as a contemporary Clarkian or Marshallian approach to the derived demand for labour; and he was quick to move on from simple marginal productivity explanations of wage determination in the labour market equilibrium state. Instead the competitive wage bargaining process involving negotiation and strategic interaction was emphasized. The long-run wage outcomes of these interactions between employers and employees might be consistent

SUMMARY AND CONCLUSIONS

with marginal productivity explanations, but there was nothing perfectly competitive about the process of reaching this state. Like Menger and Wieser, Böhm-Bawerk was uneasy reasoning with the notion that competitive processes be regarded as terminated; the task of the Austrians was to explain in detail how competition might eventually be completed. Their explanations turned on the idea that the knowledge content of decisions taken in rivalrous situations had to generate plan co-ordination among market participants. These explanations supplemented other contemporary neoclassical branches which analysed the properties of equilibrium states. In Wieser's study of the institutional aspects of competition between social groups, the observable outcome of competition conceived in these terms was social conflict and much discoordination among market participants. There were no counterparts to Wieser's analysis in other branches of contemporary neoclassicism.

Capital and distribution theory

Our final points of comparison between founding Austrian microeconomics and other emerging branches of neoclassicism turn on respective concepts of capital, interest and general distribution theory. Böhm-Bawerk's concept of capital as produced material instruments of production, coupled with the notion of capital as a 'fund' built up in the past and advanced into the future over some production interval, was clearly classical in origin. The entrepreneur's role in this theory was to choose the optimal length of the production period. Jevons also formulated a similar conception, with Jevonian capital theory based on the twin ideas of a subsistence fund of capital *advanced* over a definite period of time. Right up to the fourth and final edition of the *Positive Theory of Capital*, Böhm-Bawerk (1959b: 34–66) quibbled over the differences between his concept of the nature of capital and those of other contemporary neoclassicists – Jevons, Marshall, J. B. Clark and Fisher. There were indeed important differences in the definition of capital between these economists. Overall, Böhm-Bawerk's theory of capital had much more in common with Jevons than any other. And Knut Wicksell fused Böhm-Bawerkian capital theory with the general equilibrium ideas of Léon Walras; Wicksell produced a hybrid, advances theory of capital in the early Swedish branch of neoclassicism during the 1890s and early 1900s. (Blyth 1987; Garrison 1990: 144–53).

So while there were important intellectual linkages between Böhm-Bawerk's theory of capital and that of other neoclassicists outside the founding Austrian branch, Menger, by contrast, offered a capital concept which was unique. Menger was the first among emerging neoclassicists to emphasize that the meaning of capital must be obtained by insight into the minds of everyday decision-makers who use capital. Capital for Menger was not an aggregate of physical or social instruments of production, as Böhm-Bawerk and many other neoclassicists regarded it. In the entrepreneur's mind capital was a monetary fund of prospective values flowing from consumers' valuations of goods produced by entrepreneurs' assets. These assets are specially allocated into capital combinations with the intention to produce specific consumer goods. Like Böhm-Bawerk, Wieser and some other neoclassicists, Menger developed a forward-looking notion of capital, but Menger above all stressed the *exclusively* forward-looking nature of capital. Capital combinations were created by entrepreneurs' plans. Capital formation and the production it entailed were not ultimately technical or engineering phenomena; they were highly subjective activities orientated towards an uncertain future and relying on the creative imagination of entrepreneurs who responded to the prospective demand for consumers' goods. Likewise Menger hinted that interest on capital was a subjective phenomenon – in keeping with developments in the American branch of neoclassical economics led by F. A. Fetter which made time preference a central element explaining interest.[11]

Wieser departed from contemporary neoclassical ideas on the nature of capital by rejecting identification of capital with a monetary sum or with a subsistence fund made up of the aggregate instruments of production. It is noteworthy, as pointed out in Chapter 10, that Wicksell (and later Hayek) adopted Wieser's expression of the form and content of capital; capital comprised exhaustible natural resources *and* the technically produced means of production. Wieser's attempt to impute the return on capital did not employ the standard Marshallian abstraction of a market-supply schedule of capital. Furthermore, in Wieser's distribution theory taken as a whole the following typically founding Austrian emphases were observed:

1 There were manifold, uniquely distinguishable indivisible factor inputs associated with the production of specific consumer goods – hence the Wieserian (and Mengerian) reluctance to aggregate factors into homogeneous classes.

SUMMARY AND CONCLUSIONS

2 Factor complementarity was strongly associated with the wide diversity of capital combinations, and the possibility of smooth factor substitutability was not integrated fully into the imputation of factor values.
3 The valuation of factor inputs was an equilibrating process involving unidirectional causal sequences beginning with consumers' marginal utility valuations of outputs; mutual determination of input and output values in a general equilibrium sense *à la* Walras was inadmissible.

We had occasion to remark in Chapters 9 and 10 that other contemporary neoclassicists, including Edgeworth, Marshall and J. B. Clark, found objectionable one or other of these aspects of Austrian distribution theory. But there were other aspects of this theory in keeping with the general trend of neoclassical thought at this time: assumed 'fixed' nature of factor supplies, however 'fixity' was conceived; given technical co-efficients of production in each industry or production process; a loose notion of the marginal product of an input; and given output values. However, the Austrians, especially Menger, were more guarded about the latter in preferring to state output values as always prospective and therefore uncertain.

When considering Wieser's theories of capital and distribution in a 'progressing economy' in Chapter 10, we observed how some of the uniquely Mengerian themes noticed in earlier chapters came to the fore yet again. Wieser allowed for equilibrating processes, and the prominent position he gave to the capital-using plans of entrepreneurs provided fine examples of his founding Austrian heritage. To be sure, the most arresting element, which remained in the Austrian branch of neoclassicism from its earliest beginnings, was, as Kirzner (1994b: xix) stated it, a recognition of 'the role of the entrepreneurial market *process* in transmitting consumer valuations of consumer goods to the resources from which those consumer goods are produced' (his emphasis). In Wieser's work this idea lived on in his distribution theory and was mixed with many other classical and non-Austrian neoclassical ideas which had obviously influenced him up to the writing of *Social Economics* in 1914.

ENDURING CONTINUITIES IN FOUNDING AUSTRIAN ECONOMICS

It should now be established that Menger, Wieser and Böhm-Bawerk offered a distinctive version of neoclassical microeconomics, despite intermittent similarities with other contemporary branches of neoclassical economics. What, then, were the enduring threads that unified the founding Austrians into a theoretical tradition within the emerging neoclassical movement? When enumerated by extracting the theoretical points of commonality from each of the foregoing chapters, the complementarities between founding Austrian contributions prove to be substantial.

Conceptions of economics

1 German economic thought in the nineteenth century was their common heritage, even if they made differential use of that intellectual background. But their common intention to study the administration of resources in all its forms, and that of goods in particular, served as a basis for the Austrian science of national and human economy.
2 Although there were differences in their conceptions of economic theory at the margin, we demonstrated in Chapter 2 that their reasoning styles embodied both 'exact-theoretical' and 'empirical-theoretical' components. The three founding Austrians used different terminology to classify their theoretical endeavours, and all were tolerant of the different types of economic analysis: theoretical work at different levels of abstraction; historical-statistical work; and applied, policy-orientated economics.
3 The prime objective was to offer a sounder micro-theoretical foundation for economic science.
4 The individual decision to value and use goods formed the starting-point for Austrian microeconomics.

Economizing behaviour

5 There was a general appreciation of how a formal logic-of-choice may be constructed to analyse choice, but all three founding Austrians provided additional foundations for a broader analysis. They used interdisciplinary perspectives, from psychology, biology and ethics, to comment on valuation processes, the nature, structure and growth of needs, and the ends of economizing behaviour.
6 Menger and Wieser considered subjective value or utility as an intrinsically ordinal notion, as did Böhm-Bawerk – although Böhm-Bawerk flirted with the idea of an objective measurement scale for the intensity of utility.

SUMMARY AND CONCLUSIONS

7 There was generous allowance for the development of a non-mechanistic science of choice, the first general principle of which was an intrapersonal, genetic-causal valuation process. Valuation originated in the individual's creative imagination.

Price formation

8 By reasoning in terms of price ranges, the founding Austrians studied the process of price formation in terms of bargaining in auction market settings. Their illustrations often involved a small number of bargainers, and significantly indivisible goods available for exchange.
9 Transaction prices (exchange values) were produced by bargaining or, in modern Austrian language, by human action.
10 Illustrations of price formation allowed for extensive knowledge problems or, alternatively expressed, for different information structures. Subsequent bid–offer interaction and trading on markets had game-theoretic connotations.
11 Dynamic equilibrating processes were treated at length; equilibrium end-states were recognized but not greatly elaborated.

Competition

12 Competition for the founding Austrians was a form of rivalrous, strategic behaviour. It was always changing market circumstances; some strategies inevitably falter, others are successful. Competition generated changes in knowledge (or changes in competitors' plans).
13 Personalized bargaining was the essence of competition, and bargaining presupposed dispersion, rather than uniformity, of information among market participants.
14 Perfect competition as a formal structure or end-state did not figure prominently. In all illustrations (as compared with the theory of perfect competition) the number of bargainers is relatively small.
15 Diverse competitive arrangements are a feature of founding Austrian discussion: bilateral monopoly, large monopoly-type situations, oligopsony and more organized competitive activities on auction markets. All these situations were regarded as potentially changeable through time. Market depth, time and space considerations were critical; sometimes they led to price

variance for the 'same' goods consistently with the Austrian theory of price ranges.

Capital and distribution theory

16 Capital is created by forward-looking entrepreneurs.
17 Capital is a combination of complementary goods used by entrepreneurs who plan to produce outputs in response to the *prospect* of consumers' valuing those outputs. Uncertainty associated with future consumers' valuations makes entrepreneurs' plans contingent, heterogeneous and revisable. Hence the capital structure of a production process (and an economy) may change with the creation of new, diverse capital combinations.
18 Production processes in time do not exhibit smooth factor substitutability; quantities of factors were not conceived as being distributed along schedules relating quantities and prices in functional form. The impulse for discrete changes in a factor combination issued from the subjective filter of the entrepreneur's mind.
19 The imputation of factor values started with consumers' subjective valuation of outputs. Consumers' valuations are the ultimate causes of factor values. The unidirectional causal sequence from consumer valuation to output valuation was preferred over the concept of mutual determination.

There were many other ideas, presented in previous chapters, which, far from suggesting a common position on specific microeconomic matters, showed much diversity among the founding Austrians. This was hardly unusual. Theoretical diversity was also a feature of all other branches of emerging neoclassicism up to the 1930s. Given the points of continuity presented above, specific instances of disagreement among the founding Austrians are not evidence of a general lack of theoretical cohesiveness in the Austrian branch of neoclassicism. That Böhm-Bawerk and Wieser lacked the more thoroughgoing subjectivism of Menger, for example, seems to be a modern Austrian complaint. Such complaints may be valid (in respect of Böhm-Bawerk, for instance, as we saw in Chapter 9), but they should not detract from all the piquant insights in the microeconomics of Wieser and Böhm-Bawerk which have been bequeathed to us.

SUMMARY AND CONCLUSIONS

For modern Austro-American market process theorists, 'the work of Menger, Böhm-Bawerk and Wieser was historically significant primarily in that it *pointed beyond itself to a more fully subjectivist tradition* which that work was to generate' (Kirzner 1994a: xxvi; emphasis added). The founding Austrians may not, as a group, have seen the 'fully subjectivist' outcome before its time. As founders of one branch of neoclassicism they certainly did not predict the direction which the mainstream of neoclassicism would take from the mid-twentieth century, which proved to be hostile to many of their ideas. It has been the object of this book to bring out all the indications and suggestions that 'pointed beyond' their contributions, towards further research in a distinctive Austrian tradition: on the scope and method of economics, economizing behaviour, price theory, competition, and capital and distribution theory. According to an old story, Menger began writing his *Principles* with much excitement. We complete this study with a sense of the intellectual excitement which Menger was able to impart to Wieser, Böhm-Bawerk and beyond.

NOTES

1 IN WHAT SENSES WERE THE FOUNDING AUSTRIANS 'NEOCLASSICAL' ECONOMISTS?

1 See Kirzner 1992: 57–138 on the emergence of the Austrian perspective out of Menger's seminal work in 1871.
2 In the following chapters of this book, unless otherwise stated, all references to the *Principles of Economics* will be to the 1950 translation, which was reprinted by New York University Press in 1976.
3 See Kirzner 1994c: ix–xi.
4 The best general source on the marginalist revolution is still Black et al. 1973. The 'Mengerian roots' of the modern resurgence of Austrian economics are examined by Vaughn 1990.
5 On the origins of the term 'neoclassical' in economics, see Aspromourgos 1987.
6 See, for example, Stigler 1941; Schumpeter 1954.
7 There is an extensive literature on the 'classical liberal' ideological outlook of the Austrian school taken as a whole, some of which ignores important differences between leading Austrians since Menger. See Boehm 1985; Kirzner 1990a; Cubeddu 1993; Raico 1994; Boettke 1995.
8 For a devastating rebuttal of the main points in Mirowski 1984, see Hollander 1989. Hollander demonstrated that Mirowski did not give systematic attention to detail in classical and neoclassical texts. Mirowski was therefore guilty of isolating specific utterances in those texts from which he uncritically generalized.
9 But see Fritz Machlup's view on the essentials of Austrian economics as expounded by Kirzner 1994a: xviii–xix.
10 We may agree with Max Alter (1990a: 8) on the general point that 'Menger was a neoclassical economist despite the differences which set him off against all other neoclassical trends', but throughout this book we shall have frequent occasion to take exception to many of Alter's interpretative pronouncements on Menger's, Wieser's and Böhm-Bawerk's contributions to economic theory. See also Alter 1982; 1986; 1990b. Alter's promotion of 'the dubious idea that Menger's ideas cannot be properly discussed in English' (White 1990: 349) is without merit; the results of research reported in English in the following chapters should

persuade readers otherwise. For a scathing review of Alter 1990a, see Boettke 1992. We remain, nevertheless, sensitive throughout to Sir John Hicks's (1951: 853) warning that Menger's work 'cannot be effectively translated into English by being forced into terminology which is strange to it, and which – at its best – it transcends'.

11 Our tripartite division is not useful for all purposes. The simple division is made here to draw out general differences between the emerging branches of neoclassicism on matters of economic theory. It is indisputable that there were significant differences within these branches as they emerged and matured by the mid-twentieth century.

2 THE FOUNDING AUSTRIAN CONCEPTIONS OF ECONOMICS

1 See, for example, Grassl and Smith 1986; Milford 1990; Birner 1990; Mäki 1990; Alter 1990a; Cubeddu 1993.
2 See Bostaph 1978; 1994.
3 Such examinations have been conducted extensively elsewhere. See White 1985; Hutchison 1953: 145–51 and 1981: 176–202 and the Bostaph articles referred to in n. 2 above.
4 For an informative debate on the origins and uses of the terms 'economics' and 'political economy', including various continental European uses, see Groenewegen 1985; 1987; Arndt 1984; 1985.
5 This may be an accurate depiction of cameralistic literature prior to the nineteenth century, but see Tribe 1988 for a systematic analysis of the transformation of German cameralism in the nineteenth century.
6 See Menger's 1876 lectures to Crown Prince Rudolf of Austria where this point is made clear (Menger [1876] 1994: 32–3). In those lectures, Menger did not provide a place for the historical and statistical branch of political economy, although he refers to the practical study of economic policy which utilizes 'experiences gathered over time' (ibid.: 31).
7 Hutchison (1981: 198) observed that, for Menger, '*Einseitigkeit* [one-sidedness] on whatever side or in whatever direction, was the intellectual sin that Menger was specially and constantly concerned to condemn; and on most of the broad controversial questions that he discussed, he himself never resorted to an extreme or exclusivist position, on issues as to which economists' views have often become unreasonably polarized.'
8 In fact, Menger's theory of price formation in the *Principles* is a superb illustration of his recommendation that both exact-theoretical and empirical-theoretical research must be used in tandem. See Chapter 5 below.
9 For recent critical appraisal of Menger's classification, especially with reference to the problem of theory evaluation in the Mengerian system, see Milford 1990; Birner 1990. For a more sympathetic, modern reconstruction of Menger's methodology which argued that Menger can be interpreted as espousing 'realism' in all its different forms, see Mäki 1990.

NOTES

10 Menger's correspondence with Walras on this matter is discussed by Jaffé 1976: 520–2.
11 For Wieser, economic theory 'is not conceived unempirically' ([1914] 1927: 6). And elsewhere Wieser ([1911] 1994b: 294) claimed that 'the assumptions which the psychological school uses are all empirical'.
12 Donald Winch (1972: 331) interpreted Menger's exact-theorizing as a process seeking 'direct understanding of the reasons for the existence of objects [and presumably human actions] and proceed[ing] by constructing exact types and typical relations between them'. Wieser's theories of the 'natural economy' ([1889] 1930) and of the 'simple economy' ([1914] 1927) were completely in accord with Menger's exact-theorizing, even if Wieser's classification of the types of economic theory was less detailed and less sophisticated than Menger's.
13 Max Alter (1990a: 222–4) made much of the differences which are regarded here as mostly terminological. Alter gives these differences a deeper philosophical and methodological significance. According to Alter, 'in several important aspects of Menger's scientific conception of social reality' the founding Austrians diverged (ibid.: 223). To be sure, Wieser departed from Menger in distinguishing sharply between the methods of the natural sciences, and those of the social sciences which included economics. While granting this difference, it makes no substantial difference to our expositions of the contributions of Menger and Wieser to important aspects of economic theory in the following chapters.
14 This claim contrasts sharply with the standard history-of-economic-thought version of Menger's *Principles*. For instance, according to Hennings (1987: 225), in 'his *Grundsätze der Volkswirtschaftslehre* (1871), Menger had developed an atemporal theory of value, allocation and exchange' (emphasis added). Zuidema (1988: 22) read the *Principles* differently: 'In Menger's view the evaluation of the consumer has a time dimension.' The latter view comes close to many specific interpretations advanced in the following chapters.
15 Menger used the term *Güterordnungen*. See Menger 1871: 8.
16 Of course there was little that was completely new about Menger's theory of goods and his theory of the hierarchy of goods. German textbook writers – Roscher and Rau in particular – began by discussing the theory of goods rather than the theory of price determination as neoclassical texts usually do now. The influence of Roscher and Rau on Menger has already been mentioned; their influence on specific aspects of his early work, especially on Menger's drafts of the *Principles*, is explored by Yagi 1993: 703–7.
17 Cf. also Böhm-Bawerk's comment that 'we must seek to understand the laws, according to which we pursue our interests when they are entangled with the interests of others' (1891: 379).
18 As an aside, ostensibly distinguishing the Austrian perspective from that of Marshall, Böhm-Bawerk proceeded to chide any 'eclectic vacillation' turning on supply-and-demand explanations for the value of producers' goods. By Böhm-Bawerk's analogy, Marshall's position was like having 'the earth turning about the sun and the sun turning

NOTES

about the earth alternately'. Later he referred to the 'shibboleth of "supply and demand"' (Böhm-Bawerk 1891: 371, 382).

3 CARL MENGER'S ANALYSIS OF CHOICE

1 F. W. Fetter, an Austro-American writer was also mentioned (Robbins [1932] 1984: 16 n. 1) In the *Essay*, Robbins included frequent references to the work of other Austrian economists, including Wieser, Böhm-Bawerk, Amonn, Hayek, Kaufmann, Mayer, Morgenstern, Rosenstein-Rodan and Schönfeld.
2 In a review of Strigl 1923, Haberler ([1923–4] 1994: 223) neatly summarized Strigl's formulation of the pure logic of choice: 'the data must be constant and the scale of values must have a special form. Present and future needs must be equally highly valued – otherwise it is not possible that the same economic sequence will repeat itself year in, year out.'
3 As Addleson (1984a: 518) observed, Robbins and Mises held in common the view that 'enquiries into "causes" of ends take us out of the realm of economics into the field of psychology'.
4 These explorations, among other things, opened up a sharp doctrinal division prior to 1930 between Menger, Wieser and Böhm-Bawerk, and 'second-generation' Austrians including Mayer, Mises, Rosenstein-Rodan and Strigl. As one contemporary familiar with Austrian economics concluded, there were 'two quite distinct lines of development among those who professed allegiance to the established [Austrian] tradition' (Sweezy 1934: 176; see also Kauder 1965: 105).
5 All page references to the *Principles* refer to Menger [1871] 1950, the English translation of the original 1871 edition, unless otherwise stated. Menger 1871 is used for 'equivalent' German terms where necessary. Menger 1923 will also be referred to where there are significant changes from Menger [1871] 1950.
6 Jaffé 1976: 522, Pribram 1983: 290 and Endres 1984 have seen Menger's non-maximization principle as setting Menger apart from other leading marginalists, Jevons and Walras. Procrustean histories of economic thought which classify Menger's concept of economizing as a mere verbal and/or imprecise version of sophisticated mathematical marginalist-choice models of Jevons, Walras and Pareto will no longer suffice.
7 This point is explored at length by Alter 1990a: 199–201.
8 According to McCulloch (1977: 250), Menger's 'starting point for inferences about the subjective importance of goods is a subjective rank ordering of the set of all wants which arranges them in the order of their importance to the individual'.
9 The editors of these lectures, E. Streissler and M. Streissler, note that this 'is the only time that the idea of (marginal) utility decreasing with increasing wealth crops up' (Menger [1876] 1994: 37 n. 14). Perhaps so, but it was marginal utility of a loose, ordinal type despite the use of the mathematical notion of proportionality. The historical background to this idea of marginal utility in nineteenth-century German economics is

also elaborated in the editors' note. It should be added that the 'Rudolf Lectures' are the written record of Prince Rudolf who, in effect, wrote through the influence of Menger.

10 This interpretation is also consistent with Hutchison 1953: 141, and High and Bloch 1989: 351.

11 These phrases are also used at other points in the *Principles*. See Menger [1871] 1950: 128, 131, 180, 192. It is notable that 'maximization' finds no place in these passages.

12 See Ekelund, Furubotn and Gram 1972: 82–4; Mansfield 1982: 70 n. 12.

13 Compare Yagi 1993: 619, whose study of early drafts of the *Principles* yielded the conclusion that Menger was 'an innovator in economic theory [to the extent that]...he...developed *the maximization theorem* of consumption...on the basis of the subjective valuation of the utility of goods' (emphasis added). Later in the same article Yagi attributed to Menger a theorem of the 'maximization of the satisfaction of wants' (ibid.: 710, 711). In private correspondence Professor Yagi (1994) moved to qualify his previously published statements on this matter: 'You asked me whether Menger in the manuscript [of the *Principles*] has the concept of the differential calculus.... My guess is negative. His use of the inverted triangles suggests that he was trained in the classical Euclidean geometry.'

14 Originally, Mises [1933] 1960: 167–73, followed by Lachmann 1977: 48; Vaughn 1978: 61; White 1985: xiii–xiv.

15 Most historians of economic thought have ignored this aspect of Menger's work, being content instead to praise his suggestive but inchoate comments on the nature of needs. Menger is invariably considered to have advanced this aspect of the subject further than Jevons and Walras (Howey 1960: 25; Jaffé 1976: 519). Marshall (1920: 77n.) recognized Menger's achievement when he noted that 'Menger gave great impetus to the subtle and interesting studies of wants and utilities by the Austrian school of economists'.

16 Also Menger's biologistic interpretation of macro-social formations as 'organic' – that is, as unintended consequences of the actions of individuals – has not gone unnoticed in the literature (Alter 1982: 154). Few researchers have noticed Menger's call for developing links between microeconomics and biology, which would advance beyond the use of mere organicist metaphors.

17 Jaffé (1976: 522) was unrestrained in his praise of Menger's proposals to 'discover the laws governing market phenomena *which can be traced to their ultimate genetic determinants in man's physiological and social nature*' (emphasis added).

18 As well, there is no evidence available to support the claims first of Myrdal (1953: 16) and later of Grassl (1986: 148) that Menger turned towards psychology as a consequence of realizing the shortcomings of psychological hedonism. Their claims may have been true of Menger's followers, but not of Menger.

19 Kauder (1965: 13) referred to a weak unidirectional influence of pure psychological analysis on first-generation Austrian economics. In fact Menger's work also influenced the development of Austrian psycholo-

NOTES

gical studies. Fabian and Simons 1986 have given due attention to this matter.
20 Banfield [1848] 1973 carried this idea from German- to English-speaking economists. It is well known that Alfred Marshall's theory of the relationship of economic *activities* to the expansion of needs adjusted to, or created by, them was drawn from Banfield, Hermann and other influential German economists (see Parsons 1931). Menger's perspective on the growth of needs also hailed from German sources.
21 The *Principles* do not always employ the assumption of 'constant tastes' (Alter 1982: 156; cf. Endres 1984). Howey (1960: 154) and Lachmann (1978: 58) maintained that Menger's analysis of economizing was generally static. Streissler (1972), on the other hand, appreciated Menger's attempt to formulate a dynamic, developmental theory of demand.
22 O'Driscoll and Rizzo (1985: 28) defined static subjectivism as a situation where economizers ranked needs ordinally with full knowledge of prices and choice constraints.

4 WIESER, BÖHM-BAWERK AND THE GOALS OF ECONOMIZING BEHAVIOUR

1 Kauder (1965: 13, 125) noted Menger's wavering in the *Principles* between pronouncing on the ends of economizing or remaining noncommittal about them.
2 Cf. Drakopoulos 1990: 362, which, without any substantiation, equated Menger's economizer with an 'explicitly hedonist economic agent'.
3 While not mentioning Wieser, Kauder pointed out that the 'cleansing of utility from egotistical, altruistic and ethical motives was favored by economists inside and outside the Austrian camp' (1965: 128). He listed Slutsky, Rosenstein-Rodan and Mises as supporters of neutral utility. Robbins's *Essay* is full of praise for Austrian economists who, by contrast to Jevons, showed that utility theory was 'capable of being defended in absolutely non-hedonistic terms' (Robbins [1932] 1984: 85). As we shall demonstrate below, Wieser rejected hedonism, but that is not to say that he rejected other ethical connotations which may conceivably arise from the explication of utility theory.
4 It is rare to find one kind word for any Austrian economist in Myrdal 1953, but on this point Myrdal congratulated Wieser: 'without value judgements the whole notion of social conduct of economic affairs is meaningless. It is v. Wieser's greater merit to have seen this clearly' (1953: 154). Wieser also held that such judgements were necessary for analysing individual conduct in the simple economy case.
5 Wieser's utility theory was coloured by an ascetic outlook the political roots of which were enunciated in Kauder 1958: 421–3.
6 This distinction was developed by the Austrian psychologist–philosopher C. von Ehrenfels in the 1890s. On Ehrenfels, see Eaton 1930. Böhm-Bawerk (1959b: 421) cited Ehrenfels.
7 See also Fabian and Simons 1986: 86. Rosenstein-Rodan ([1927] 1960: 101) accepted that in the struggle against hedonism 'Böhm-Bawerk

NOTES

himself pronounced against it', as if a mere pronouncement was sufficient to neutralize his utility-theory from hedonist linkages. In the *Essay*, Robbins ([1932] 1984: 84) also accepted Böhm-Bawerk's pronouncement at face value.

8 Why should ordinary bread-and-butter needs be described as banal? Kauder (1958: 422) demonstrated that the intellectual and political influences on Böhm-Bawerk led him to advocate 'social quietism': that is, social stability ahead of economic progress. This entailed both that the rich should desist from spending on luxuries, and a steady unchanging consumption among the masses.

9 Böhm-Bawerk (1959c: 139) complained of the 'disturbing influence which the unsettled dispute of hedonism' exerted on his work.

10 Ehrenfels's intrinsic–extrinsic distinction was soon discarded by other contributors to the Austrian school of psychology (Fabian and Simons 1986: 87).

11 See Rosenstein-Rodan [1927] 1960: 80, who reported that, altogether, Wieser proposed that utility was non-measurable 'to some extent'. Rosenstein-Rodan had classified Wieser among those who believed that 'utilities are not measurable but can be compared'. Presumably, Rosenstein-Rodan meant ordinal comparisons.

12 This is perhaps the source of McCulloch's (1977: 274) comment that the 'Austrian literature is full of contradictory statements as to whether utility is expressible cardinally'.

13 According to Kauder's (1965: 197) reading of Böhm-Bawerk's argument, 'exact [cardinal] measuring is not possible [presumably in practice] but *approximate* measuring is' (emphasis in original).

14 Similarly, Bonar (1913: 243) was exaggerating when he maintained that 'the whole edifice' of Böhm-Bawerk's work depended on the '*cardinal* principle of final utility' (emphasis added).

15 Kirzner (1994a: xxvii) proposed that Čuhel's mostly psychological insights represented the mental process of utility comparisons along ordinalist lines and were the consequence of 'his subjectivist (introspective) appreciation of the nature of human preferences and choices'. It is difficult to disagree with this conclusion.

16 The term 'mechanical' is in fact used here following Böhm-Bawerk's ([1912] 1994: 342) summary of Čuhel's argument. Čuhel 'declares it to be "non-essential" that we can apply *mechanically* a certain standard to the magnitude to be determined like we apply a ... measuring tape in measuring levels' (emphasis added).

17 This practical psychology was apparently what Böhm-Bawerk (1959b: 195) was referring to when he stated that economists must 'plumb only the shallower depths, as it were, of psychological waters'. He then mentioned Wieser's views on the potency of introspection.

18 One later example is Schumpeter's position that the pure 'theory of economic equilibrium', except for some minor phraseological similarities, had no dependence on what he called 'professional psychology'. He insisted that economics did not inquire into the facts that shaped choices; it had no brief to investigate the psychological bases of evalua-

NOTES

tion. For example, economists accepted scales of demand price as ultimate facts (Schumpeter 1954: 27–8, 796–8, 1057–9).

19 In a revealing comment drawing on the advice of Ludwig Lachmann, Addleson (1984a: 518–19), stated that in 'order to keep the disciplines [of economics and psychology] separate, [praxeological] economics must treat ends as "given". This argument unfortunately led Mises to a position which borders on behaviourism.' Runde (1987: 103–5) developed a similar perspective on Misesian praxeology, considering it a static explanatory scheme – even though Mises himself may not have intended it to be constructed that way.

5 CARL MENGER'S THEORY OF PRICE FORMATION

1 Stigler (1937: 241) set the scene by mentioning Menger's price theory *en passant* in his oft-quoted study of the 'Economics of Carl Menger'. One might therefore be excused for mistakenly believing that Menger's 'interest was in developing a theory of subjective value, not a price-theory' (Bell 1953: 426).
2 Painstaking research on Menger's early manuscripts of 1867 and 1868 by Yagi (1992) supports Hayek's view.
3 Vaughn (1978: 63) speculates: 'perhaps...Menger did not believe that the theory of price was central to economics'. Whether it was 'central' for Menger or not, Menger aimed to develop a price theory, however rudimentary or flawed that theory may have been. If 'Menger simply was not concerned with describing predictable equilibrium prices' (Vaughn 1991: 559), then it remains for us to explain what precisely he was concerned with in the theory of price formation.
4 As Birner (1990: 245) observed; 'the economic theory of the *Principles* is an exact theory'. Working with more sedulous attention to detail, Alter (1990a: 159, 169, 178–9) considered that there are some exceptions, especially in the chapter on price. We shall have cause to return to this matter in due course.
5 Notable in the *Investigations* is the absence of any statement regarding the exact analyst's knowledge of preference scales. In the *Principles*, published some twelve years before the *Investigations*, Menger does not explicitly formulate these assumptions for an exact theory of price formation. As we shall see, Chapter 5 of the *Principles* modifies the content of the axioms regarding market participants' knowledge to allow for different trading protocols.
6 Menger does not dispense with appeals to real cases as a rough inductivist way of justifying exact results. Milford (1990: 232–4) and Birner (1990: 248–52) explore the logical and epistemological problems that beset Menger's distinction between exact-theoretical and empirical-theoretical economics. Menger's 'justificationism-cum-inductivism', as Birner (1990: 252) called it, is unpersuasive; it is nevertheless necessary to recognize Menger's distinction between exact and empirical economics, with all its limitations, as a preliminary to apprehending his price theory.

NOTES

7 Alter (1990a: 175) used the term 'accidental', which is acceptable. However, Alter then proceeded unjustifiably to concentrate on Menger's theory of 'accidental' price formation where 'accidental' is used in the sense of 'probabilistic', as if Menger's study of price formation is predominantly a realistic, empirical exercise. White (1990: 354) objected to Alter's reading. The offending sentence in the original reads: '*Die Preise sind hiebei aber lediglich Erscheinungen, Symptome des ökonomischen Ausgleiches zwischen menschlichen Wirthschaften*' (Menger 1871: 172; cf. Menger [1871] 1950: 191).

8 In Mengerian mode, Hayek (1952: 41) cites recurring price formation processes as important examples of the generation of a spontaneous order, the result of independent actions of individuals which produces an order that is no part of their intentions. 'It makes no difference', Hayek writes, 'whether the process extends over a long period of time...as in the case of the formation of prices.' For Menger, as we shall see in his illustrations of price formation, the 'period of time' is purely *conjectural*; it has no real, historical basis. See also Menger ([1883] 1985: 158).

9 This leaves aside the case where there are no price quotations on either demand side or supply side; price theory would then have no obvious jurisdiction.

10 When prices are conceived as *ex post* barter ratios in a world in which all traders' plans are co-ordinated and all relevant information is acquired and disseminated, they will not serve any function. See Cowen and Fink 1985: 867.

11 In modern economics, the word 'equilibrium' suggests a state which, if left alone, would not move. An equilibrium is a state in which mutual consistency of the various actions has been achieved. See Machlup 1958: 9–10.

12 Several commentators have proposed otherwise: originally Morgenstern 1927, and, more recently, Moss 1978: 24. Whether or not recontracting excluded actual transactions in Edgeworth's analysis is now controversial (Negishi 1987: 594–5). I am obliged to Lawrence White for assistance with the following comparisons between Menger's and Edgeworth's analyses of bilateral exchange.

13 See Menger's remark in the 'Preface' to the *Principles* ([1871] 1950: 48), which predicts that his investigation of the exact laws of price will turn on the price limits of a range.

14 A geometric average of the two price limits is one of many other conceivable outcomes (see Chipman 1965: 43–4; Moss 1978: 26; White 1990: 355 n. 3). It would be inappropriate to belabour this fault in Menger's formulation rather than to recognize that it is the 'range of indeterminacy within which price formation takes place' (Menger [1871] 1950: 199) that constitutes his principal contribution.

15 Cf. Kirzner 1990a: 102, which described Menger's 'economic' prices as those 'which would prevail in the absence of error' in a world inhabited by 'omniscient economizing individuals' (Kirzner 1992: 78). In accurately summarizing the literature on this matter, Vaughn (1990: 383 n. 7) noted that 'Menger consciously abstracted from error and ignorance in

his theory of competitive price'. But in fact Menger's abstraction referred to in this passage is introduced explicitly at two points later in the chapter on price; it has a specific meaning only at these points, as we shall demonstrate below; it should not be read as applying *throughout* his theorizing on economic price formation, or, in particular, to the case of price formation in isolated exchange.

16 Menger's solution is tediously prolix but worth noting nevertheless, if only to demonstrate that it does not differ in principle from case two: 'Price formation takes place between limits that are set by the equivalent of one unit of the monopolized good to the individual least eager and least able to compete who still participates in the exchange and the equivalent of one unit of the monopolized good to the individual most eager and best able to compete of the competitors who are economically excluded from the exchange' ([1871] 1950: 207). See Tables 3 and 4 below.

17 According to Granger and Morgenstern 1970: 2, Carl Menger's 'price theory... has strong features [in common with] the derivation of auction prices – a similarity which has not been followed up by many later writers'. The Mengerian auction deserves elaboration because it differs from the Walrasian price-auction market.

18 Negishi (1985: 161–5) develops the long-side and short-side principles, and he indicates that they are nascent in Menger's theory of the marketability of commodities, developed later in the *Principles*.

19 Menger's treatment could have been more sophisticated here: the bidder who has a valuation of 80 may want to consider the probability that there is another bidder whose valuation of the first horse is close to his so that a transaction may not take place just below 80.

20 As Knight ('Introduction' to Menger [1871] 1950: 22) complained, in Menger's *Principles* there is an 'absence of any... explicit recognition of a demand relation'. Figure 1 demonstrates that Knight's complaint is unwarranted. Knight conceded that Menger uses the term *Nachfrage* on some occasions, but there 'is no hint of intersection of curves or functions showing consumption or production as "functions" of price'.

21 This notion of demand is formally developed much later in Morgenstern (1948; 1972: 1177). Morgenstern explains that bids are alternatives in the sense that they are 'mutually exclusive at the moment of an intended transaction'.

22 A modern example of such temporally sequential price discrimination might be the marketing of movies – first run at high-priced cinemas, next at cheaper cinemas and on premium cable television, and last on videocassette. (I am obliged to Lawrence White for suggesting this example.)

23 That Menger was familiar with traditional Marshallian-type schedules and curves of demand cannot be doubted. He was familiar, for instance, with Rau's demand curve formulated as early as 1841 (Streissler 1990b: 48 n. 62). It is pertinent to remember, given our attribution of a restricted type of 'intramarginal' demand relation to Menger's buyers, that Rau's demand curve 'assumes each individual buying one unit of a commodity, the typical case for reservation price analysis and thus for "price bounds"' (ibid.: 57).

NOTES

24 While Kirzner's account over-generalizes in this matter, it does report accurately that Menger did not provide an adequate theory of price equilibration in modern neo-Austrian (Kirznerian) mode, because there is no allowance for a learning process and for entrepreneurial alertness to arbitrage opportunities.

25 That these assumptions pertaining to demand were perhaps wanting in empirical content would not have fazed Menger. After all, as he stressed so often in the *Investigations*, 'Nothing is so certain as that the results of the exact orientation of theoretical research appear insufficient and unempirical in the field of economy... when measured by the standard of realism. This is, however, self-evident, since the results of exact research... are true only... with presuppositions which in reality do not always apply' (1985: 69).

26 This conclusion confirms Streissler's reading (1972: 440). See also Streissler 1990a: 180–1.

6 BÖHM-BAWERK'S VALUE AND PRICE THEORY

1 Oskar Morgenstern papers, 9 November 1940, Duke University; quoted in Rellstab 1992: 83. See also Mirowski 1992: 129. These remarks suggest that Böhm-Bawerk's ideas on price formation had historical significance in the development of game theory. Unfortunately, none of the contributions to Weintraub 1992a considers Böhm-Bawerk's work in any detail, however rudimentary that work may now seem in comparison with the contributions of other luminaries in economic theory in the late nineteenth century.

2 For a recent critique of Alter's understanding of Menger's economics, see White 1990; Boettke 1992.

3 Indeed Böhm-Bawerk (1959b: 421) cites Ehrenfels. On Ehrenfels's contribution, see Fabian and Simons 1986: 71–5, 84–6.

4 All references to Böhm-Bawerk's *Positive Theory of Capital* hereafter refer to the 1959 Huncke translation (Böhm-Bawerk 1959b). The 1959 Sennholz translation of Böhm-Bawerk's *Further Essays on Capital and Interest* will also be cited (Böhm-Bawerk 1959c).

5 We resist the temptation at this point to consider Böhm-Bawerk's flirtation with hedonistic notions; that matter has been treated elsewhere. See Endres 1991b: 294–5, and Chapter 4 above.

6 With Böhm-Bawerk's approval, Bonar (1888: 13) embarked on a study of Austrian value theory to clarify it for Anglo-American scholars. Bonar rightly insisted that both subjective and objective value in exchange 'are deeply rooted in the common language of men' and are therefore retained as distinct concepts in Böhm-Bawerk's writings. Bonar (ibid.: 25n.) notes that Böhm-Bawerk 'read the manuscript' of his paper. See Böhm-Bawerk 1891: 368n. for an expression of approval. Cf. Alter 1990a: 227, who complains of Böhm-Bawerk's 'ambivalence in his use of subjective value' without recognizing that Böhm-Bawerk expressly discusses the laws of value formation on two different expositional levels.

NOTES

7 Green's criticism is valid as far as it goes, but it fails to recognize Böhm-Bawerk's (and Wieser's) distinction between objective value *per se* and the *laws which determine* objective value; the latter, as we shall demonstrate below, have 'causal' foundations which are completely subjective.
8 Joseph Schumpeter, the Austrian turned Walrasian, cannot be exonerated on this score. As Kirzner (1960: 80, 81) explained, Schumpeter's concept of exchange leaves 'human behaviour to the psychologists, the economist is merely to examine the *results* of behaviour in terms of related variations in the quantities of goods and prices.... Price to Schumpeter meant simply a parameter governing simultaneous variations in the quantities of goods' (his emphasis). Böhm-Bawerk did not share Schumpeter's position on these matters.
9 In the *Theory of Money and Credit*, first published in 1912, Mises ([1934] 1981: 53–4) drew on the support of Čuhel in criticizing the suggestion in Böhm-Bawerk's early work (1959b: 196–200) that intrapersonal acts of valuation could have an objective, cardinally measurable dimension and that these valuations could be carried over into the objectification of exchange value. Böhm-Bawerk's response to Čuhel in an article 'On the "Measurability" of Sensations' (1959c: 124–36) makes it clear that while Böhm-Bawerk may have wavered on these matters in his early work, he assumed a more consistently subjectivist position in his later work. See also Chapter 4 above.
10 The 'genetic-causal' tradition in economic theorizing has its roots in early Austrian economics and was carefully examined by Hans Mayer in 1932. Mayer's important 1932 article was recently translated by P. Camiller. See Mayer [1932] 1994. For a modern statement of genetic-causal theorizing, see Cowan and Rizzo 1991.
11 Böhm-Bawerk frequently remarked on developments in psychology which had the potential to advance our understanding of 'fundamental psychic processes' (e.g. 1959c: 140). Bonar (1888: 24) complained that those 'discussions of the relation of wants...to the means of satisfaction seem too easily apt...to convert economical discussion into psychological. Even Böhm-Bawerk...does not, in practice, avoid a blending of psychology with economics.'
12 In his *Habilitationschrift* of 1881, Böhm-Bawerk described economizing as an acquired habit, but he did not elaborate (Böhm-Bawerk 1962: 87).
13 See 1959b: 263–4; Böhm-Bawerk 1962: 90–2. For comments on this remarkable achievement, see Streissler 1972: 434; 1990a: 174.
14 In any case, we concur with Streissler (1972: 430 n. 15) that 'it is just because he admired Walras so much that Schumpeter is such a bad guide to the real Austrian achievement which has always been in complete contrast to Walras'.
15 We shall use Böhm-Bawerk 1959b (first published in 1889) rather than some very similar horse-trading auctions (which use an interesting triangular exposition) presented in his early 1881–2 Innsbruck lectures. On these lectures, see Tomo 1987: esp. 6, 47–50.
16 On the connections between game theory and Edgeworthian recontracting, see Shubik 1959; Morgenstern and Schwödiauer 1976: 218. Of

NOTES

course, Edgeworth possibly held several concepts of recontracting, but that need not detain us here (see Creedy 1980).

17 According to Böhm-Bawerk (1959b: 216), an 'exchange is economically possible only between persons whose valuations of the good and of the medium of exchange *differ* and, indeed, differ in opposite direction' (emphasis added; the quotation is italicized in the original).

18 Our market demand and supply relation for Böhm-Bawerk's market differs from that produced in Schotter 1974: 200. Schotter's graphical depiction is not a faithful representation of Böhm-Bawerk's intention to rule out bids and offers which are equal to buyers' and sellers' valuations respectively – hence the open-ended circles denoting valuations in our Figure 3.

19 On the German classicals and reservation price analysis, see Streissler 1990b: 48.

20 Indeed, Menger's disapproval of some aspects of Böhm-Bawerk's theory of capital and interest signalled a fundamental tension in Böhm-Bawerk's thought. It is now well established that Böhm-Bawerk made a decisive break from the Mengerian sect of the Austrian tradition at least in his formulation of a capital and interest theory (Streissler and Weber 1973: 231; Endres 1987a; 1991a; Garrison 1990). See also Chapters 8 and 9 below.

7 THE PROCESS OF COMPETITION IN FOUNDING AUSTRIAN ECONOMIC THEORY: I, MENGER'S *PRINCIPLES*

1 See O'Driscoll and Rizzo 1985: 97–102; Lavoie 1985: 172.
2 Schumpeter's ideas on competition have been dealt with extensively elsewhere. For the latest survey, see Boudreaux 1994.
3 On competition the exception is McNulty's article on 'Competition: Austrian Conceptions' (1987), but unfortunately he begins with Schumpeter, thus leaving out of account other contributions in the Austrian tradition before Hayek (and Mises) on the subject.
4 McNulty's (1987: 536) inclusion of Clark 1961 in an article on Austrian conceptions of competition is difficult to justify. More difficult to understand in the light of extensive research on the Austrians is Backhouse 1990: 63, which only considered Schumpeter's 'dynamic...evolutionary' ideas on competition. Dennis (1977: vii) admitted that he 'only skimmed the surface of the German literature [on competition] with passing reference to the writings of...von Wieser'.
5 Harris (1988: 141) reinforced Morgan's 'stylization' of neoclassical competition, which might, at first sight, seem to be a caricature.
6 It was recently stated confidently that the 'differences between neoclassical theorists and adherents of the Austrian approach could scarcely be more marked than in the field of economic analysis concerning competition' (Veit 1990: 103). Whether this statement may be applied to the contributions of the founding Austrians is far from clear.

NOTES

7 Cf. Boehm 1992: 16: 'Harking back to Menger...the starting point for Austrian analysis is not "the market" as such, but individual trades.'
8 According to Hayek (1934: 400), all Mengerian economic activity, including exchange, involves planning for the future.
9 Thus, as Streissler (1972: 433) reported, Mengerian market participants are 'constantly trying to increase [their] knowledge'. For Menger the 'acquisition of knowledge was an integral part of the economic problem' (Vaughn 1990: 381).
10 According to Stigler (1947: 24), 'In everyday usage...competition is used in a very personalized sense.... [And] economic relationships are never perfectly competitive if they involve any personal relationships between economic units' (his emphasis). This insight was also noted approvingly by Hayek 1948: 97n.
11 O'Driscoll and Rizzo (1985: 84) noticed the importance of Morgenstern 1935 in the development of Austrian market process analysis. Perlman's (1986: 277) suggestion that the Austrians in general had a strong belief in perfect competition does not seem to be well founded, because it neglects the important caveats on knowledge which Menger entered at a very early stage in the Austrian tradition.
12 For the latest survey on modern Austrian interpretations of non-price rivalry, see Reekie 1994.
13 Compare Vaughn 1994: 19, who speculated that some examples in Menger's work 'without much stretch of the imagination could be construed as perfectly competitive'. No justification for stretching the imagination in this manner is provided in this chapter.
14 In Mengerian mode, Mayer ([1932] 1994: 50, 60–1) remarked on the 'process of economic cognition', the 'mental factors making up demand' and the 'significance of the subjective factor' in causal-genetic theories which distinguish them from functional theories of exchange, competition and price.
15 Price 'variance' is used here and in the following discussion in place of Menger's term price 'fluctuations' ([1871] 1950: 255). Menger wrote that some commodities 'are subject to violent fluctuations' of price (ibid.: 255–6).
16 Another possibility is that Menger meant by 'transactions taking place at higher and lower prices' trades in markedly different quantities from the 'hundredweight' mentioned at the beginning of his description of the wool market. The text gives us no warrant to restrict his meaning in this manner.

8 THE PROCESS OF COMPETITION IN FOUNDING AUSTRIAN ECONOMIC THEORY: II, WIESER AND BÖHM-BAWERK

1 Mayer's article offered a critique of 'functional' theorizing from the point of view of the genetic-causal approach avowedly common to the Austrians. He devoted the article to Wieser (Mayer [1932] 1994: 49).

NOTES

For a modern discussion of causal-genetic theorizing, see Cowan and Rizzo 1991.

2 Mayer ([1932] 1994: 109) mentioned the method of 'decreasing abstraction' which was purportedly adopted by 'Austrian theorists'. According to Mayer, this method corresponded to the idea that the theorist could use successive approximation to deal with complexity.

3 The high profile we give to *Social Economics* in this chapter is consistent with the views of Streissler (1986: 8), who described the book as a 'monumental textbook in economic theory', and Schumpeter (1951: 300), who believed that the book contained Wieser's 'last and ripest message on pure theory'.

4 Streissler (1986: 103–4; 1990b: 176) discussed Wieser's moralizing about the need for a stable basis for calculation in the social economy; prices arrived at socially are 'just' because they are stable, and stability for Wieser necessarily implied that these prices permitted 'computational efficiency' or signalled resource-allocative efficiency.

5 See also Ekelund 1970: 186 et passim.

6 It is in this special sense that Wieser saw 'competition as a dangerous rather than a beneficient force' (Hutchison 1953: 159). Hutchison did not qualify this statement as we would.

7 While it is patently correct to report that 'Böhm-Bawerk followed Menger in emphasizing the ever-changing nature of [market] circumstances' (Hennings 1986: 232), Böhm-Bawerk's remarks on the behaviour of entrepreneurs are tantalizingly brief and he had little to say on the behaviour of business firms.

8 His appreciation of Walras's *Elements* was probably limited because of his attitude to mathematical methods. None the less, he absorbed some influences from the Lausanne School (Hayek 1992: 51).

9 See Boudreaux 1994 for discussion of the treatment of competition as a process in the work of Schumpeter and Kirzner. See also Kirzner 1973.

10 On Hayek's multi-market or general equilibrium analysis, which has as its centrepiece the problem of co-ordination, see O'Driscoll 1977.

11 For an appreciation of the general influence of Wieser on Schumpeter's work, see Samuels 1983.

12 Robert Hébert (1994: 389) remarked that the concept of competition accepted by Austrian economists was a 'therapeutic notion...[which] recognizes error and ignorance as part of the human condition, and searches for palliatives'. Perhaps so. If we wish to be more specific, however, the founding Austrians presumed that error and especially ignorance were the *sine qua non* for a genuine competitive process. And plan divergence was the catalyst for this process.

13 Without considering the work of the founding Austrians on competition, Addleson (1984b) reached a similar conclusion. He compared *modern* Austrian approaches to competition with twentieth-century general equilibrium economics and concluded that 'the Austrian paradigm appears to offer the best prospects for developing a theory of competition' (1984b: 169).

NOTES

14 See Vaughn (1990; 1994) and references cited in Garrouste 1994: 270 for further evidence on differences among members of the Austrian tradition – both within each generation and between generations.

9 CAPITAL IN FOUNDING AUSTRIAN ECONOMIC THEORY: MENGER VERSUS BÖHM-BAWERK

1 Wieser (1891: 115) and Seager (1893: 239 n. l) state that Menger and Böhm-Bawerk had rival interest theories. See also Hutchison 1953: 138, 152; Kauder 1965: 105. Cf. Hayek's (1934: 410) softer version that Menger 'did not quite agree' with Böhm-Bawerk's definition of capital. Without providing information on the basis of this disagreement, Hayek implies that the difference was one of opinion on a mere terminological matter.
2 This is not to say that other scholars have not given some attention to the problem. Most discussions are, however, brief and fleeting: for example, Seligman 1963: 281; and Hicks 1976a: 139.
3 The history of this publication is clearly described by Carl von Weizsäcker (1984: 133): 'In 1879, Eugen von Böhm-Bawerk submitted to the University of Vienna an habilitation thesis, with the title *Kritische Beiträge zur Volkswirtschaftslehre vom Gute und von Güternutzung* ("Critical Contributions to the Theory of Economic Goods and their Utility"). Four months later the thesis was deemed to meet the regulations by the examiners appointed by Faculty, Carl Menger and Lorenz von Stein. The latter, however, a great Hegelian political scientist, accompanied his approval with a biting, even hostile critique of the young scholar's work. The original version of Böhm-Bawerk's thesis has been lost, but it was published in an obviously condensed form in 1881 in Innsbruck, where he had in the meantime been appointed to his first Chair, under the title *Rechte und Verhältnisse vom Standpunkte der Volkswirtschaftlichen Güterlehre* ("Rights and Relations from the Aspect of the Economic Theory of Goods").'
4 Böhm-Bawerk's first publication was translated by G. D. Huncke as 'Whether Legal Rights and Relationships are Economic Goods' in Böhm-Bawerk (1962). Later Böhm-Bawerk (1891: 238) said of this work that it gives 'many plain, if cautious hints of my leading ideas'. Streissler (1969: 251) was right in proclaiming that the *Rights* 'has been forgotten unjustly'. Kuenne (1971), in a special study of Böhm-Bawerk's economics, failed to mention the work. In more recent literature, Weizsäcker 1984, Endres 1987a (from which this chapter draws heavily) and Leen 1989 have investigated the importance of Böhm-Bawerk's *Rights*.
5 All subsequent page references to the *Rights* will be to G. D. Huncke's translation in Böhm-Bawerk (1962).
6 See Menger [1871] 1950: 51–113.
7 Böhm-Bawerk says he will 'supplement' Menger's findings ([1881] 1962: 41).

NOTES

8 In another place Menger stated that an individual commands a good 'if he is in a position to employ it for the satisfaction of his needs' ([1871] 1950: 109 n. 12).
9 Menger and Böhm-Bawerk use *Verhältnisse* regularly. Following translators Dingwall and Hoselitz (of Menger) and Huncke (of Böhm-Bawerk), 'relationships' has been chosen even though there is no English word or phrase that is capable of expressing the same meaning as *Verhältnisse* in this context. 'Intangibles' or 'claims' may be suitable alternatives. Originally, it appears that Hermann (1832) first coined the word 'relations' or 'relationships' in the economics literature. See Weizsäcker 1984: 134.
10 Hayek (1973: 8) characterized Menger's subjectivist *method of analysis* as one that relies on *Verstehen*: 'Menger believes that in observing the actions of other persons we are assisted by a capacity of *understanding* the meaning of such actions in a manner in which we cannot understand physical events' (his emphasis). Wieser (not Böhm-Bawerk) followed Menger's suggested method more closely. See Hutchison 1981: 205.
11 Menger [1871] 1950: 67–71, 216, 224; [1883] 1963: 69, 214; Alter 1982; and Chapter 3 above.
12 Only later does Böhm-Bawerk refer to various orders of goods.
13 Böhm-Bawerk's neglect of the role of these factors in the functioning of the economic process is noted in Kauder 1958: 422. By contrast, Menger's intense interest in these factors is discussed in Streissler 1973.
14 His precise words in this connection were: 'des Widerspruches, in welchem Böhm's Grundauffassung zur Erfahrung steht' (Menger [1915] 1935: 301).
15 See Burns 1974: 147.
16 Menger's first citation in the *Principles* was of Aristotle on goods ([1871] 1950: 52 n. 2). See also wider knowledge of Aristotle's writings demonstrated in Menger's *Untersuchungen* (Menger [1883] 1985: esp. 220–2 passim). On Menger's wide appreciation of Aristotle, see Kauder 1958; Alter 1982. On the originally unplanned nature of reciprocity in Menger's work, see Schneider's comments in Menger [1883] 1963: 7.
17 This is suggested rather obliquely by Menger ([1871] 1950: 162; also 74, 80, 103, 109, 249). Menger regularly used the phrases 'progress of civilization' and 'organized market'.
18 Moss (1978: 20) notes that this knowledge 'becomes highly prized' by Menger's traders.
19 Menger ([1871] 1950: 90–2) discussed, for instance, the development of a professional class of persons whose task it is to compile and disseminate information about the quality and quantity of goods available.
20 For example, see Blaug 1978: 498–505; Hicks 1973; Ahmad 1991: 117–22.
21 On this point, see Pellengahr 1986.
22 We ignore here Böhm-Bawerk's attempt to capture the relationship between the various maturity classes in Figure 4 with a single measure of capital, the average period of production. This attempt was made at a later stage in *Positive Theory*. This macroeconomic measure combined the effect of both the quantity of inputs used as capital, and the length

NOTES

of time for which it was used. Menger would surely have disapproved of this macroeconomic construct, but he did not comment on it explicitly. As Garrison (1990: 141) maintained, the 'attempt to stipulate just how such an average period could be calculated led Böhm-Bawerk away from Menger's forward-looking vision in which (subjective) values are to be gauged by entrepreneurs'. See also Kirzner 1976a: 38; Lewin 1994: 210–13.

23 There is a resemblance here, not altogether coincidental, between Menger's distinction (items of wealth/capital) and J. B. Clark's ([1899] 1924) distinction between capital goods as technical productive instruments, and capital as an abiding fund of value. Menger's and Clark's concepts derived from German sources.

24 See Menger ([1876] 1994: 61–5). According to Menger, from a strictly theoretical viewpoint, 'assets are *all* of a person's *economic* goods; these may consist of money, houses, farms, objects of all kinds, stocks, domestic animals, etc. It is the sum total of belongings in the widest sense' (ibid.: 61, his emphasis). By contrast, capital 'denotes any stock of assets' (ibid.: 65) which is 'the continuing foundation of any income' (ibid.: 63). It deserves noting that Menger included 'a person's labour potential' as capital (ibid.: 63).

25 Menger's article was published in Conrad's *Jahrbücher* and is reprinted in Menger [1888] 1935: 133–83. Scholars may have been misled by Frank Knight's 'Introduction' to Menger 1950 (30 n. 12), where they are informed that this article makes 'no substantial contribution'. *Per contra* see Hayek (1934: 410–11); Wicksell (1958: 188). Streissler and Weber (1973: 231) make the interesting claim that Menger's objective in this article was to 'forestall Böhm's publication [*Positive Theory*] by a further elaboration of his own theory of capital, which is evidently a veiled criticism of what he knew that Böhm would soon publish'.

26 Menger is much closer to the German classical economics tradition than Böhm-Bawerk on this point (and not only this point). Mangoldt and Hermann before him include land under the heading of capital: see Hennings 1980: 664 n. 21. Böhm-Bawerk would certainly have disputed Wieser's ([1889] 1930: xxxiv) comment that 'the German school long ago formulated the conceptions, leaving us only the task of filling them out by adequate observation'.

27 Menger ([1888] 1935: 174). His precise words were: 'Der Realbegriff des Kapitals umfaßt das Vermögen der Erwerbswirtschaft, welcher technischen Natur dasselbe an sich auch sein mag, insofern sein Geldwert Gegenstand unseres ökonomischen Kalküls ist, d. i. wenn dasselbe sich uns rechnungsmäßaig als eine werbende Geldsumme darstellt'. See also ibid.: 173, 178, passim.

28 John Hicks (1974) coined the term 'fundism' to describe the essence of this forward-looking capital concept. In this connection he classified the English classicists and 'the Austrians' as fundists (ibid.: 313). But see Kirzner 1976a for a more discriminating analysis in respect of the Austrian economists.

29 Detailed studies of the entrepreneurial function in Menger's work have been completed by Martin (1979) and Kirzner (1978).

NOTES

30 We agree with Martin (1979: 279) that Menger's entrepreneur 'creates goodwill' which adds to the capital stock of the economy. This message is, however, only implicit in Menger's work.
31 This translation was made by Karl Polanyi (1971: 18). In the following paragraph we draw heavily on Polanyi 1971 and the translations contained therein.
32 Even in his obituary of Böhm-Bawerk, Menger ([1915] 1935: 300–1) referred to Böhm-Bawerk's lack of respect for *Erfahrung*, by which he appeared to mean knowledge derived from empirical data, experience or empirical-theoretical research.
33 Wieser ([1889] 1930: 125 n. l) recognized Menger's defence of 'the popular as against the scientific concept of capital' but chose the safe side and remained respectfully equivocal.
34 O'Driscoll (1986: 603) concluded that in 'his microeconomic analysis of money, Menger adopts a subjectivist perspective to explain the emergence of a commonly accepted medium of exchange. *The analysis is predicated on pervasive uncertainties facing commodity traders*' (emphasis added). See also ibid.: 608–9.
35 Entrepreneurial actions which result in capital formation will always be influenced by knowledge about technological conditions of production, and such knowledge can be acquired. However, knowledge of demand conditions is particularly difficult to acquire once and for all.
36 Wicksell (1958: 196) regretted, as we do, that Menger did not see fit to debate the theory of interest with Böhm-Bawerk.
37 On this point, see Wicksell 1958: 195–6.
38 Böhm-Bawerk's reasons for interest remain controversial. For a survey of all the important critiques, see Bernholz 1993. See also Heijman 1988.
39 Kirzner's (1966) first contribution in the field should also be consulted, because it demonstrated a strong Misesian influence. See also Zuidema 1988: 70–1.

10 MENGERIAN DISTRIBUTION THEORY: WIESER'S CONTRIBUTION

1 For two recent general appreciations of Wieser and his work, see Streissler 1986; 1987.
2 For example, Hutchison (1953: 153) argued that Wieser ([1889] 1930) bore 'strong family resemblances to Menger's *Grundsatze*'. Rothschild (1973: 209) submitted that 'Wieser built on his [Menger's] foundations.'
3 See also the 'Preface' in Wieser [1889] 1930: xxiv–xxxv.
4 Cf. Knight 1950: 31, who praised Wieser's capital-theory, regarding it as 'sounder' than both Menger's and Böhm-Bawerk's views on the subject. Knight (1935: 158) also paid tribute to Wieser's theory of interest.
5 Two exceptions in recent literature are Rothschild 1973 and Streissler 1987, which touch *tangentially* on matters of concern in this chapter. Zuidema 1988 and Lewin 1994 ignored Wieser's work.
6 To be sure, Streissler and Weber (1973: 229) alluded, all too briefly, to one crucial theoretical point of separation between Menger and Wieser:

NOTES

Menger's 'vision of production was a time consuming multi-stage process – an approach that did not appeal to Wieser'.

7   On Menger's concept compared with Böhm-Bawerk's, see Endres 1987a, and Chapter 9 above.
8   Compare Schumpeter's ([1911] 1934: 120–1) remarks on Menger's concept. For Schumpeter, capital included various means of payment and other circulating media which serve to provide entrepreneurs with control over capital goods.
9   In drawing a distinction between capital and non-capital, Wicksell rejected Böhm-Bawerk's division between the aggregate of intermediate goods (social capital) and a national subsistence fund (national capital) in favour of Wieser's view that capital 'must be more related to the "consumability and mobility" and therefore ready availability and utilization of capital-goods in the narrower sense' (1958: 105).
10 The stationary and progressing cases were often discussed side by side in Wieser's work. For example, see the discussion of capital value and interest in *Natural Value* (Book 4) and in *Social Economics* ([1914] 1927: 29–35).
11 Wieser came dangerously close to assuming what he originally aims to prove at this point. See Böhm-Bawerk's criticisms of Wieser's procedure, detailed in the final section of this chapter.
12 As Rothschild (1973: 219) observed, Wieser could be regarded as a forerunner of economists in the twentieth century who reasoned in terms of a finite number of production plans and in terms of discontinuities or 'corners' in aggregate production functions (e.g. Leontief, linear-activity analysts).
13 Mathematical refinement and 'analytical sophistication' may well have allowed Wieser to produce a more determinate equilibrium (even Wicksellian) solution for his imputation theory, as Rothschild (1973: 220–3) demonstrated. Considering what Wieser ([1914] 1927) had to offer, it is seriously to be doubted whether Wieser would have been comfortable with intellectual concentration on the stationary economy and the general imputation theory with which stationariness was associated. Wieser's *Social Economics* hardly showed unstinting devotion to equilibrium theorizing.
14 Wieser's concept of stationariness was therefore criticized in Edgeworth 1925: 51–2. Rothschild (1973: 216) gave a more recent critical account of this matter: 'once we allow factor supplies to vary the distribution problem acquires new aspects. Though the connection between final utilities and factor values does not disappear, we can no longer explain the latter *exclusively* by the former' (his emphasis).
15 Cf. one of Dobb's (1973: 196) suggested interpretations of Wieser's procedure, where it is conjectured that it resembled Marshallian short-period equilibrium analysis. Again, this interpretation cannot be sustained, since the Marshallian short period allowed producers' decisions to *alter* quantities of inputs supplied with respect to price and marginal cost (Marshall 1920: 314–15, 412).
16 That the asserted technical productivity of capital is neither a necessary nor a sufficient condition for explaining the existence of a positive rate

NOTES

of interest in a stationary economy (following Irving Fisher) is now very well known, and need not detain us here. For a standard textbook treatment, see Blaug 1978: 531–2.

17 This conclusion is in broad agreement with Wieser's theory of imputation, which uses fixed co-efficients. Every form of capital of better quality than another has a higher return imputed to it. In comparing qualities of capital, it is the net return that decides the imputation ([1889] 1930: 131–3).

18 All this relates to interest on productive capital. Interest on consumption loans cannot be explained by productivity as Wieser (1891: 116n.) expressly recognized. Wieser explained interest on consumption loans in psychological terms, comparing the needs of debtors with those of creditors.

19 Wieser's *Social Economics* was careful to distinguish between 'money-capital' and money used for property purchases. Thus money 'loses the characteristics of capital whenever it is used by anyone who is not an entrepreneur: [as] when an individual uses it to buy a dwelling.... In the hands of a builder or contractor a house is capital; in the hands of one who purchases it [as a dwelling]...it is no longer capital. It becomes property.... When an estate is not purchased with the object of resale, it is not regarded as capital' ([1914] 1927: 290).

20 Incidentally, Hilferding's *Das Finanzkapital* (2nd edn) is listed among Wieser's references in the section on money and credit ([1914] 1927: 238).

21 On the disjunction between 'interest' and 'profit' (or the rate of return on producers' capital) in the history of economic thought, see Panico 1987.

22 For an account of Menger's departure from equilibrium economics in the strict sense, see Streissler 1972; Mirowski 1984: 370–2; Vaughn 1990; and Chapter 5 above.

23 As Streissler (1986: 98) read *Social Economics*, Wieser 'explained how technical progress changes the whole spectrum of production processes. It is evident that he thought...even in terms of process analysis.'

24 Ethical reasons for saving are instead brought to account, viz., the 'spirit of self denial' and 'deprivation' (Wieser [1914] 1927: 300). An interest rate factor is mentioned *en passant* much later (ibid.: 350).

25 Wieser's position is remarkably close to Menger's on this matter. Both appreciate the function of money as a mediator and as a potential obstacle to the trade in capital goods. See Menger [1892] 1936: 59. It is disappointing, as Roll (1936: 456) correctly reported, that Menger's 'description of the role of money in the capital market is...not as suggestive of further analysis as other parts' of Menger's work on money.

26 Cf. Schumpeter 1934, originally published in 1911, which is not mentioned in Wieser's references (e.g. [1914] 1927: 30) where it might have been expected. Schumpeter, by the way, labelled the classical line of the secular trend of interest a 'dogma' ([1911] 1934: 210).

27 Cf. also Wieser [1914] 1927: 350: 'the rate of interest is lowered owing to the continuous increase of capital'.

NOTES

28 As Wieser ([1889] 1930: xxxiv) admitted in respect of the German classical school, 'in great part, the German school long ago formulated the conceptions, leaving for us only the task of filling them out'.
29 Streissler and Weber (1973: 229) concurred with Hennings in so far as they maintained that Wieser would not have liked Menger's view of production as a time-consuming, multi-stage process.
30 According to Streissler 1986: 101, 'Wieser became a neoclassical author, an author who blended the old classical tradition with the ideas of the marginal revolution.'
31 We therefore differ from Stephan Boehm (1992: 4), who remarked that Wieser's *Social Economics* was 'a highly personal statement far removed from Menger's concerns with "pure" theory'. This remark may have been accurate in respect of some of the more institutional aspects of *Social Economics* – for example, those concerned with competition (as we explained in Chapter 8 above) – but it was not a valid generalization applicable to the pure theoretical content of Wieser's ideas on distribution in that book.

11 THE FOUNDING AUSTRIAN VERSION OF NEOCLASSICAL MICROECONOMICS: SUMMARY AND CONCLUSIONS

1 According to Kirzner (1994a: xii), in the post-Misesian revival of Austrian economics from the 1970s 'it would become apparent that the Mengerian legacy would generate developments in the theory of market process which would be thoroughly inconsistent with the central content of the neoclassical orthodoxy (as that orthodoxy developed organically from the mainstream economics of the pre-Keynesian era)'.
2 See Boehm 1992. The influence of the Mayer circle on Ludwig Lachmann should not be forgotten. On this point, refer to Kirzner 1994b: xv.
3 One starting reference might be noted here on controversies over other branches of early neoclassicism: on Marshall and Marshallian economics, and on Walras and Walrasian economics in the early years, see the relevant chapters in Hennings and Samuels 1990.
4 What, for instance, can be made of the following statement if the *development* of neoclassical economics is not laid out in context: 'Menger's claim to being a founder of neoclassical economics, while genuine, reflects only part of his message' (Vaughn 1994: 33)?
5 According to Bürgenmeier (1994: 342), 'in mainstream economics Walras is portrayed as a neoclassical, mathematical economist, but in fact he was interested in economics in a broader sense which is not much discussed today'.
6 Letter no. 569, in Jaffé 1965: 772, translated in Bürgenmeier 1994: 350. It should be added, in fairness to W. S. Jevons, that he too saw the importance of many-sidedness in economics – going by his achievements in statistics and his applied work on labour, population and social reform.

NOTES

7 See also Hennings 1985: 267. Vaughn's (1994: 9) characterization of 'neoclassical' would in fact rule out Marshall. For Vaughn, neoclassical economics 'explains *all* human action as variation on constrained maximization where preferences are considered to be given, well-ordered and stable, and where there is widespread knowledge of constraints' (emphasis added). It is difficult strictly to label many leading marginalist economists or emerging neoclassicists up to the 1920s as 'neoclassical' on these terms – perhaps excepting Wicksteed. If there are any doubts about Walras, see Bürgenmeier 1994; Van Daal and Jolink 1993.
8 Unfortunately Streissler and Weber (1973: 228) generalize too freely in concluding that 'in contrast to Walras and even Jevons he [Menger] was a stranger to the very notion of equilibrium'.
9 Of course we may now ask under what conditions such equilibrating tendencies were possible, and about the determinateness, existence, uniqueness and stability of equilibrium as well as convergence towards a perceived equilibrium outcome, but these neoclassical questions postdate the contributions of the founding Austrians.
10 See Koslowski 1990: 12–14, 20 on the importance of equilibrating process in the modern market-theoretical framework developed by Kirzner. For Kirzner's version at source, see Kirzner 1973; 1979.
11 Fetter's important essays on this matter are collected in Fetter 1977; see also Pellengahr 1986.

BIBLIOGRAPHY

Addleson, M. S. (1984a) 'Robbins's Essay in Retrospect: On Subjectivism and an "Economics of Choice"', *Rivista Internazionale di Scienze Economiche e Commerciale* 31: 506–23.
—— (1984b) 'General Equilibrium and "Competition": On Competition as Strategy', *South African Journal of Economics* 52, 2: 156–71.
—— (1986) '"Radical Subjectivism" and the Language of Austrian Economics', in I. M. Kirzner (ed.), *Subjectivism, Intelligibility and Economic Understanding*, London: Macmillan.
—— (1994) 'Competition', in P. J. Boettke (ed.), *The Elgar Companion to Austrian Economics*, Aldershot: Edward Elgar.
Ahmad, S. (1991) *Capital in Economic Theory: Neoclassical Cambridge and Chaos*, Aldershot: Edward Elgar.
Alter, M. (1982) 'Carl Menger and "Homo Oeconomicus"', *Journal of Economic Issues* 16: 149–60.
—— (1986) 'Carl Menger, Mathematics, and the Foundation of Neo-Classical Value Theory', *Quaderni di storia dell' economia politica* 4, 3: 77–87.
—— (1990a) *Carl Menger and the Origins of Austrian Economics*, Boulder, Colo.: Westview Press.
—— (1990b) 'What do We Know About Menger?', in B. J. Caldwell (ed.), *Carl Menger and His Legacy in Economics*, Durham, NC: Duke University Press.
Arndt, H. W. (1984) 'Political Economy', *Economic Record* 60: 266–73.
—— (1985) 'Political Economy: A Reply', *Economic Record* 61: 752.
Aspromourgos, T. (1987) 'Neoclassical', in J. Eatwell et. al. (eds), *The New Palgrave: A Dictionary of Economics*, III, London: Macmillan.
Backhouse, R. (1990) 'Competition', in J. Creedy (ed.), *Foundations of Economic Thought*, Oxford: Blackwell.
Banfield, T. ([1848] 1973) *The Organisation of Industry*, New York: Ronald Press.
Bell, J. F. (1953) *A History of Economic Thought*, New York: Ronald Press.
Bernholz, P. (1993) 'The Importance of Böhm-Bawerk's Theory of Capital and Interest From a Historical Perspective', *History of Economic Ideas* 1, 2: 21–58.

Bianchi, M., and Moulin, H. (1991) 'Strategic Interactions in Economics: The Game Theoretic Alternative', in N. De Marchi and M. Blaug (eds), *Appraising Economic Theories*, Aldershot: Edward Elgar.

Birner, J. (1990) 'A Roundabout Solution to a Fundamental Problem in Menger's Methodology and Beyond', in B. J. Caldwell (ed.), *Carl Menger and His Legacy in Economics*, Durham, NC: Duke University Press.

Black, R., Coats, A., and Goodwin, C. (eds) (1973) *The Marginal Revolution in Economics*, Durham, NC: Duke University Press.

Blaug, M. (1978) *Economic Theory in Retrospect*, 3rd edn, Cambridge: Cambridge University Press.

——(1990) 'Comment on O'Brien's "Lionel Robbins and the Austrian Connection"', in B. J. Caldwell (ed.), *Carl Menger and His Legacy in Economics*, Durham, NC: Duke University Press.

——(1992) 'Comment', in B. J. Caldwell and S. Boehm (eds), *Austrian Economics: Tensions and New Directions*, Boston, Mass.: Kluwer.

Bliss, C. (1987) 'Distribution Theories: Neoclassical', in J. Eatwell et. al. (eds), *The New Palgrave: A Dictionary of Economics*, IV, London: Macmillan.

Blyth, C. (1987) 'Wage Fund Doctrine', in J. Eatwell et. al. (eds), *The New Palgrave: A Dictionary of Economics*, IV, London: Macmillan.

Boehm, S. (1985) 'The Political Economy of the Austrian School', in P. Roggi (ed.), *Gli economisti e la political economica*, Naples: Edizioni Scientifiche Italiene.

——(1992) 'Austrian Economics Between the Wars: Some Historiographical Problems', in B. J. Caldwell and S. Boehm (eds), *Austrian Economics: Tensions and New Directions*, Boston, Mass.: Kluwer.

Boettke, P. J. (1992) [Review of M. Alter, *Carl Menger and the Origins of Austrian Economics*], Journal of Economic History 52: 519–20.

——(1994) 'Introduction', in P. J. Boettke (ed.), *The Elgar Companion to Austrian Economics*, Aldershot: Edward Elgar.

——(1995) 'Why Are There No Austrian Socialists? Ideology, Science and the Austrian School', *Journal of the History of Economic Thought* 17, 1: 35–56.

Böhm-Bawerk, E. von ([1881] 1962) 'Whether Legal Rights and Relationships are Economic Goods', repr. in *Shorter Classics of Eugen v. Böhm-Bawerk*, South Holland, Ill.: Libertarian Press.

——([1884] 1932) *Capital and Interest: A Critical History of Economical Theory*, 1st edn, trans. W. A. Smart, New York: G. E. Stechert & Co.

——([1889] 1923) *Positive Theory of Capital*, 1st edn, trans. W. A. Smart, New York: G. E. Stechert & Co.

——(1890) 'The Historical Versus the Deductive Method in Political Economy', *Annals of the American Academy of Political and Social Sciences* 1: 243–71.

——(1891) 'The Austrian Economists', *Annals of the American Academy of Political and Social Sciences* 2: 361–84.

——(1894) 'The Ultimate Standard of Value', *Annals of the American Academy of Political and Social Sciences*, repr. in *Shorter Classics of Eugen v. Böhm-Bawerk*, South Holland, Ill.: Libertarian Press.

BIBLIOGRAPHY

—— (1895) 'The Positive Theory of Capital and its Critics', *Quarterly Journal of Economics* 9: 113–31.

—— ([1896] 1962) 'Unresolved Contradictions in the Marxian Economic System', repr. in *Shorter Classics of Eugen v. Böhm-Bawerk*, South Holland, Ill.: Libertarian Press.

—— ([1912] 1994) 'On the Measurability of Sensations', in I. M. Kirzner (ed.), *Classics in Austrian Economics: The Founding Era*, I, London: William Pickering.

—— ([1914] 1962) *Control or Economic Law?*', repr. in *Shorter Classics of Eugen v. Böhm-Bawerk*, South Holland, Ill.: Libertarian Press.

—— (1959a) *Capital and Interest I: History and Critique of Interest Theories*, 4th edn (1921), trans. G. D. Huncke, South Holland, Ill.: Libertarian Press.

—— (1959b) *Capital and Interest II: Positive Theory of Capital*, 4th edn (1921), trans. G. D. Huncke, South Holland, Ill.: Libertarian Press.

—— (1959c) *Capital and Interest III: Further Essays on Capital and Interest*, 4th edn (1921), trans. by G. D. Huncke, South Holland, Ill.: Libertarian Press.

—— (1962) *Shorter Classics of Eugen v. Böhm-Bawerk*, South Holland, Ill.: Libertarian Press.

Bonar, J. (1888) 'The Austrian Economists and Their Views of Value', *Quarterly Journal of Economics* 3: 1–31.

—— (1913) [Review of E. von Bohm-Bawerk's *Capital and Interest*, Part II of the 3rd edn], *Economic Journal* 23: 241–6.

Bostaph, S. H. (1978) 'The Methodological Debate Between Carl Menger and the German Historicists', *Atlantic Economic Journal* 6, 3: 3–16.

—— (1994), 'The *Methodenstreit*', in P. J. Boettke (ed.), *The Elgar Companion to Austrian Economics*, Aldershot: Edward Elgar.

Boudreaux, D. (1994) 'Schumpeter and Kirzner on Competition and Equilibrium', in P. J. Boettke and D. Prychitko (eds), *The Market Process: Essays in Contemporary Austrian Economics*, Aldershot: Edward Elgar.

Brems, H. (1986) *Pioneering Economic Theory, 1630–1890: A Mathematical Restatement*, Baltimore, Md: Johns Hopkins University Press.

—— (1988) 'Time and Interest: Böhm-Bawerk and Åkerman–Wicksell', *History of Political Economy* 20, 4: 565–81.

Bürgenmeier, B. (1994) 'The Misperception of Walras', *American Economic Review* 84, 1: 342–52.

Burns, T. (1974) 'On the Rationale of the Corporate System', in R. Marris (ed.), *The Corporate Society*, London: Macmillan.

Caldwell, B. J. (ed.) (1990) *Carl Menger and His Legacy in Economics*, Durham, NC: Duke University Press

Campus, A. (1987) 'Marginalist Economics', in J. Eatwell et. al. (eds), *The New Palgrave: A Dictionary of Economics*, II, London: Macmillan.

Chipman, J. S. (1965) 'The Nature and Meaning of Equilibrium in Economic Theory', *Annals of the American Academy of Political and Social Sciences* 75: 35–64.

Clark, J. B. ([1899] 1924) *The Distribution of Wealth*, New York: Macmillan.

Clark, J. M. (1961) *Competition as a Dynamic Process*, Washington DC: Brookings Institution.

BIBLIOGRAPHY

Coase, R. (1975) 'Marshall on Method', *Journal of Law and Economics* 18, 1: 25–31.

Cowan, R. (1994) 'Causation and Genetic Causation in Economic Theory', in P. J. Boettke (ed.), *The Elgar Companion to Austrian Economics*, Aldershot: Edward Elgar.

Cowan, R. and Rizzo, M. J. (1991) *The Genetic-Causal Moment in Economic Theory*, C. V. Starr Centre For Applied Economics, Economic Research Reports no. 91–13, New York: New York University.

Cowen, T. and Fink, R. (1985) 'Inconsistent Equilibrium Constructs: The Evenly Rotating Economy of Mises and Rothbard', *American Economic Review* 75: 866–9.

Creedy, J. (1980) 'Some Recent Interpretations of *Mathematical Psychics*', *History of Political Economy* 12, 2: 267–76.

Cubeddu, R. (1993) *The Philosophy of the Austrian School*, London: Routledge.

Čuhel, F. ([1907] 1994) 'On The Theory of Needs', in I. M. Kirzner (ed.), *Classics in Austrian Economics, I: The Founding Era*, London: William Pickering and Chatto Publishers.

Dehez, P., and Drèze, J. H. (1984) 'On Supply Constrained Equilibria', *Journal of Economic Theory* 33: 172–82.

Dennis, K. (1977) *Competition in the History of Economic Thought*, New York: Arno Press.

Dobb, M. (1973) *Theories of Value and Distribution since Adam Smith*, Cambridge: Cambridge University Press.

Drakopoulos, S. A. (1990) 'Two Levels of Hedonistic Influence on Microeconomic Theory', *Scottish Journal of Political Economy* 34, 4: 360–78.

Eaton, H. (1930) *The Austrian Philosophy of Values*, Norman, Okla.: University of Oklahoma Press.

Edgeworth, F. Y. (1892) [Review of Böhm-Bawerk, *Positive Theory of Capital*], *Economic Journal* 2: 328–36.

—— (1925) *Papers Relating to Political Economy*, 3 vols, New York: Burt Franklin.

Ekelund, R. B. (1970) 'Power and Utility: The Normative Economics of Friedrich von Wieser', *Review of Social Economy* 28: 179–96.

Ekelund, R. B., Furubotn, E. G., and Gramm W. P. (eds) (1972) *The Evolution of Modern Demand Theory*, Lexington, Ky: D. C. Heath.

Endres, A. M. (1984) 'Institutional Elements in Carl Menger's Theory of Demand: Comment', *Journal of Economic Issues* 18: 897–904.

—— (1987a) 'The Origins of Böhm-Bawerk's "Greatest Error": Theoretical Points of Separation from Menger', *Journal of Institutional and Theoretical Economics* 143, 2: 291–309.

—— (1987b) 'Subjectivism, Psychology and the Modern Austrians: Comment', in P. Earl (ed.) *Psychological Economics: Issues, Tensions and Prospects*, Boston, Mass.: Kluwer Academic Publishers.

—— (1991a) 'Austrian Capital and Interest Theory: Wieser's Theory and the Menger Tradition', *Review of Austrian Economics* 5, 1: 67–91.

—— (1991b) 'Menger, Wieser, Böhm-Bawerk and the Analysis of Economizing Behaviour', *History of Political Economy* 23, 2: 279–99.

BIBLIOGRAPHY

—— (1991c) 'Marshall's Analysis of Economizing Behaviour with Particular Reference to the Consumer', *European Economic Review* 35: 333–42.
—— (1995) 'Carl Menger's Theory of Price Formation Reconsidered', *History of Political Economy* 27, 2: 261–88.
—— (1996) 'Some Microfoundations of Austrian Economics: Böhm-Bawerk's Version', *European Journal of the History of Economic Thought* 3: 87–109.
Fabian R., and Simons, P. (1986) 'The Second Austrian School of Value Theory', in W. Grassl et. al. (eds), *Austrian Economics: Historical and Philosophical Background*, London: Croom Helm.
Fetter, F. A. ([1914] 1977) 'Interest Theories, Old and New', in F. A. Fetter, *Capital Interest and Rent*, ed. M. Rothbard, Kansas City: Sheed Andrews and McMeel.
—— ([1927] 1977) 'Interest Theory and Price Movements', in F. A. Fetter, *Capital Interest and Rent*, ed. M. Rothbard, Kansas City: Sheed Andrews and McMeel.
—— (1977) *Capital, Interest and Rent*, ed. M. Rothbard, Kansas City: Sheed Andrews and McMeel.
Fisher, I. (1906) *The Nature of Capital and Income*, New York: Macmillan.
Fisher, R. (1986) *The Logic of Economic Discovery: Neoclassical Economics and the Marginal Revolution*, Brighton: Wheatsheaf Books.
Fraser, L. (1937) *Economic Thought and Language*, London: A. & C. Black.
Garrison, R. W. (1985) 'A Subjectivist View of a Capital-Using Economy', in G. O'Driscoll and M. Rizzo, *The Economics of Time and Ignorance*, Oxford: Blackwell.
—— (1990) 'Austrian Capital Theory: The Early Controversies', in B. J. Caldwell (ed.), *Carl Menger and His Legacy in Economics*, Durham, NC: Duke University Press.
Garrouste, P. (1994) 'Menger and Hayek on Institutions: Continuity and Discontinuity', *Journal of the History of Economic Thought* 16, 2: 270–91.
Georgescu-Roegen, N. (1966) *Analytical Economics: Issues and Problems*, Cambridge, Mass.: Harvard University Press.
—— (1968) 'Utility', in D. L. Sills (ed.), *International Encyclopaedia of the Social Sciences*, 16, New York: Pergamon Press, pp. 271–96.
Gram H., and Walsh V. C. (1976) 'Menger and Jevons in the Setting of Post-von Neumann–Sraffa Economics', *Atlantic Economic Journal* 6: 46–56.
Granger, C., and Morgenstern, O. (1970) *Predictability of Stock Market Prices*, Lexington, Ky: D. C. Heath.
Grassl, W. (1986) 'Markets and Morality: Austrian Perspectives on the Economic Approach to Human Behaviour', in W. Grassl and B. Smith (eds), *Austrian Economics*, London: Croom Helm.
Grassl, W., and Smith B. (eds) (1986) *Austrian Economics: Historical and Philosophical Background*, London: Croom Helm.
Green, D. I. (1895) 'Wieser's Natural Value', *Annals of the American Academy of Political and Social Sciences* 5: 512–30.
Groenewegen, P. D. (1985) 'Professor Arndt on Political Economy: A Comment', *Economic Record* 61: 744–51.

BIBLIOGRAPHY

—— (1987) 'Political Economy and Economics', in J. Eatwell et. al. (eds), *The New Palgrave: A Dictionary of Economics*, III, London: Macmillan.
Haberler, G. ([1923–4] 1994) 'Economics as an Exact Science', in I. M. Kirzner (ed.) *Classics in Austrian Economics II: The Interwar Period*, London: William Pickering and Chatto.
—— (1951) 'Joseph Alois Schumpeter, 1883–1950', in S. E. Harris (ed.), *Schumpeter, Social Scientist*, Cambridge, Mass.: Harvard University Press.
Harris, D. J. (1988) 'On the Classical Theory of Competition', *Cambridge Journal of Economics* 12: 139–67.
Hayek, F. A. (1934) 'Carl Menger', *Economica* 1: 393–420.
—— ([1934] 1976) 'Carl Menger' [Introduction to the LSE reprint of Menger's *Grundsätze*], repr. in C. Menger, *Principles of Economics*, New York: New York University Press.
—— (1941) *The Pure Theory of Capital*, Chicago, Ill.: Chicago University Press.
—— (1948) *Individualism and the Economic Order*, London: Routledge.
—— (1952) *The Counter Revolution of Science*, Glencoe Ill.: Free Press.
—— (1973) 'The Place of Menger's *Grundsätze* in the History of Economic Thought', in J. Hicks and W. Weber, *Carl Menger and the Austrian School of Economics*, Oxford: Clarendon Press.
—— (1978) *New Studies in Philosophy, Politics, Economics and the History of Ideas*, London: Routledge.
—— (1992) *The Fortunes of Liberalism: The Collected Works of F. A. Hayek*, IV, Chicago, Ill.: Chicago University Press.
—— (1994) *Hayek on Hayek: An Autobiographical Dialogue*, ed. S. Kresge and L. Wenar, London: Routledge
Hébert, R. F. (1994) 'Advertising', in P. J. Boettke (ed.), *The Elgar Companion to Austrian Economics*, Aldershot: Edward Elgar.
Heijman, W. (1988) 'Böhm-Bawerk on Time Preference: Economic Action Based on Future Needs', *Journal of Economic Studies* 15: 79–91.
Hennings, K. H. (1980) 'The Transition from Classical to Neoclassical Theory: Hans von Mangoldt', *Kyklos* 33: 658–81.
—— (1985) 'The State of Microeconomics', in L. Samuelson (ed.), *Microeconomic Theory*, Boston, Mass.: Kluwer.
—— (1986) 'The Exchange Paradigm and the Theory of Production and Distribution', in M. Baranzini and R. Scazzieri (eds), *Foundations of Economics: Structures of Enquiry and Economic Theory*, Oxford: Blackwell.
—— (1987) 'Böhm-Bawerk, Eugen von (1851–1914)', in J. Eatwell et. al. (eds), *The New Palgrave: A Dictionary of Economics*, I, London: Macmillan, pp. 254–9.
Hennings, K. H., and Samuels, W. J. (eds) (1990) *Neoclassical Economic Theory 1870–1930*, Boston, Mass.: Kluwer.
Henry, J. F. (1990) *The Making of Neoclassical Economics*, Boston, Mass.: Unwin Hyman.
Hermann, F. W. (1832) *Staatswirthschaftliche Untersuchungen*, Munich: Von Hermann.
Hicks, J .R. (1951) [Review of C. Menger, *Principles of Economics*], *Economic Journal* 61: 852–3.

BIBLIOGRAPHY

—— (1973) 'The Austrian Theory of Capital and Its Rebirth in Modern Economics', in J. R. Hicks and W. Weber (eds), *Carl Menger and the Austrian School of Economics*, Oxford: Clarendon Press.

—— (1974) 'Capital Controversies: Ancient and Modern', *American Economic Review* 64: 307–16.

—— (1976a) 'Some Questions of Time in Economics', in A. M. Tang et. al. (eds), *Evolution, Welfare and Time in Economics*, Lexington, Ky: D. C. Heath.

—— (1976b) '"Revolutions" in Economics', in S. Latsis (ed.), *Method and Appraisal in Economics*, Cambridge: Cambridge University Press.

High, J., and Bloch, H. (1989) 'On the History of Ordinal Utility Theory 1900–1932', *History of Political Economy* 21, 2: 351–65.

Hollander, S. (1989) 'On P. Mirowski's Physics and the "Marginalist Revolution"', *Cambridge Journal of Economics* 13: 459–70.

Howey, R. S. (1960) *The Rise of the Marginal Utility School 1870–1889*, Lawrence, Kan.: University of Kansas Press.

Hutchison, T. W. (1953) *A Review of Economic Doctrines 1870–1929*, Oxford: Clarendon Press.

—— (1981) *The Politics and Philosophy of Economics*, Oxford: Blackwell.

Jaffé, W. (1976) 'Menger, Jevons and Walras Dehomogenized', *Economic Inquiry* 14: 511–24.

—— (1983) 'Léon Walras and His Conception of Economics', in D. A. Walker (ed.), *William Jaffé's Essays on Walras*, Cambridge: Cambridge University Press.

Jevons, W. S. (1879) *Theory of Political Economy*, 2nd edn, London: Macmillan.

Kauder, E. (1958) 'Intellectual Roots of the Older Austrian School', *Zeitschrift für Nationalökonomie* 17: 411–25.

—— (1965) *A History of Marginal Utility Theory*, Princeton, NJ: Princeton University Press.

Kirzner, I. M. (1960) *The Economic Point of View*, Princeton, NJ: D. van Nostrand.

—— (1966) *An Essay on Capital*, New York: A. M. Kelley.

—— (1973) *Competition and Entrepreneurship*, Chicago, Ill.: Chicago University Press.

—— (1976a) 'The Theory of Capital', in E. G. Dolan (ed.), *The Foundations of Modern Austrian Economics*, Kansas City, Kan.: Sheed Ward.

—— (1976b) 'Ludwig von Mises and the Theory of Capital and Interest', in L. S. Moss (ed.), *The Economics of Ludwig von Mises: Toward a Critical Appraisal*, Kansas City, Kan.: Sheed Andrews and McMeel.

—— (1978) 'The Entrepreneurial Role in Menger's System', *Atlantic Economic Journal* 6, 3: 31–45.

—— (1979) *Perception, Opportunity and Profit*, Chicago, Ill.: Chicago University Press.

—— (1982) 'Uncertainty, Discovery and Human Action', in I. M. Kirzner (ed.), *Method, Process and Austrian Economics*, Lexington, Ky: D. C. Heath.

—— (1990a) 'Menger, Classical Liberalism, and the Austrian School of Economics', in B. J. Caldwell (ed.), *Carl Menger and His Legacy in Economics*, Durham, NC: Duke University Press.

BIBLIOGRAPHY

—— (1990b) 'Commentary', in K. Hennings and W. Samuels (eds) *Neoclassical Economic Theory 1870–1930*, Boston, Mass.: Kluwer.
—— (1992) *The Meaning of the Market Process: Essays in the Development of Modern Austrian Economics*, London: Routledge.
—— (ed.) (1994a) *Classics in Austrian Economics: The Founding Era*, London: William Pickering.
—— (ed.) (1994b) *Classics in Austrian Economics: The Interwar Period*, London: William Pickering.
—— (ed.) (1994c) *Classics in Austrian Economics: The Age of Mises and Hayek*, London: William Pickering.
Knight, F. H. (1916) 'Neglected Factors in the Problem of Normal Interest', *Quarterly Journal of Economics* 30: 279–310.
—— (1934) 'Capital, Time and the Interest Rate', *Economica* 1: 257–86.
—— (1935) *The Ethics of Competition and Other Essays*, 2nd edn, London: Allen and Unwin.
—— (1950) 'Introduction', in C. Menger, *Principles of Economics*, trans. J. Dingwall and B. Hoselitz, Glencoe, Ill.: Free Press.
Koslowski, P. (1990) 'The Categorical and Ontological Presuppositions of Austrian and Neoclassical Economics', in A. Bosch, P. Koslowski and R. Veit (eds), *General Equilibrium or Market Process*, Tübingen: J. C. B. Mohr.
Kregel, J. A. (1976) *Theory of Capital*, London: Macmillan.
Kreps, D. (1990) *A Course in Microeconomic Theory*, Brighton: Wheatsheaf.
Kuenne, R. E. (1971) *Eugen von Böhm-Bawerk*, New York: Columbia University Press.
Lachmann, L. (1956) *Capital and Its Structure*, London: Bell and Sons.
—— (1977) *Capital, Expectations and the Market Process, Essays on the Theory of the Market Economy*, Kansas City, Kan.: Sheed Andrews and McMeel.
—— (1978) 'Carl Menger and the Incomplete Revolution of Subjectivism', *Atlantic Economic Journal* 6: 57–9.
—— (1982) 'The Salvage of Ideas: Problems of the Revival of Austrian Economic Thought', *Zeitschrift für die gesamte Staatswissenschaft* 138: 629–45.
—— (1986) *The Market as an Economic Process*, Oxford: Blackwell.
Lavoie, D. (1985) *Rivalry and Central Planning: The Socialist Calculation Debate Reconsidered*, Cambridge: Cambridge University Press.
—— (1994) 'Introduction: Expectations and the Meaning of Institutions', in D. Lavoie (ed.), *Expectations and the Meaning of Institutions: Essays in Economics by Ludwig Lachmann*, London: Routledge.
Leen, A. R. (1989) 'Böhm-Bawerk's Goods Characteristics Reactivated for Modern Austrians', *Journal of Economic Studies* 16, 2: 109–20.
Lewin, P. (1994) 'Capital Theory', in P. J. Boettke (ed.), *The Elgar Companion to Austrian Economics*, Aldershot: Edward Elgar.
McCulloch, J. H. (1977) 'The Austrian Theory of Marginal Use and of Ordinal Marginal Utility', *Zeitschrift für Nationalökonomie* 37: 249–80.
McNulty, P. J. (1968) 'Economic Theory and the Meaning of Competition', *Quarterly Journal of Economics* 82: 639–66.

BIBLIOGRAPHY

—— (1987) 'Competition: Austrian Conceptions', in J. Eatwell et. al. (eds), *The New Palgrave: A Dictionary of Economics*, I, London: Macmillan.

Machlup, F. (1952) *The Economics of Sellers' Competition*, Baltimore, Md: Johns Hopkins University Press.

—— (1958) 'Equilibrium and Disequilibrium: Misplaced Concreteness and Disguised Politics', *Economic Journal* 68: 1–24.

Mäki, U. (1990) 'Mengerian Economics in Realist Perspective', in B. J. Caldwell (ed.) *Carl Menger and His Legacy in Economics*, Durham, NC: Duke University Press.

Maloney, J. (1987) 'Real Cost Doctrine', in J. Eatwell et. al. (eds), *The New Palgrave: A Dictionary of Economics*, I, London: Macmillan.

Mansfield, E. (1982) *Microeconomics: Theory and Applications*, 4th edn, New York: W. W. Norton.

Marshall, A. (1920) *Principles of Economics*, 8th edn, London: Macmillan.

—— (1961a) *Principles of Economics*, 8th edn, ed. W. Guillebaud, London: Macmillan.

—— (1961b) *Principles of Economics Variorum*, 8th edn, ed. W. Guillebaud, London: Macmillan.

Martin, D. T. (1979) 'Alternative Views of Mengerian Entrepreneurship', *History of Political Economy* 11, 2: 271–85.

Mayer, H. (1932) *Der Erkenntniswert der Funktionellen Preistheorien*, Vienna: Springer Verlag.

—— ([1932] 1994) *Der Erkenntniswert der Funktionellen Preistheorien* (1932), trans. as 'The Cognitive Value of Functional Theories of Price', in I. Kirzner (ed.), *Classics in Austrian Economics II*, London: William Pickering.

Menger, C. (1871) *Grundsätze der Volkswirtschaftslehre*, Vienna: Wilhelm Braumüller.

—— ([1871] 1950) *Principles of Economics*, trans. J. Dingwall and B. Hoselitz, Glencoe, Ill.: Free Press.

—— ([1871] 1976) *Principles of Economics*, trans. J. Dingwall and B. Hoselitz, New York: New York University Press.

—— ([1875] 1935) 'Wilhelm Roscher', reprinted in F. A. Hayek (ed.), *The Collected Works of Carl Menger*, III, London: London School of Economics Reprints of Scarce Tracts.

—— ([1876] 1994) *Carl Menger's Lectures to Crown Prince Rudolf of Austria*, ed. E. W. Streissler, trans. M. Streissler with the assistance of D. F. Good, Aldershot: Edward Elgar.

—— ([1883] 1963) *Problems of Economics and Sociology*, trans. F. J. Nock, Urbana, Ill: University of Illinois Press.

—— ([1883] 1985) *Investigations into the Method of the Social Sciences with Special Reference to Economics*, trans. F. J. Nock, ed. L. White, New York: New York University Press.

—— (1888) 'Zur Theorie des Kapitals', *Jahrbücher für Nationalökonomie und Statistik* 17: 1–49.

—— ([1888] 1935) 'Zur Theorie des Kapitals', reprinted in F. A. Hayek (ed.), *The Collected Works of Carl Menger*, III, London: London School of Economics Reprints of Scarce Tracts.

—— ([1889] 1994) 'Toward a Systematic Classification of the Economic Sciences', in I. Kirzner (ed.), *Classics in Austrian Economics*, I, London: William Pickering.
—— ([1892] 1936) 'Geld', repr. in F. A. Hayek (ed.), *The Collected Works of Carl Menger*, IV, London: London School of Economics Reprints of Scarce Tracts.
—— ([1915] 1935) 'Eugen Böhm-Bawerk', reprinted in F. A. Hayek (ed.), *The Collected Works of Carl Menger*, III, London: London School of Economics Reprints of Scarce Tracts.
—— (1923) *Grundsätze der Volkswirtschaftslehre*, 2nd edn, Vienna:- Hölder.
Milford, K. (1990) 'Menger's Methodology', in B. J. Caldwell (ed.), *Carl Menger and His Legacy in Economics*, Durham, NC: Duke University Press.
Milgrom, P. (1989) 'Auctions and Bidding: A Primer', *Journal of Economic Perspectives* 3, 2: 3–22.
Mirowski, P. (1984) 'Physics and the "Marginalist Revolution"', *Cambridge Journal of Economics* 8: 361–79.
—— (1992) 'What Were von Neumann and Morgenstern Trying to Accomplish?', *History of Political Economy* 24 (Supplement): 113–50.
—— (1994) 'What Are the Questions?', in R. E. Backhouse (ed.), *New Directions in Economic Methodology*, London: Routledge.
Mises, L. von. ([1933] 1960) *Epistemological Problems of Economics*, trans. G. Reisman, Princeton, NJ: Princeton University Press.
—— ([1934] 1981) *The Theory of Money and Credit*, trans. H. E. Bateson, Indianapolis, Ind.: Liberty Classics.
—— (1949) *Human Action: A Treatise on Economics*, London: W. Hodge.
—— (1978) *Notes and Recollections*, trans. H. F. Sennholz, South Holland, Ill.: Libertarian Press.
Morgan, M. (1993) 'Competing Notions of "Competition" in Late Nineteenth-Century American Economics', *History of Political Economy* 25, 4: 563–604.
Morgenstern, O. (1927) 'Francis Y. Edgeworth', *Zeitschrift für Volkswirtschaft und Sozialpolitik* 5: 261–90.
—— (1935) 'Vollkommene Voraussicht und Wirtschaftliches Gleichgewicht', *Zeitschrift für Nationalökonomie* 6, 3: 337–57.
—— (1948) 'Demand Theory Reconsidered', *Quarterly Journal of Economics* 62: 165–99.
—— (1972) 'Thirteen Critical Points in Contemporary Economic Theory', *Journal of Economic Literature* 10, 4: 1163–89.
—— (1976) 'The Collaboration between Oskar Morgenstern and John von Neumann on the Theory of Games', *Journal of Economic Literature* 14: 805–16.
Morgenstern O., and Schwödiauer G. (1976) 'Competition and Collusion in Bilateral Markets', *Zeitschrift für Nationalökonomie*, 36: 217–45.
Moss, L. S. (1978) 'Carl Menger's Theory of Exchange', *Atlantic Economic Journal* 6: 17–29.
Myrdal, G. (1953) *The Political Element in the Development of Economic Theory*, London: Routledge.

Negishi, T. (1985) *Economic Theories in a Non-Walrasian Tradition*, Cambridge: Cambridge University Press.
—— (1987) 'Tâtonnement and Recontracting', in J. Eatwell et. al. (eds), *The New Palgrave: A Dictionary of Economics*, IV, London: Macmillan.
Niehans, J. (1990) *A History of Economic Thought: Classic Contributions, 1720–1980*, Baltimore, Md: Johns Hopkins University Press.
Noyes, C. (1948) *Economic Man in Relation to His Environment*, 2 vols, New York: Columbia University Press.
Nyblén, G. (1951) *The Role of Summation in Economic Science*, Lund: Gleerup.
O'Brien, G. P. (1988) *Lionel Robbins*, London: Macmillan.
O'Driscoll, G. P. (1977) *Economics as a Co-ordination Problem: The Contributions of Friedrich Hayek*, Kansas City, Kan.: Sheed Andrews and McMeel.
—— (1986) 'Money: Menger's Evolutionary Theory', *History of Political Economy* 18, 4: 601–16.
O'Driscoll, G. P., and Rizzo, M. (1985) *The Economics of Time and Ignorance*, Oxford: Blackwell.
Panico, C. (1987) 'Interest and Profit', in J. Eatwell et. al. (eds), *The New Palgrave: A Dictionary of Economics*, II, London: Macmillan.
Pantaleoni, M. ([1898] 1957) *Pure Economics*, trans. T. Boston Bruce, New York: Kelly and Millman.
Parsons, T. (1931) 'Wants and Activities in Marshall', *Quarterly Journal of Economics* 46: 101–40.
Pellengahr, M. (1986) 'Austrians Versus Austrians I', and 'Austrians Versus Austrians II' in M. Faber (ed.), *Lecture Notes in Economics and Mathematical Systems: Studies in Austrian Capital Theory, Investment and Time*, Heidelberg: Springer Verlag.
Perlman, M. (1986) 'Subjectivism and American Institutionalism', in I. M. Kirzner (ed.), *Subjectivism, Intelligibility and Economic Understanding*, New York: New York University Press.
Pigou, A. C. (ed.) (1925) *Memorials of Alfred Marshall*, London: Macmillan.
Polanyi, K. (1971) 'Carl Menger's Two Meanings of "Economic"', in G. Dalton (ed.), *Studies in Economic Anthropology*, Washington, DC: American Anthropological Association.
Preiser, E. ([1959] 1971) 'Property, Power and the Distribution of Income', in K. Rothschild (ed.), *Power in Economics*, Harmondsworth: Penguin.
Pribram, K. (1983) *A History of Economic Reasoning*, Baltimore, Md: Johns Hopkins University Press.
Raico, R. (1994) 'Classical Liberalism and the Austrian School', in P. J. Boettke (ed.), *The Elgar Companion to Austrian Economics*, Aldershot: Edward Elgar.
Reekie, W. D. (1994) 'Non-Price Rivalry', in P. J. Boettke (ed.), *The Elgar Companion to Austrian Economics*, Aldershot: Edward Elgar.
Rellstab, U. (1992) 'New Insights into the Collaboration Between John von Neumann and Oskar Morgenstern on the *Theory of Games*', *History of Political Economy*, 24 (Supplement): 77–95.
Rima, I. (1977) 'Neoclassicism and Dissent', in S. Weintraub (ed.), *Modern Economic Thought*, Oxford: Blackwell.

BIBLIOGRAPHY

Robbins, L. (1930) 'On a Certain Ambiguity in the Concept of Stationary Equilibrium', *Economic Journal* 40: 194–214.
—— (1932) *An Essay on the Nature and Significance of Economic Science*, London: Macmillan.
—— ([1932] 1984) *An Essay on the Nature and Significance of Economic Science*, 3rd edn, London: Macmillan.
—— (1976) *Political Economy Past and Present*, London: Macmillan.
Rogin, L. (1956) *The Meaning and Validity of Economic Theory*, New York: Columbia University Press.
Roll, E. (1936) 'Menger on Money', *Economica* 3, 455–60.
Roscher, W. (1878) *Principles of Political Economy*, New York: Holt.
Rosenstein-Rodan, P. ([1927] 1960) 'Marginal Utility', *International Economic Papers* 10: 71–106.
Rothbard, M. N. (1956) 'Toward a Reconstruction of Utility and Welfare Economics', in M. Rothbard (ed.), *On Freedom and Free Enterprise: Essays in Honor of Ludwig von Mises*, Princeton, NJ: Van Nostrand.
—— (1962) *Man, Economy and State: A Treatise on Economic Principles*, Princeton, NJ: Van Nostrand.
—— (1976) 'New Light on the Prehistory of the Austrian School', in E. G. Dolan (ed.), *The Foundations of Modern Austrian Economics*, Kansas City, Kan.: Sheed Andrews and McMeel.
—— (1987) 'Time Preference', in J. Eatwell et. al. (eds), *The New Palgrave: A Dictionary of Economics*, IV, London: Macmillan.
Rothschild, K. (1973) 'Distributive Aspects of the Austrian Theory', in J. Hicks and W. Weber, *Carl Menger and the Austrian School of Economics*, Oxford: Clarendon Press.
Runde, J. (1987) 'Subjectivism, Psychology, and the Modern Austrians', in P. Earl (ed.), *Psychological Economics: Issues, Tensions, Prospects*, Boston: Kluwer.
Samuels, W. J. (1983) 'The Influence of Friedrich von Wieser on Joseph A. Schumpeter', *History of Economics Society Bulletin* 4, 2: 5–19.
—— (1990) 'Introduction', in K. Hennings and W. Samuels (eds), *Neoclassical Economic Theory 1870–1930*, Boston: Kluwer.
Samuelson, P. A. (1952) 'Economic Theory and Mathematics: An Appraisal', *American Economic Review, Papers and Proceedings* 42: 56–66.
Schotter, A. (1974) 'Auctioning Böhm-Bawerk's Horses', *International Journal of Game Theory* 5, 4: 195–215.
—— (1992) 'Oskar Morgenstern's Contribution to the Theory of Games', *History of Political Economy* 24 (Supplement): 95–112.
Schumpeter, J. ([1911] 1934) *The Theory of Economic Development*, Cambridge, Mass.: Harvard University Press.
—— (1942) *Capitalism, Socialism and Democracy*, London: Unwin.
—— (1951) *Ten Great Economists From Marx to Keynes*, Oxford: Clarendon Press.
—— (1954) *History of Economic Analysis*, New York: Oxford University Press.
Seager, H. R. (1893) 'Economics at Berlin and Vienna', *Journal of Political Economy* 1: 236–62.

BIBLIOGRAPHY

Seligman, E. R. (1963) *Main Currents in Modern Economics*, New York: Columbia University Press.

Shubik, M. (1959) 'Edgeworth Market Games', in R. Luce and A. W. Tucker (eds), *Contributions to the Theory of Games*, Princeton, NJ: Princeton University Press.

—— (1987) *A Game Theoretic Approach to Political Economy*, Boston, Mass.: MIT Press.

Silverman, P. (1990) 'The Cameralistic Roots of Menger's Achievement', in B. J. Caldwell (ed.), *Carl Menger and His Legacy in Economics*, Durham, NC: Duke University Press.

Slutsky, E. (1927) 'Zur Kritik der Böhm-Bawerkschen Wertbegriffs und seiner Lehre von der Messzbarkeit des Werts', *Schmollers Jarbuch für Gesetzgebung* 51: 541–60.

Souter, R. (1933) 'The Nature and Significance of Economic Science in Recent Discussion', *Quarterly Journal of Economics* 48: 377–413.

Spann, O. (1930) *Types of Economic Theory*, London: Allen and Unwin.

Stegmüller, W. (1973) *Entscheidungslogik (rationale Entscheidungstheorie)*, Berlin: Springer Verlag.

Stigler, G. (1937) 'The Economics of Carl Menger', *Journal of Political Economy* 45: 228–50.

—— (1941) *Production and Distribution Theories*, New York: Macmillan.

—— (1947) *The Theory of Price*, New York: Macmillan.

Streissler, E. (1969) 'Structural Economic Thought: The Significance of the Austrian School Today', *Zeitschrift für Nationalökonomie* 3–4: 237–66.

—— (1972) 'To What Extent Was the Austrian School Marginalist?', *History of Political Economy* 4: 426–41.

—— (1973) 'Menger's Theories of Money and Uncertainty – A Modern Interpretation', in J. Hicks and W. Weber, *Carl Menger and the Austrian School of Economics*, Oxford: Clarendon Press.

—— (1983) 'Schumpeter and Hayek: On Some Similarities in Their Thought', in F. Machlup, G. Fels and H. Müller-Groeling (eds), *Reflections on a Troubled World Economy*, New York: St Martin's Press.

—— (1986) 'Arma Virumque Cano – Friedrich von Weiser, the Bard as Economist', in N. Leser (ed.), *Die Werner Schule der Nationalökonomie*, Vienna: H. Böhlau.

—— (1987) 'Wieser, F. von.', in J. Eatwell et. al. (eds), *The New Palgrave: A Dictionary of Economics*, IV, London: Macmillan.

—— (1990a) 'Menger, Böhm-Bawerk and Weiser: The Origins of the Austrian School', in K. Hennings and W. Samuels (eds), *Neoclassical Economic Theory 1870–1930*, Boston, Mass.: Kluwer.

—— (1990b) 'The Influence of German Economics on the Work of Menger and Marshall', *History of Political Economy* 22 (Supplement): 31–68.

—— (1994) 'German Predecessors of the Austrian School', in P. J. Boettke (ed.), *The Elgar Companion to Austrian Economics*, Aldershot: Edward Elgar.

Streissler, E. and Weber, W. (1973) 'The Menger Tradition', in J. Hicks and W. Weber, *Carl Menger and the Austrian School of Economics*, Oxford: Clarendon Press.

Strigl, R. (1923) *Die ökonomischen Kategorien und die Organisation der Wirtschaft*, Jena: G. Fischer.
Sweezy, A. (1934) 'The Interpretation of Subjective Value Theory in the Writings of the Austrian Economists', *Review of Economic Studies* 1: 176–85.
—— (1935) 'Collected Works of Carl Menger', *Quarterly Journal of Economics* 50: 719–30.
Tomo, S. (1987) *Early Lectures on Economics by Böhm-Bawerk (A Transcript of Nationalökonomie nach Prof. Dr. Eugen von Böhm)*, Tokyo: Hitotsubashi Centre for Historical Social Science Literature.
—— (1995) 'Beyond Roscher Or Not? A Reappraisal of Menger's and Böhm-Bawerk's Contributions to the Theory of Interest', *Journal of Economic Studies* 22: 127–33.
Tribe, K. (1988) *Governing Economy: The Reformation of Economic Discourse 1750–1840*, Cambridge: Cambridge University Press.
Varian, H. R. (1987) 'Microeconomics', in J. Eatwell et. al. (eds), *The New Palgrave: A Dictionary of Economics*, III, London: Macmillan.
Van Daal J., and Jolink, A. (1993) *The Equilibrium Economics of Léon Walras*, London: Routledge.
Vaughn, K. I. (1978) 'The Reinterpretation of Carl Menger: Some Notes on Recent Scholarship', *Atlantic Economic Journal* 6.3: 60–4.
—— (1987) 'Carl Menger', in J. Eatwell et. al. (eds), *The New Palgrave: A Dictionary of Economics*, II, London: Macmillan.
—— (1990) 'The Mengerian Roots of the Austrian Revival', in B. J. Caldwell (ed.), *Carl Menger and His Legacy in Economics*, Durham, NC: Duke University Press.
—— (1991) [Review of M. Alter, *Carl Menger and the Origins of Austrian Economics*], *History of Political Economy* 23: 558–60.
—— (1994) *Austrian Economics in America: The Migration of a Tradition*, Cambridge: Cambridge University Press.
Veblen, T. (1920) *The Place of Science in Modern Civilization, and Other Essays*, New York: Viking Press.
Veit, R. (1990) 'Neoclassical and Austrian Theory of Economic Policy', in A. Bosch, P. Koslowski and R. Veit (eds), *General Equilibrium and Market Process: Neoclassical and Austrian Theories of Economics*, Tübingen: J. C. B. Mohr.
Von Neumann, J., and Morgenstern, O. (1947) *Theory of Games and Economic Behaviour*, 2nd edn, Princeton, NJ: Princeton University Press.
Walras, L. (1954) *Correspondence and Related Papers*, 2 vols, ed. W. Jaffé, Amsterdam: North Holland.
—— (1965) *Elements of Pure Economics*, trans. W. Jaffé, London: Allen and Unwin.
Weintraub, E. R. (1991) *Stabilizing Dynamics: Constructing Economic Knowledge*, Cambridge: Cambridge University Press.
—— (ed.) (1992) *Toward a History of Game Theory*, Durham, NC: Duke University Press.
Weizsäcker C. C. von. (1984) 'Rights and Relations in Modern Economic Theory', *Journal of Economic Behavior and Organization* 5: 133–57.

BIBLIOGRAPHY

White, L. (1985) 'Introduction' in C. Menger, *Investigations into the Method of the Social Sciences*, New York: New York University Press.

—— (1990) 'Restoring an "Altered" Menger: Comment', *History of Political Economy* 22 (Supplement): 349–58.

Wicksell, K. ([1924] 1958) 'The New Edition of Menger's *Grundsätze*', *Ekonomisk Tidskrift*, (1924); repr. in K. Wicksell, *Selected Papers on Economic Theory*, London: Allen and Unwin.

—— (1958) *Selected Papers on Economic Theory*, London: Allen and Unwin.

Wieser, F. A. ([1876] 1994) 'On the Relationship of Costs to Value', in I. M. Kirzner (ed.), *Classics in Austrian Economics: The Founding Era*, I, London: William Pickering.

—— (1884) *Über den Ursprung und die Hauptgesetze des wirthschaftlichen Werthes*, Vienna: Hölder.

—— ([1889] 1930) *Natural Value*, trans. C. Malloch, London: Macmillan.

—— (1891) 'The Austrian School and the Theory of Value', *Economic Journal* 1: 108–21.

—— ([1911] 1994) 'The Nature and Substance of Theoretical Economics', trans. W. Kirby, in I. M. Kirzner (ed.), *Classics in Austrian Economics: The Founding Era*, I, London: William Pickering.

—— ([1914] 1927) *Social Economics*, trans. A. F. Hinrichs, New York: Adelphi.

—— (1923) 'Carl Menger', in *Neue österreichische Biographie*: 1815–1918, Vienna: Amalthea-Verlag.

—— (1929) *Gesammelte Abhandlungen*, ed. F. A. Hayek, Tübingen: Mohr.

Winch, D. M. (1972) 'Marginalism and the Boundaries of Economic Science', *History of Political Economy* 4, 2: 325–43.

Yagi, K. (1983) *Böhm-Bawerk's First Interest Theory, with C. Menger–Böhm-Bawerk Correspondence 1884–85*, Tokyo: Hitotsubashi Centre for Historical Social Science Literature.

—— (1992) 'Carl Menger as Editor: Significance of Journalistic Experience for his Economics and for his Later Life', *Revue européenne des Sciences Sociales*, 30: 93–108.

—— (1993) 'Carl Menger's *Grundsätze* in the Making', *History of Political Economy* 25, 4: 695–725.

—— (1994) [Personal communication, 3/7/94].

Zuidema, R. P. (1988) 'On the Austrian Contribution to Capital Theory', *Journal of Economic Studies* 15: 64–78.

INDEX

Addleson, M. 36
advertising 119
aggregation 13, 77, 79, 104–5, 123, 160, 163, 170, 220
Alter, M. 6, 145
altruistic needs 34–5
arbitragers 82, 121
Aristotle 11, 156, 159
asceticism 46–7, 50
auction 71–2, 74, 77–8, 94–6, 100, 102, 106, 116–17, 120, 127, 135, 216, 223
auctioneer 100, 124
Austrian economic theory 9; as branch of neoclassicism 8
Austrian philosophy 9, 190, 213
Austrian psychologists 37, 48, 87
Austrian School 11, 109, 207; pre-history 11

Banfield, T. 35
bargaining 66–70, 74, 83, 99, 101, 106, 115–17, 135–8, 140–1, 143, 217, 223; see also rivalry; strategic behaviour
Bertrand-type equilibrium 73
bilateral exchange 67–70, 114–15
bilateral monopoly 112–13, 120, 122, 218, 223
biology 36, 58, 223
Blang, M. 4, 109
Blyth, C. 219
Boehm, S. 207, 215
Böhm-Bawerk, E. 1–2, 5, 15, 22–3, 25, 37, 51, 57–9, 83, 109–10, 125–6, 141–7, 176–8, 191, 193, 200–5, 207, 222, 224–5; and capital concept 162–72, 219–20; competition 134–41, 218–19; cost 23; economizing 47–50, 90–4, 222; equilibrium concept 100–5; and game theory 98–100; on goods 23, 147–53, 176; and interest concept 172–6; on introspection 55; his methodology 18–19, 22–3, 94, 140; theory of markets 90–100; 216; on utility measurement 50–7; his value theory 86–100; on Wieser's capital and interest theory 201–2
Boettke, P. 2
Bonar, J. 28
Brems, H. 189
business connections and relationships 155, 161, 163, 170, 176
buyers' competition 117, 120, 126, 135–6; see also competition

Cameralism 11
Campus, A. 4
capital concepts 162–72, 180–2, 220
capital formation 165–6, 171, 177, 198, 220
capital productivity 164–5, 174–5, 183–4, 192–3, 203
capital structure 166, 224
capital theory 164, 219–21, 224–5
capital using 147, 174, 177, 205

INDEX

causal theorizing 26, 33, 91–3, 101–2, 120–1, 129, 137, 151–2, 161, 186, 189, 221, 224; *see also* genetic-causal analysis
certainty equivalence 93, 147
Chamberlin, E. 108, 133
choice 24–31, 93, 140, 213–15
Clark, J.B. 103–4, 162, 203, 219, 221
Clark, J.M. 110
classical economics: English 5, 10, 169, 199–200, 204, 212; German, 12–13, 199, 212–13
competition 82, 108–45, 195, 223–5; atomistic 112, 122, 126, 135; behavioural aspects 111–5, 133–4, 142, 144; as conflict 126, 129–33, 143; as dynamic process 82, 108, 110, 118–19, 121–3, 132–4, 145; Hayekian 141–3, neoclassical 110–1, 218
competitive equilibrium 108–9, 139
complementarity between goods and factors 35, 152–3, 167, 170, 173, 186, 203, 221; between plans 177; structural 177
conjectural theorizing 70, 81–2
consumer surplus 77, 127
copyrights 153, 155, 159
costs 81, 83
Cournot, A. 79, 218
credit 155–6, 195, 198
Crown Prince Rudolf 28, 30, 32
Crusoe economy 22–3, 87, 134, 159, 165
Čuhel, F. 54–7, 215

demand: curves 75, 80; relation 75–6; 98–9, 216; schedules 95, 102, 128, 190, 204, 213; stratified 129
diminishing returns 183, 193
distribution theory 7, 139, 189, 219–21, 225
Dobb, M. 185

Dutch auction 77
dynamic subjectivism 40, 214–15

economic philosophy 3
economic prices 65, 69, 82–3, 122
economic profit 81
economic progress 80; *see also* progress
economizing behaviour 25–6, 105, 171, 209, 213, 225; as activity or process 26, 38, 63, 112; in Böhm-Bawerk 47–50, 92–4; in Cameralism 12; in Menger 27–40, 149, 151, 214; in Wieser 41–7, 189, 205
Edgeworth, Y. 54, 69, 90, 95–6, 102, 108, 215–18, 221
egotistical needs 34–5
empirical-theoretical method 13, 15, 17–18, 39, 62, 66, 69, 73, 151, 157, 212, 214, 222
egence 54–5
entrepreneurship 109, 119, 177, 224; in Böhm-Bawerk 135–7, 166, 175; in Menger 167–73, 176, 220–1; in Wieser 132–3, 197–8, 205
equilibrating process 61, 64–6, 82–3, 104–5, 140–1, 186, 204, 215–16, 223
equilibrating tendencies 61, 73–4, 77, 86, 100, 217–18
equilibrium price 61, 66, 80, 106, 134, 197
equilibrium states 64–6, 103, 105, 114, 125, 127, 136, 138–9, 188, 215, 218, 223; *see also* general equilibrium; partial equilibrium
equimarginal principle 45, 101
ethics 25, 41, 44, 46, 57–8, 172, 222
exact laws 40
exact-theoretical method 13, 15, 17–18, 39, 62, 69–70, 73, 75, 80–2, 214, 222
exchange 5–6, 45, 63, 87, 106, 113, 120–1, 125, 128, 140, 218
expected utility 93
externalities 162

INDEX

Fetter, F.A. 162, 174, 203, 220
financial rights 154, 157; see also credit
Fisher, I. 162, 219
Fisher, R. 4
Fraser, L. 25

game theory 79, 84–6, 99–100, 106, 110, 116, 135, 217, 223; see also Morgenstern, O.
Garrison, R. 166, 176, 219
general equilibrium 60–1, 90, 124, 136, 143, 215–16, 219, 221; see also equilibrium
genetic-causal analysis 14, 66, 93, 105, 120, 126, 141, 190, 213, 216, 223; see also causal theorizing
Georgescu-Roegen, N. 28, 35
German psychologists 50
goodwill 146, 153, 155–8, 160, 170–1
Gossen, H. 44
Gossen's law 44
Green, D. 89
Gross, H. 109

Haberler, G. 208
Hayek, F. 2, 29, 36, 60, 62, 108–11, 115–16, 119, 122, 140–3, 145, 160, 181–2, 208, 220
hedonism 41, 46–7, 49, 57
Hennings, K. 5, 95, 203–4
Henry, J. 3
Hermann, F.B. 35
Hermann, F.W. 109
Hicks, J. 5, 120
historical economics 8–9, 13–14, 212
homo oeconomicus 33
Howey, R. 53, 86
human capital 149

ideology 3
imaginary goods 32–3, 49, 161
imagination 53, 55, 86, 93, 160, 171, 215, 223
imperfect competition 108
imputation 182, 184, 192, 201–3, 224

indivisibilities 67, 70, 72, 75, 95, 106, 117, 122, 186, 198, 216
information asymmetries 69, 116, 218
information dispersion 124, 217
information structure 70–1; see also knowledge
institutional economics 8
intangible goods 32, 151, 153–4, 159, 169–70, 173, 176
interest: productivity explanations 174–5; as return on loanable funds 174; see also time preference; rate of interest
intra-marginal demand schedules 78, 83
introspection 37, 50, 55–6, 192, 201–2
invention 197, 200

Jaffé, W. 5, 29–30, 60, 111
Jevonian branch of neoclassicism 5, 31, 90, 169, 219
Jevons, W. 8, 15, 27–8, 34, 38, 54, 57, 107, 108, 111, 145, 181, 196, 212, 215–16, 219

Kauder, E. 50, 57
Kirzner, I. 1, 3, 80, 109, 119, 136, 140, 145, 177, 208–9, 211, 221
Knies, K. 42
Knight, F. 203
knowledge 70, 81, 90, 93, 109, 124, 141–4, 214; in Böhm Bawerk 136–8, 148–9; in Hayek 141–3; in Menger 20, 26, 31, 33–4, 38, 40, 62, 65, 112–19, 159–62, 167–8; in Wieser 128, 201
knowledge dynamics 58; see also knowledge
Kreps, D. 206
Kudler, J. 35

Lachmann, L. 34, 177, 208
Lavoie, D. 8, 111, 127
law of one price 130, 195, 204
Lewin, P. 166–76

INDEX

logic-of-choice 25–6, 34, 40, 41, 47, 56, 58, 209, 213–15, 222
logic of valuation 41, 43

Machlup, F. 120, 208
macroeconomics 104–6, 157
Maloney, J. 95
marginal pairs 97, 135
marginal productivity 7, 131, 137–9, 184, 218–19
marginal revolution 2, 5, 15, 206
marginal utility 27, 30, 40, 44, 48–9, 134, 186, 189, 207; stratified marginal utility 129, 133
marginalist economics 2–5, 29–30, 204
market clearing 74–5, 83, 97, 216
market depth 122, 223
market organization 73, 122–4, 161
market process 33, 84, 135, 138, 140, 162, 216, 219, 221, 225
marketability of commodities 81, 121
Marshall, A. 6, 30, 79, 91, 102–3, 107–8, 212, 214–16, 221
Marshallian branch of neoclassicism 3, 6, 7, 8, 26, 31, 60, 75, 85–6, 93, 95, 103, 106, 109, 139, 145, 185, 206–7, 209–10, 216–18
Marx, K. 137, 200
material needs 32
materialism 31–2, 34, 147, 162, 179
mathematics 15, 28, 30–1, 52, 75, 90, 213, 215
maximization 26–7, 30, 214–15
Mayer circle 141, 208–9
Mayer, H. 66, 126
McCulloch, J.H. 28
McNulty, P. 111–12
measurement 15, 29, 50, 53–7, 169, 215, 222
Menger, C. 1–2, 5–6, 8–10, 14–18, 24, 41–2, 44, 51, 56–9, 89, 106, 126, 128, 140–51, 165, 176–8, 181, 189–91, 196, 204–5, 207, 222, 224–5; on capital 167–72, 220; on competition 108–25, 218–19; on choice 24–40, 222; on economic progress 37–40; on economic research fields 10–11, 14, 212–13; on equilibrium 63–7, 114; on goods 20, 150–3, 156–62, 165–8; on imputation 202; on interest 173–6; on knowledge 20, 31, 38–40; his microeconomics 20; his needs hierarchy 20–1; on price formation 60–84, 216; on research fields in economics 10–11, 14, 212–13; on scope of economics 12; his subjectivism 31–5, 56, 124, 149, 174, 224
mental evaluation 29, 31, 51, 53, 55–6, 58, 87
mercantilist 169
Methodenstreit 9, 13, 41, 212
methodological individualism 7
methodology of Austrian economics 9, 212–13
Mill, J.S. 103
Mirowski, P. 6
Mises, L. von 2, 24, 32–3, 56–8, 124, 160–1, 174, 177, 208
monetary calculation 37, 170, 198–9, 204
monetary economy 37, 167, 169, 171–2
monopoloidal competition 133
monopoly 75–80, 110, 114, 118, 120, 137–8, 143, 145, 150
monopsony 138–9
Morgan, M. 110–11
Morgenstern, O. 79, 85, 110, 115–17, 208
Moss, L. 80, 113

national economy 14, 19, 222
needs-hierarchy 27–8, 33–4, 37, 57
needs-satisfaction 26–9, 43, 105
needs: categories 34; growth 26, 37–40, 58–9; structure 26, 33–7, 58–9; time dimension 26
neoclassical economics 2–8, 61, 109, 111–12, 215; Austrian

INDEX

branch 8; distribution theory 139; Hicks-Stigler version 7; mainstream theory 209–10, 225; and optimization 7, 27; Paretian branch 7; *see also* Jevonian branch, Marshallian branch and Walrasian branch of neoclassicism
non-economic factors 17, 43, 69, 75, 135, 139
non-price rivalry 119, 132–3, 143
numéraire price 63, 65
Nyblén, G. 86

O'Driscoll, G. 40
oligopsony 120–1, 223
opportunity cost 188, 193, 209

Pantaleoni, M. 79–80
Pareto, V. 30, 57, 116, 144, 213, 218
Pareto-efficiency 68
partial equilibrium 60–1, 106, 136; *see also* equilibrium
patents 153, 155, 159, 163
perfect competition 108, 110–12, 120, 133–4, 136, 143, 218–19, 223
period of production 194
physics 6
physiological requirements 34–5, 38–9, 44
political economy 9–10, 13, 21–2, 32
praxeology 58
preferences 24, 66–7
Preiser, E. 138
Pribram, K. 36–7
price bounds 67, 97, 101–2, 129
price discrimination 77–8, 82, 114, 116, 130, 217
price dispersion 80, 121
price duels 61, 70–3, 134–5
price formation 60–86, 94, 101–2, 106, 115, 120–1, 134, 140, 143, 217
price range 69–70, 72–3, 78, 95, 223–4

price taking 118
price variance 122–4, 128
price war 115–16, 120, 122, 128, 131
private values assumption 71–2, 95–6
process analysis 118; *see also* market process; equilibrating process
product innovation 118, 143
progress: in Menger 34, 37–9, 159, 161; in Wieser 182–3, 191, 194, 199–200, 204, 221
property rights 151–3, 176
psychology 25, 36–7, 45, 47, 50, 54–5, 57–9, 202, 222

rate of interest 104, 182, 191, 195, 198–200; *see also* interest
rational reconstructions 4, 217
Rau, K. 12, 35, 70, 213
recontracting 68, 96, 217
reserve price 74
Ricardo, D. 103
Rima, I. 3
rivalry 108, 115, 119, 122, 127–8, 131, 145; *see also* non-price rivalry
Rizzo, M. 40
Robbins L. 10, 24–5, 36, 58, 103–4, 184, 208–9
Robinson, J. 108, 133
Rogin, L. 155
Roscher, W. 9 13, 35, 64, 156
Rosenstein-Rodan, P. 41
Rothbard, M. 58, 174
Rothschild, K. 139
roundabout methods of production 165

Samuels, W. 6
Samuelson, P. 60
satiation 75
Say's law 155
Schäffle, A. 35, 38, 109, 157
Schmoller, G. 9
Schotter, A. 100
Schullern-Schrattenhofen, H. von 109

Schumpeter, J. 16, 50–1, 60, 93, 103, 109, 132–3, 140, 143, 146, 176, 205, 208
science of national economy 14
self-interest 26, 40, 94, 134, 161
sellers' competition 80–2, 132, 135; *see also* competition
speculators 82, 121
sequential transactions 78
serial chain of causality 91
Shubik, M. 99–100
Silverman, P. 11, 33
Slutsky, E. 50
Smith, A. 141
Souter, R. 24–5
Spann, O. 146
spontaneous order 118
static subjectivism 40, 214
stationary economy 181–3, 185, 187–94, 201, 203
stationary state 105
statistics 14, 16
Stigler, G. 27, 60, 180, 183, 185, 188, 190
strategic behaviour 74, 77, 97–100, 116, 120, 138–9, 145, 217; *see also* bargaining; game theory; rivalry
Streissler, E. 5, 65, 146–7, 162, 179–80, 196, 200, 207
Strigl, R. 17, 24–5, 213
subjectivism 124, 142
subsistence fund 181
substitution 186–9
supply relation 98–9, 216
supply schedule 102–3, 183–5, 190, 204, 213, 220

tâtonnement 61, 72, 114
Thünen, J. von 202
theorem of non-equivalence 140
theory of market structures 120–5
theory of value 7, 61, 90; *see also* value
time 20, 91, 165, 171, 194, 198, 223; horizons 195; intervals 183, 193; lapses 80
time preference 174–6, 182, 191, 194, 203, 220
Tomo, S. 101, 173
total utility 27; *see also* utility
trademarks 153

uncertainty 38, 93, 137, 172, 177, 198
utility 25, 44, 47, 53, 128, 153, 86, 214–15; cardinal measurement 29, 52–5, 215; ordinal measurement 29, 51, 57, 222

value 86–94, 106; exchange value 88–90, 94; extrinsic and intrinsic 47–8, 87; subjective value formation 87–90
value theory 179
Vaughn, K. 207, 211
Veblen, T. 38
Verstehende method 36–7
von Neumann, J. 85, 110

Walras, L. 6, 8, 15, 27–8, 30, 38, 57, 60, 64–5, 90, 102, 107–8, 111, 116, 144, 190, 196, 212–13, 215–16, 218–19, 221
Walrasian branch of neoclassicism 3, 6–8, 16, 26, 31, 60, 70, 74–5, 85–6, 90, 93, 106, 109, 131, 139, 144–5, 185, 206–7, 209–10
Walrasian price-auction theory 83, 97
wealth computation 153–62
Weber, W. 146, 179
Weintraub, E. 104–5
Weiser, F. 1–2, 5, 15–18, 25, 37, 51, 56–9, 101, 109, 15, 135, 141–5, 178–9, 207, 221–2, 224–5; his capital concept 180–2; on capital, interest and imputation in a stationary economy 182–90; on competition 126–34, 218–19; on economizing 41–7, 222; on introspection 16, 45–6; his methodology 21, 126; on price conflict 123; on

INDEX

Schumpeter's method 16; his theory of interest 190–4, 204; his theory of the simple economy 23, 127

White, L. 7, 15, 34

Wicksell, K. 81, 104, 180, 219–20
Wicksteed, P. 213
Winch, D. 8

Yagi, K. 51, 70, 173